DIXIE SPIRITS

DIXIE SPIRITS

True Tales of the Strange and Supernatural in the South

Christopher K. Coleman

CUMBERLAND HOUSE
Nashville, Tennessee

DIXIE SPIRITS
SECOND EDITION
PUBLISHED BY CUMBERLAND HOUSE PUBLISHING INC.
431 Harding Industrial Drive
Nashville, Tennessee 37211

Copyright © 2002 by Christopher K. Coleman

First edition published 2002. Second edition 2008

ISBN-13 978-1-58182-671-5 (paperback : alk. paper)
ISBN-10 1-58182-617-0 (paperback : alk. paper)

Cover design: Gore Studio, Inc.
Text design: John Mitchell

The Library of Congress has cataloged the first edition as follows:

Coleman, Christopher Kiernan, 1949-
  Dixie spirits : true tales of the strange and supernatural in the south / Christopher K. Coleman.
    p. cm.
  ISBN 1-58182-293-6
  1. Ghosts—Southern States. 2. Haunted places—Southern States. I. Title.
BF1472.U6 C6477 2002
  133.1'0975—dc21

                                                                        2002006455

Printed in Canada

1 2 3 4 5 6 7—14 13 12 11 10 09 08

*To my devoted wife Veronica, whose love and support
has been of inestimable value, and whose great beauty
continues to haunt my waking dreams—
a haunting I hope never to be free of.*

Contents

Foreword 9
Introduction 11

ALABAMA APPARITIONS
1. The Face in the Courthouse Window 15
2. Athens Apparitions 21
3. Graveyard Shift:
The Haunting of Sloss Furnaces 25

ARKANSAS ARCANA
4. Crescent Hotel Hauntings 35
5. Fouke Lore 41
6. The Day the Devil Came Down to Arkansas 49

GHOSTS AND HAUNTS OF GEORGIA
7. The Barnsley Curse 55
8. Savannah Specters 65
9. The Haunted Pillar 73

TRANSYLVANIA TALES
10. Mysteries of Mammoth Cave 79
11. The Happy Hollow Horror 87
12. The Late Mrs. Varick:
The Gray Ghost of Liberty Hall 93

LOUISIANA LORE AND GORE
13. The 'Most Haunted' Myrtles 101
14. The Witch Queen of New Orleans 107
15. At the Werewolves Ball 119

MISSISSIPPI MYSTERIES
16. The Great International Hoodoo Conspiracy
and Other Tales of the Black Art 129
17. Curse of the Singing River 135
18. The Devil's Backbone: Ghosts and Haunts
of Natchez and the Natchez Trace 141

MYSTIC MISSOURI
19. The Devil's Promenade:
The Hornet Ghost Light *153*
20. The Lemp Curse: Lavender Lady, Monkey Boy
and the Bucolic Brewmeisters *159*

HAINTS OF THE OLD NORTH STATE
21. The White Doe: The Mystery of Virginia Dare *167*
22. Belinda and the Brown Mountain Lights *173*
23. A Night on Bald Roan Mountain *181*

SOUTH CAROLINA SPIRITS
24. An Affair of Honor *189*
25. The Gray Man *195*
26. South Battery Hauntings:
The Battery Carriage House Inn *201*

TENNESSEE TERRORS
27. The Haunting of Reelfoot Lake *209*
28. Clara and Lizzie: A Memphis Mystery *217*
29. The Oak and the Hackberry *229*

VIRGINIA: THE DARK DOMINION
30. The Devil's Dominion *239*
31. The Haunted Homes of Robert E. Lee *247*
32. The Trouble with Martha *255*

WEST VIRGINIA WEIRDNESS
33. Cornstalk's Curse: The Mothman Enigma *263*
34. Incident at Flatwoods:
Close Encounter of the Weird Kind *277*

Appendix:
Haunted Hotels of Dixie *287*

Foreword

Since the original edition of Dixie Spirits, many changes have taken place which made this new edition advisable. The growth in interest in the paranormal has continued unabated, and media coverage of it has exploded—although not always for the better. There are any number of documentary shows on television dealing with the paranormal and especially with "haunted history." Moreover, the growth of ghost tours in cities throughout the South has been enormous, and many sites open to the public that formerly avoided discussion of their ghosts are now far more forthcoming. All this indicates a growing popular interest in the subject.

In addition, I have been aware that some of the information I included in the first edition has become dated. Therefore, wherever possible in this new edition I have tried to give the most up-to-date and accurate information on locations and accessibility. I have added sections for those who may wish to visit the locations featured, as well as a sampling of similar haunted sites in each state, including places where one may spend the night with a resident ghost or two. I trust all these additions will prove useful to those who travel through Dixie's haunted realms.

I also would like to thank the staff of Cumberland House for their efforts on my behalf to make this book a success, as well as the many informants and historic sites that provided me with information.

If you do go ghost hunting, however, please remember that folks in Dixie value courtesy greatly. They extend it to you as a matter of course and expect the same in return. Just because someone is on a quest to find ghosts does not give them the right to trespass on private property. There are many genuine haunts mentioned in this book that remain private, and it is just common courtesy to respect the owner's privacy. With that in mind, however, anyone exploring the haints and haunts of Dixie should have an enjoyable time—and perhaps have some interesting adventures along the way. Good hunting.

Introduction

What is it about the South that makes it so congenial to the supernatural? Is it those long, languid, moonlit nights, redolent with the scent of honeysuckle and magnolia, that mesmerize the senses? Is it Dixie's turbulent and tragic past that has roused so many restless spirits? Or is it something less tangible, less definable, that stirs the Southern soul and draws the darkness near?

Whatever the cause, the fact remains that, from the brooding swamps of the Delta to the mist-enshrouded heights of Appalachia, scenes supernatural and oddities unexplained confront the wayfarer at almost every turn. Haunted hotels, ghost-infested mansions, family curses, mysterious monsters, and assorted other fey and fearsome phenomena—nearly every city, town and whistle-stop can lay claim to one such strangeness or another.

Some communities revel in their uncanny aura; New Orleans, for instance, takes particular pride in its reputation as the "Voodoo Capital of America." Other towns are more circumspect about their haunting heritage; Nashville, best known for its music, is chock full of ghosts of various ilk, yet folks there are often close-mouthed when it comes to their encounters with the paranormal. Still other cities, such as staid Richmond, Virginia, and sedate Charleston, South Carolina, seem to have come to terms with their spectral side, to the point of hosting ghost tours for visitors.

Native-born residents of Dixie are proud—and justly so—of their heritage. Some call it the Spirit of Dixie—an awareness of the distinctive culture, customs, and history of the lands below the Mason-Dixon line. Yet there is another aspect of this heritage, more whispered than spoken, which outsiders are rarely privy to. This is the realm not of the Spirit of Dixie but of Dixie Spirits.

While Southerners are proud of their heritage and the glory of the land that gave them birth, that pride and glory have not come without a price. Beyond the beauty of the land and the charm of its people, there lies a darker side of Dixie. For if there is pride, there has also been prejudice; if there is music and laughter, there have also been dirges and tears; and if Dixie seems to be a land of bountiful light and life, it also has had strife and darkness in measure far beyond its fair share.

This darker side of Dixie has inspired generations of Southern writers. From Poe and Bierce to Faulkner and Anne Rice, writers have been driven to craft tales of terror and imagination. Yet, in truth, no fiction can compare in strangeness with the true accounts of horror, hauntings, and hellfire with which the South has been so amply endowed.

More than a century ago another sojourner in the South, Ambrose Bierce, posed the question, "Can such things be?" If, at the dawn of a new millennium, we are still in quest of answers to that question, it ought to be remembered that oftentimes the journey itself is of greater worth than the destination.

Let us go, then, and explore those darker byways and shadowy back alleys of the South. For if Dixie is no longer simply the land of cotton, old times there are still far from forgotten, especially by its more spectral citizens. They have stories to tell us still, if we have the wit to listen. On this journey we may yet hope to unravel their messages—and at times heed their warnings—and in the process illumine in part these dark, dark corners of Dixie.

DIXIE SPIRITS

1

The Face in the Courthouse Window

N APRIL 1865 YANKEE CAVALRY were making their way from Tuscaloosa to Columbus, Alabama, when they paid a visit to the little town of Carrolton. They had instructions to seize a Confederate commissary there to deny supplies to the enemy. For good measure, however, they burned down the Pickens County Courthouse, which stood proudly in the center of the town square.

It was one atrocity among many and certainly not the worst the Yankees committed during the War Between the States. But for the folks in Carrolton, it was bad enough.

As was the case with other communities throughout the South, the county courthouse was more than just four walls housing the local law court. The courthouse, in the center of the county seat, was a place to meet for folks high and low. It was the political nexus of the county, a place where local disputes were settled, deals were made, gossip shared, acquaintances renewed, tall tales swapped, and much time wasted. It was, in essence, the heart and soul of the community.

After the war, the residents of Pickens County rebuilt their courthouse, even as they suffered through the hard, lean years of Yankee occupation and Reconstruction. Things were beginning to look up by 1876 as the new courthouse was completed and Reconstruction was ending. Then, one dark night, the new courthouse burned down.

In the early hours of Thursday, November 16, fire broke out in several places inside the building. There was no doubt the fire had been set deliberately.

Memories of the Yankee atrocity in 1865 were still fresh in everyone's minds in Carrolton, and in the hardscrabble years after the war it had been no easy matter to gather the money and resources to rebuild the courthouse. Now someone had burned down the new building as well. Needless to say, feelings were hard, very hard, about the whole matter.

No arrests were made immediately, but there were suspects in the case. In particular, the shadow of suspicion fell on a "rowdy black man" by the name of Henry Wells, who lived on the edge of town.

A former slave, Wells had already had a number of run-ins with the law: arrests for burglary, carrying concealed weapons, assault, and the like. In fact, Henry was already under indictment in the county for previous offenses, and as the authorities looked closer at the case, Henry Wells loomed larger in their eyes as a suspect.

Henry, it was believed, had gone on a "burglary spree" and broken into the courthouse with an accomplice. Whether they set the fire to cover up a robbery, or whether Henry simply set the fire to destroy court records of his indictments and thereby prevent his prosecution, is not certain. But the sheriff was certain of one thing: He was sure he had his man, and arrested Wells on arson charges.

On January 29, 1878, Henry Wells, case 971, was arraigned by Bill Burkhalter on charges of committing arson. Henry was not granted bail—either because of the seriousness of the crime, or perhaps because Henry simply lacked the money. Either way, however, it proved just as well that Henry wasn't released on bail.

The old courthouse had been rebuilt the preceding year at no little expense, but the affront to the community ran deeper than just the cost.

As word spread about Wells's arrest for arson, people began gathering in town, and the crowd started getting larger and uglier. There was talk of getting "satisfaction" without waiting on the legal system to dispense justice.

As a precaution, the sheriff moved Henry from the town jail to a room in the attic of the new courthouse. The old jail was strong enough to keep prisoners from getting out, but the sheriff felt the new three-story brick courthouse would be better suited to keeping folks from getting in.

From his garret window on the top level of the new courthouse, Henry could peer out a lone small window at the mob gathering below.

The situation on the town square was becoming very ugly indeed. The authorities were determined to observe the letter of the law, but the crowd had other ideas. Perhaps the turbulent emotions building in front of the courthouse distracted them from the storm brewing just on the horizon.

Regardless of whatever crimes Wells may have committed previously, Henry adamantly denied burning down the Pickens County Courthouse. And as he stared out at the angry mob below, Wells repeated his protestations of innocence, adding, "If you kill me, I will be with you always."

Suddenly, a violent thunderstorm broke over Carrolton. Henry was peering out the garret window, his face expressing a mix of emotions—fear, pain, sorrow—and other thoughts known only to God. Just then a lightning bolt flashed, striking the top of the courthouse.

Wells was not lynched, but it was a very near thing. Curiously, the lightning bolt from above burned the image of Henry's face into the pane of glass he was peering through. The violent storm also dampened the bloodlust of the mob, and both the storm and the lightning bolt were taken as a kind of divine sign.

Although the mob dispersed, the sheriff still felt it would be wiser to move Wells to a larger city where passions were not running so high and the jail was more stoutly built.

Because resources were limited, the sheriff could not transport the prisoner himself, so he deputized a local bounty hunter, John Hunnicutt, to take Henry Wells to Tuscaloosa for safekeeping.

What happened next remains somewhat murky. One account claims that Wells died four days later, "from the infection of a gunshot wound suffered long ago." A local lawyer, recalling local tradition, said that Henry had attempted to escape and was shot dead. Hunnicutt himself claimed he had found Wells hiding out in Tuscaloosa County and brought him back to Carrolton.

Hunnicutt had been a boy when Sutherland's Yankees descended on Alabama, but the soldiers stole his prize possession, his horse, and he neither forgot nor forgave the offense. Like many poor whites in the South, Hunnicutt's family had not particularly benefited from the institution of slavery, but poor whites had often borne the brunt of suffering during both the war and Reconstruction.

John L. Hunnicutt, therefore, did not have much use for either Yankees or blacks. By his own admission, Hunnicutt was something of a rounder and had even been a member of the Ku Klux Klan. It seems likely, therefore, that Hunnicutt returned Wells to Carrolton with a terminal case of lead poisoning.

Henry Wells never had his day in court, and whether he was innocent or guilty of arson remains a moot dispute. But his presentiment, "I will be with you always," proved only too true.

With Wells dead and buried, the residents of Carrolton would just as soon have forgotten the whole ugly incident. But when the courthouse custodian went to clean the garret window in the room where Wells had been held, he found something unusual: No amount of scrubbing with soap and water could remove the image inscribed upon it.

A number of attempts were made to wipe off the image, and even gasoline was used. But no solvent seemed able to erase the face, no matter what the authorities tried.

Other things about the image are curious as well. Viewed close up from the inside of the room, it appears to be only a slight discoloration of the glass. No face is apparent. It is only when the window is viewed from ground level from the north side of the courthouse that the image of Henry Wells becomes visible. In essence, it is only when the window is viewed from the spot where the lynch mob once stood that Henry's face appears.

On December 30, 1927, a severe hailstorm tore through the northern part of Pickens County, causing a great deal of damage. Every window in the courthouse was broken by the storm except one: The window bearing the image of Henry Wells was preserved from destruction while all other window panes in the courthouse were destroyed.

Was it just coincidence, or was it an act of God that the garret window was spared? In any case, folks in Carrolton came to believe that there was some sort of supernatural power protecting Wells's image from harm.

Whether it is a manifestation of the natural or supernatural, the "face in the window" has evolved over the years from an uncomfortable reminder of an ugly incident into a local attraction and wonderment.

The 1960s—like the 1860s—were a difficult time in Dixie, with much racial turmoil and bitter feelings on both sides. There was some concern among the residents of Carrolton that some hothead might vent his rage on the face in the courthouse window. But through it all the image of Henry Wells endured, eventually becoming an icon for the whole community.

Whenever lawyers came to town to plead a case, the local probate judge would act as unofficial tour guide and tell them the story behind the face in the window.

One time, a teacher from Birmingham called the judge, telling him that her class was studying folklore and asking if he would mind talking to the students about the strange image. He said that he would be glad to talk with the youngsters.

On the appointed day, the chartered buses pulled up and the children stepped off and entered the courthouse. They were from an inner-city school in Birmingham and were predominantly African-Americans. Seeing them gave the judge pause to think, not just about what to say but about the meaning of the face in the window itself.

The judge told the students the story as he had always heard it told. He then offered the opinion that the window and its strange image were a reminder to everyone that such a thing should never happen again.

When one of the children asked how he could tell the face was that of a black man, the judge was brought up short. He realized, for the first time, that the race of the man belonging to the face in the window could not be determined. It was simply the image of a man, neither white nor black, staring in terror at what was occurring in the town square below him—a man who had been denied his day in court.

To this day in Carrolton, on dark and stormy nights, when the wind howls through the eaves of the old courthouse like a banshee's baleful wail, the gloom is often pierced by the flash of a thunderbolt. And when lightning descends from the heavens, it is said that the spirit of Henry Wells is re-animated by means of the uncanny image in the glass and that his ghost can be seen moving about the garret cell.

It is almost as if the ghost of Henry Wells is trying to tell us, "I am innocent. If you kill me, I will be with you always."

PICKENS COUNTY COURTHOUSE
11 Courthouse Square • P.O. Box 382
Carrollton, AL 35447

(Carrollton is 30 miles west of Tuscaloosa, at the intersection of Highways 17 and 86.)

2

Athens Apparitions

THENS, ALABAMA, IS A SLEEPY little college town some twenty miles
west of Huntsville. Nothing much happens in Athens—and for the
most part people there like it that way. The last time anything of
note happened was during the War Between the States, when the Yankees looted the town. Since then, it's been mostly quiet—except, of
course, for the haints that inhabit Athens State University.

Athens State, although neither as large nor as famous as its sister
institutions in 'Bama, nevertheless possesses a venerable pedigree.
Founded in 1822 as a finishing school for young Christian ladies, it
has endured war, Reconstruction, and modernization.

The oldest building on Athens State's campus is Founder's Hall, a
grand antebellum structure. The four Ionic columns screening the
main entrance are named Matthew, Mark, Luke, and John—a custom
that dates back to the days when the school was run by the Methodist
Church. According to tradition, a barrel of whiskey is still hidden
within one of the columns—stashed there by a tippling worker in
1822 to hide it from his teetotaling foreman.

During the Civil War, the college was saved from destruction by its headmistress, Madame Jane Hamilton Childs. Yankee troops, irate that local bushwhackers had fired on them, had threatened to burn down the town. Col. Basil Vasili Turchinoff—a Union officer, originally a Russian from the Don region—resorted to Cossack tactics, allowing his men to loot the town. The incident became known as the "Rape of Athens." But when they came to the gates of the college, they met a far more formidable foe than any Confederate army—they ran afoul of Headmistress Jane Childs.

Standing between rampaging Yankee looters and a dormitory full of the fairest flowers of Alabama femininity, Madame Childs produced a note from the folds of her voluminous black dress. The note was allegedly written by none other than Abraham Lincoln himself and attested to the loyalty and fidelity to the Union of Madame Childs and her wards.

That note, plus Jane Childs's icy stare and will of iron, dissuaded the Yankees from their dastardly deed, thereby preserving Founder's Hall and—presumably—the virtue of its young female inhabitants. At least, that is the local tradition.

Another stately building on campus is Brown Hall. Built in 1912, it was named in honor of Florence Brown, the secretary to the college's president, who lived around the turn of the century. In 1909 a terrible typhoid epidemic broke out on campus. All the faculty left except Miss Brown, who bravely stayed on to watch over those girls too sick to go home. Four of the students died of the disease, as did Florence herself. Faculty and friends contributed to build the hall in her memory.

Needless to say, with such spirited ladies populating the school's history, it ought to come as no surprise that Athens State has its fair share of hauntings.

At Founders' Hall, for example, students and teachers who stay late after dark often experience strange things.

A professor, working late one night in the building, heard the jingling of keys outside the door to his office. Opening the door to see who was standing there, he saw before him a strange, fog-like entity in the hallway.

A visiting instructor, on campus for an interview some time back, stayed overnight in Founder's Hall. He swore he heard footsteps in the empty building and what sounded to him like a jingling or rattling—

as of chains. The good professor decided not to accept a position at the school, and never returned after his first visit.

It is believed the main spirit haunting Founder's Hall is the stern Madame Childs. As she did in life, Jane Childs wanders the hallways of the old dormitory, overseeing her wards, her large chain of keys jingling by her side as she makes her rounds.

There may be a male presence in this building as well, for in addition to clicking sounds and squeaky doors, students have smelled the aroma of cigar smoke. A specter sometimes has been observed peering out a third-story window and is referred to by students as "the Night Stalker."

The devoted Miss Brown may also still be in evidence on campus. She inhabits the hall that bears her name. Brown Hall formerly was used for adult education classes, and its tall Corinthian columns now guard the offices of the college's president. Although Miss Brown died before the building was erected, its dedication to her memory, and her empathy for the college administration, seems to have caused her spirit to become attracted to that place.

One adjunct instructor who taught night classes in Brown Hall discovered that objects would disappear or be moved to a different location all on their own. Once, staying late after class, he suddenly found the entire classroom going haywire about him. Objects were jostled about, there were loud knocking sounds, and pictures even began falling off the walls with no apparent cause.

Of all of Athens State's ghosts, however, perhaps the best known inhabits McCandless Hall, a squarish brick building that once served as a campus theater and performing arts center.

According to campus lore, a famous opera singer—thought to be Abigail Lylia Burns—once graced the floorboards of McCandless's auditorium. Her performance was outstanding and drew repeated ovations from the audience. Coming back for several curtain calls, and clutching a bouquet of bright red roses, she thanked the audience and vowed that she would return to the theater someday.

On her way out of town, speeding to another musical engagement, the carriage in which the diva was riding was crossing a wooden bridge when a bolt of lightning spooked its team of horses. Their wild, erratic motions caused the carriage to tip over, plunging the opera singer headlong into the river below.

True to her word, it is said, the diva returned to the campus—as a ghost. She is described as having golden hair, and always wears a formal white gown; sometimes she is also described as being bathed in an eerie white light.

Chatting over burgers and sodas in the Snack Shack in the basement of McCandless, generations of students have told of seeing visions at the windows, hearing footsteps in the building when it is empty, and smelling the distinct scent of fresh flowers.

People have been known to come all the way from Birmingham to catch a glimpse of the phantom diva at Halloween time. On May 12, 1987, the Huntsville Opera staged a memorial concert at the theater, and many expected Abigail to make a showing then. Although three psychics in the audience all claimed to sense her presence, the rest of those attending were disappointed that Abigail's apparition did not appear for an encore.

In recent years, psychic investigators have determined that Abigail Burns never visited Athens, Alabama—at least not in 1914. The identity of the dead diva thus remains a bit of a mystery. Still, the beech tree planted next to McCandless Hall in 1914 in memory of the deceased singer still grows there—proof that in the main the story is substantially true.

Educators have long had the reputation for being dedicated to their profession. Long hours, low pay, and little thanks have been the traditional rewards for their efforts. Athens State University, then, must be doubly blessed: to have educators whose devotion to their school is such that it endures even beyond the grave.

ATHENS STATE UNIVERSITY
300 N. Beatty Street
Athens, AL 35611
(205) 232-1802 • (800) 522-0272
www.athens.edu

(Athens is 20 miles west of Huntsville, just off Highway 72.)

3

Graveyard Shift:
The Haunting of Sloss Furnaces

NOT ALL OF DIXIE'S SPIRITS reside in the bucolic countryside or within the confines of some antebellum mansion. Indeed, some of the most terrifying hauntings occur in decidedly nontraditional settings. One such horror infests a modern-day iron foundry.

There has been iron smelting in the South since frontier days, but the antebellum South never put much stock in heavy industry. The Civil War, however, changed all that. The Confederacy found itself with a woeful lack of iron foundries to forge weapons, and its soldiers paid dearly for that shortcoming on the battlefield. Historians agree that the virtual absence of heavy industry in Dixie was a major factor in its defeat.

The end of the war saw the South in shambles. King Cotton was dead, and if Dixie was to survive, those who wanted to see it rise from the ashes needed to do something radically different.

In the area around the hamlet of Birmingham, Alabama, there were deposits of iron ore, limestone, and coal. It occurred to some local businessmen that there was an opportunity to develop an iron business that might be able to compete with the big iron foundries of the North.

At Oxmoor, an experimental furnace had already been built that used coke to extract iron from ore more economically than the traditional charcoal method. The first furnace in Birmingham to use this new process was known as Alice No. 1, located on the western outskirts of town.

Just two years later, James Sloss opened his own furnaces on the town's eastern limits. The enterprise soon proved a success. By the end of the century,

But progress does not come without a price—and at Sloss Furnaces, that price was often paid out in human suffering and death. Iron smelting in those days was a very dangerous business. Temperatures in the factory could reach 120 degrees or more; the hours were long and the work fatiguing; and even at the best of times, working conditions were hazardous. Add to this mix a sadistic foreman, and you had a deadly combination indeed.

James "Slag" Wormwood was an iron man through and through. He had begun smelting iron back when it was still pretty much a backwoods operation. Slag gradually worked his way up to shift foreman at Sloss Furnaces and was put in charge of the graveyard shift, supervising some 150 men.

Not much production was expected out of a graveyard shift; the workers' primary duty was to make sure the furnace remained hot enough to ensure full production on the daytime shift. But Slag was ambitious and was always looking to curry favor with management. Moreover, he knew how to get the most of even a skeleton crew—and in the days before unions and government regulations, management didn't much care how he did it, as long as he got results.

Iron workers as a rule were a burly, roughneck lot; hard-drinking, hard-fighting, and tough—they had to be to survive the infernal conditions inside the iron works. Slag Wormwood was tougher than most and twice as mean. Driving his men far harder than any other shift boss, Slag's shift managed to exceed company goals—but at a terrible cost.

During the time the Sloss Furnaces Mill was in operation, fifty-five men were killed there. Of these, forty-seven died in accidents during the graveyard shift; many more were severely maimed or permanently disabled. In that era, if a man was hurt and couldn't work, he was fired. If a worker died, his widow got nothing. Times were tough and jobs were scarce, and management could always find new men hungry enough to work the graveyard shift.

Conditions were bad enough at the furnace under normal circumstances, but Wormwood drove his crew mercilessly. Slag heaped verbal—and physical—abuse on his crew without end. He also made them take dangerous risks to speed up production, and in the mill shortcuts could be deadly. Slag made working on his shift literally a "living hell."

On October 16, 1899, James Wormwood was standing on a catwalk high above the furnace floor, overlooking the massive open-hearth cauldron filled to the brim with molten iron. According to the official accident report, Slag lost his footing and fell into the molten metal. Death would have been almost—but not quite—instantaneous.

At the time, however, there was a persistent rumor that his accidental death was not so accidental.

For one thing, Slag rarely went on the high catwalk. Wormwood's job was to supervise the workers and keep them on their toes—workers rarely had to be on the catwalk during a regular production run. So why was Slag there? And how could such an experienced iron worker suddenly have become so careless? On top of it all, there were 150 men with a strong motive to see Slag Wormwood dead.

Gossip, never confirmed, had it that Wormwood was already dead when he hit the molten metal of the fiery furnace. It was rumored that several workers, fed up with Wormwood's abuse, ganged up on the hated foreman and murdered him, then dragged his battered, lifeless body up onto the catwalk and tossed it over the railing into the fiery pit below.

In any case, police declined to investigate the incident, and the coroner labeled his death just another "industrial accident."

With Slag's demise, conditions ought to have improved on the graveyard shift. After Wormwood's death, however, workers on the night shift at Sloss began to report "strange" occurrences.

Production on the shift declined, and the men complained that an "unnatural presence" was dogging them throughout the night. Workers began to quit, and ultimately the company found it difficult to hire men who were willing to go into the mill late at night, even for extra pay. Finally, in 1901, the company discontinued the graveyard shift for good.

The problems at Sloss seemed to end with the demise of the graveyard shift. Still, reports of uncanny occurrences continued to surface over the years. In 1926, for example, a night watchman reportedly was injured after being shoved from behind. The security guard thought he heard a gruff voice behind him shout, "Get back to work!" just before he was pushed. In the 1940s several supervisors reported encountering a man who appeared to be badly burned and who shouted angrily at them.

In fact, over the years, nearly a hundred reports were officially filed with Birmingham police claiming supernatural incidents at Sloss Furnaces. Some were minor—whistles blowing on their own and the like, but others were more serious, involving actual physical assault.

The majority of these spectral encounters had several things in common. Most incidents took place during the month of September or October, and the paranormal encounters almost always occurred late at night—during what use to be the graveyard shift.

Finally, the owners of Sloss Furnaces decided to close down the aging plant and offered to donate the property to the state with the idea of turning it into a museum of industry. But the state fair board didn't want to be bothered with maintaining the mammoth complex and passed on the offer.

Yet the old steel mill in many ways symbolized the city of Birmingham and its role in the growth of the New South. Through efforts of its residents, the city took over the property, and Sloss eventually was designated a National Historic Landmark.

Since the 1970s Sloss Furnaces has operated as an open-air museum; it also serves as a venue for concerts and other public gatherings. In recent years, capitalizing on the place's supernatural reputation, part of the mill has operated as a seasonal "haunted house" attraction. Sloss Furnaces is probably the only such "haunted house" that lives up to its billing.

Over the years, in addition to being a historic site and public venue, Sloss Furnaces has also become a popular hangout for the younger set in Birmingham. Tweens and teens use the site for a late-night lover's rendezvous or a place to drink and party, and a few go there simply on a dare, to venture alone into a real haunted place.

Due in part to all this activity, an unusually large number of people claim to have had authentic encounters with the supernatural there.

One such visitor, a girl named Jessica, visited the mill alone one night. As she walked past the large abandoned furnace, she noticed the giant machinery standing eerily stark and silent in the moonlight.

Suddenly, it seemed as if the machines had all been turned on. Jessica could hear men working the foundry equipment, and then she heard a piercing scream, followed by men's voices yelling, "He fell into the furnace!" As she drew closer to the furnace, she swore she could feel searing heat coming from it and heard the sounds of workers all around her, although none could be seen.

In another instance, a carload of teenagers visited the Sloss works on a ghost-hunting expedition. Although their hobby had taken them to several old abandoned houses in search of ghosts, they had never actually seen any. Arriving after a two-hour drive to check out the complex "just as something to do," they went in and started walking around.

As they were proceeding across a catwalk, a whistle went off, spooking the group. The farther they went into the mill, the more things seemed to happen around them. Several times the boys heard the clanging of metal as well as the sound of footsteps behind them. As most of us would do, they tried to rationalize these occurrences, believing it was just their imaginations playing tricks.

Then, about 3 A.M., as they were leaving, a man ran up behind them. When they turned around, they were confronted by a figure with glowing, molten-red eyes and charred-black skin that looked "melted" around the edges. The apparition shoved one of the teens from behind and shook his fist at the others, yelling at them to "get back to work!"

The boys didn't need a second warning; they high-tailed it back to their car and tore out of there. The boy who had been pushed from behind soon began complaining that his back was sore. They stopped at a nearby convenience store, and when his friends inspected his back, they saw two large burn marks—both in the distinct shape of handprints.

In the fall of 2001 a young man named Sam visited Sloss Furnaces alone out of idle curiosity. It was a cold October day, and at first he encountered nothing unusual—no fires, no sounds, no lights or electricity—nothing unusual. After Sam had seen about all he wished, he began to dismiss the entire ghostly reputation of Sloss as a hoax.

As he was leaving, however, he dropped his eyeglasses, and as Sam was groping on the ground to find them, he heard a voice. It spoke in a low whisper but seemed to be coming from all around him. He thought it was saying, "Do your part or you will be removed."

Sam found his glasses and put them back on; when he did so, he thought he saw an African-American man standing before him. The figure frightened him—all the more so when his eyes focused and he realized the man was not a Negro at all but rather appeared "fatally burned."

Sam began to run, and as he did so, he heard the Burned Man shout, "If you see three drunk Mexican men who worked here, either shoot them yourself or bring them to me."

Sam didn't wait to listen to anything more. He was convinced that he'd met the ghost of the "owner," but more importantly, he felt that the spirit was "very violent" and "definitely wants revenge."

Adventurous twenty-somethings and amorous teens are not the only ones to have encountered strange phenomena at Sloss Furnaces. In 1988 a research team from the Center for Paranormal Events investigated the site and concluded that it was "a location rife with restless souls."

More recently, a team of investigative reporters and psychic researchers sent to Birmingham by WJTV-Channel 12 of Jackson, Mississippi, came up with some interesting results as well. While no one came face to face with Slag Woodworm, the researchers did encounter some highly unusual phenomena. Their electronic equipment recorded anomalies not explainable in ordinary terms.

For example, while passing through a section of the site called the Tunnel, they began to hear the sound of footsteps other than their own. There were loud banging noises as well. The Tunnel is one part of the furnaces where visitors have often reported seeing a floating apparition.

Another psychic hotspot investigated was the catwalk. Here psychic Chris Simon reported seeing a white glowing light with no apparent source of origin. One of the reporters experienced difficulty breathing and had a definite sensation that the air had become heavy.

Janis Railey, one of the psychic investigators present, snapped some digital photos on the catwalk. Nothing was visible to the naked eye, but when the team examined the photos later, glowing orbs were visible in the shots. Railey also recorded inexplicable temperature fluctuations inside the building, ranging from hot to cold.

In another section of the factory, the camera seemed to capture the image of a face; even under close analysis, the image still seemed to be that of a human. In the Blowing Room, where an explosion in 1888 had blinded and maimed six men, videographer Darren Dedo was convinced that he heard the sound of a shifting foot coming from one corner of the room and also had an overwhelming sense that he was not alone there.

The team from WJTV's *Unexplained* show left without having a visual encounter with Sloss Furnaces' chief spook, yet there is no question that they had a number of uncanny encounters.

There are other ghosts that haunt the industrial skeletons of Birmingham's iron-mongering past; most—but not all—of them are at Sloss. One local tradition, for example, identifies someone other than Slag Wormwood as the Burned Man.

Theophilus Calvin Jowers had started in iron working at Oxmoor back in the 1870s, and in 1887 was working at the old Alice No. 1 Furnace in Birmingham as assistant foundry-man. Local lore has it that one day Jowers was trying to change out a bell on the furnace and, while using a block and tackle, lost his balance. Calvin and the bell both fell into the molten iron, and for more than twenty years thereafter, Jowers's ghost haunted the complex.

Allegedly, when the Alice furnace was closed, Jowers's ghost "roamed from furnace to furnace" until it finally settled in at Sloss Furnaces. While the story of Calvin's ghost certainly bears a strong resemblance to that of the Burned Man, there are good reasons to question that identification.

For one thing, Jowers worked and died at Alice Furnace, not at Sloss. More importantly, Jowers is described as a devoted family man who was well-liked by his fellow workers. He simply did not possess the sort of mean streak that Slag had. The Burned Man at Sloss is definitely a malevolent spirit—an apparition whose personality is far better matched by that of Slag Woodworm than by old Calvin Jowers.

Even allowing that some of the many reports of supernatural encounters at Sloss Furnaces may be due more to the expectations of the visitors than to an actual spectral presence, the weight of evidence leans heavily in favor of Sloss Furnaces' supernatural reputation being genuine.

In its heyday this industrial behemoth chewed up ore and spit out iron and steel; it chewed up and spit out men, too. Historical descriptions of the working conditions at the furnaces often use the term "hellish" to describe them. Ungodly temperatures inside the factory, infernal working conditions, and—above all—a foreman whom only Satan could love, all made for a graveyard shift in its most literal meaning.

Sloss Furnaces today stands as a monument to the birth of the New South and the transformation of agrarian Dixie into a modern industrial region. It is also a testament to the men who worked and died to make that New South a reality.

That the souls of many who helped craft that new reality may still reside among the rusting girders and silent machines of this sprawling complex is a definite possibility. As much as any decaying mansion or deserted battlefield, Sloss Furnaces is an intimate part of Dixie's haunted heritage.

By day, Sloss Furnaces is a unique historic site and open-air museum. By night, however, the graveyard shift takes over—and the Devil only knows what happens then.

You may tour the Sloss Furnaces National Historic Landmark in perfect safety during the daytime. For more information contact:

SLOSS FURNACES
P.O. Box 1178 • 20 32nd Street N.
Birmingham, AL 35202
(205) 324-1911
www.slossfurnaces.com

During the month of October, the Sloss Fright Furnace operates on the historic site at night. The popular Halloween attraction is based on the factory's very real haunted past. October is also when most reported paranormal encounters have occurred. Contact them at:

SLOSS FRIGHT FURNACE
www.frightfurnace.com
E-mail: chet@frightfurnace.com

If you go ...

More haints and haunts of Dixie to see in Alabama:

AUBURN
AUBURN UNIVERSITY
Auburn, AL 36849
(334)844-4000
www.auburn.edu

University Chapel is haunted by the ghost of a dead soldier whose spirit was disturbed when the building was used by a theater troupe in the 1960s.

MOBILE
BRAGG-MITCHELL MANSION
1906 Spring Hill Avenue
Mobile, AL 36607
(251) 471-6364
www.azaleacity.com/braggmitchell/

OAKLEIGH MANSION
300 Oakleigh Place
Mobile, AL 36604
(251) 432-1281 • (866) 390-0553
www.historicmobile.org

Described as "the perfect haunted house" with at least two ghosts, flickering lights and moving furniture.

MONTGOMERY
STATE CAPITOL BUILDING
600 Dexter Avenue
Montgomery, AL 36230
(334) 242-3935

Assorted apparitions reported by staff and visitors.

SELMA
STURDIVANT HALL
713 Mabry Street
Selma, AL 36701
(334) 872-5626
www.sturdivanthall.com

"The Ruined Banker" and a child ghost haunt the house and grounds.

Alabama Ghost Tours

SELMA
THE SELMA GHOST TOUR

Self-guided ghost tour of Selma; printed ghost tours are available from the Visitor Information Center on Broad Street. A seasonal guided tour is also offered by the Tourism and Convention Bureau in October.
P.O. Box 467
Selma, AL 36702
(334) 875-7241

4

Crescent Hotel Hauntings

THEY CALL IT "THE GRAND OLD LADY of the Ozarks," and as one draws near the gleaming white limestone walls of the Crescent Hotel, one can well understand how it earned that epithet.

The Crescent rises majestically atop a mountain summit, overlooking the north Arkansas resort town of Eureka Springs. Its gables and spires soaring above the landscape give the venerable structure the aspect of an enchanted castle—an impression that is not far off the mark. For, like many European castles, the Crescent Hotel is home to more than its fair share of ghosts—and its history is strewn with real-life ghost stories.

By modern standards, the Crescent Hotel is not very large. It has only sixty-eight guest suites available, although as a whole the hotel has an abundance of space, inside and out. The Crescent was built in an era when quality counted far more than quantity, and even today what the hotel lacks in bed space, it more than makes up for in beauty and charm.

The hotel was designed from the start to cater to the carriage set. Since the early 1800s Eureka Springs had been renowned for the curative powers of its hot springs, and by the 1880s, the town was already a popular resort destination for the wealthy. With this in mind, former Union Gen. Powell C. Clayton gained financial backing from several well-heeled investors and began building the Crescent Hotel.

Considerable effort was expended to erect this Victorian pleasure palace. Clayton selected twenty-seven prime acres atop West Mountain, which afforded a panoramic view of the Ozarks. Isaac Taylor, a noted architect from St. Louis, was commissioned to design the hotel, and no expense was spared during its construction, down to importing Irish stonemasons to hand cut the pure-white Arkansas limestone for the walls and trim.

When the Crescent opened in May 1886, it was billed as the most luxurious hotel in the country. Soon the nation's elite were coming to the Crescent to hobnob and drink the healthful waters. The age of the Gibson Girl was dawning, and elegant young ladies and socially prominent matrons mingled there at teas and cotillions with wealthy heirs and elderly but eligible millionaires. It was the golden era of the Crescent Hotel, when white gloves were as common a sight in the lobby as top hats and tails.

By the early 1900s, however, the Crescent was no longer quite the "in" gathering place for the rich, and the hotel fell on leaner times. By 1908 it was no longer able to operate full time as a hotel. To keep the business afloat, its owners began to operate a ladies finishing school at the hotel in the off-season, the Crescent College and Conservatory for Young Women. It would continue as a junior college into the 1930s.

For a number of years this arrangement seemed to work well for the hotel. But by 1934 the school closed its doors for good, a victim of the Great Depression.

However, the doors of the Grand Old Lady were not to be closed for long. In 1937 an eccentric millionaire and erstwhile inventor, Norman Baker, purchased the aging hotel and converted it into a hospital.

Baker had made his money inventing various mechanical devices, including an organ powered by compressed air. While talented enough in his own area of expertise, Baker took it into his head that he was an expert in the field of medicine as well. He fancied he could invent a cure for dread diseases where all others had failed.

Devoting his fortune to this quest, Norman Baker first opened a hospital in Iowa, where he offered terminal patients "miracle" cures. Authorities in the state soon took a dim view of "Doctor" Baker's activities; he was convicted of practicing medicine without a license, and his hospital was shut down.

Undeterred by this setback, Baker moved to Arkansas and bought the Crescent Hotel, ultimately transforming it into a cancer hospital. Given Eureka Springs' longtime reputation for the curative powers of its spring waters, there was at least a certain amount of logic behind the move.

While renovating the hotel to serve as hospital, however, Baker made a number of changes, some quite bizarre. Much of the Crescent's elegant woodwork was ripped out and other sections were painted over in garish color schemes. Baker seemed particularly fond of the color purple, painting the entire lobby in that shade, and he decorated his penthouse apartment in varying hues of lavender.

Baker's private penthouse at the Crescent was also festooned with Tommy guns on the walls—which he kept for "self-defense" against a fancied surprise attack by the American Medical Association. Nor was this the self-proclaimed physician's only oddity: "Doctor" Baker also had secret passages installed within the walls of the Crescent that would provide for a quick getaway in case of a surprise all-out assault by agents of the AMA.

Baker boasted in his ads that he could cure cancer without surgery or "dangerous" x-rays. Although his "cure"—drinking pure mountain spring water—was for the most part harmless, Baker diverted many patients who were desperate for a quick cure away from legitimate doctors who may have been able to help them.

The federal government finally caught up with "Doctor" Baker and shut down his operation for good. Norman Baker was convicted of seven counts of mail fraud and was sentenced to Leavenworth prison, closing the most bizarre chapter in the hotel's history.

The Crescent reopened as a hotel in 1946, but sadly, time had taken its toll on the Grand Old Lady. For many years it was best described as "seedily elegant." One owner followed another, and while some made attempts to maintain the "Queen of the Ozarks," most preferred to exploit the hotel however they could to make a quick profit.

Over time, needed repairs were neglected and renovations to update the hotel were not performed. It was not until 1997 that new owners finally began to rescue the Grand Old Lady from decades of neglect.

A real estate executive from Connecticut and his wife, Martin and Elise Roenigk, were passing through Eureka Springs and fell in love with the quaint Victorian spirit of the place. On an impulse, the couple decided to get into the hotel business. It wasn't until they purchased the Crescent that they realized the place's "Victorian Spirit" included several of a decidedly spectral sort.

Under the Roenigks' management the hotel has undergone a major renovation. The face-lift included everything, from new crystal chandeliers in the grand ballroom to a room-by-room restoration of the interior decor. But through all of this, one thing hasn't changed at the Crescent: its ghosts.

The gaggle of ghosts that inhabit the hotel very much reflect its checkered past. The spectral guests of the Crescent, in fact, date to the hotel's very origins.

Perhaps the best-known ghostly guest, and by far the Crescent's oldest, is the one that inhabits Room 218, known as the "Haunted Room." Over the years numerous guests have reported strange happenings while staying there. Unusual sounds often emanate from the room, and guests frequently experience odd sensations while in it.

In Room 218 doors open and slam shut on their own; some who stay overnight there even swear they are shaken awake in the middle of the night. Other guests have reported seeing hands coming out of the bathroom mirror. Visitors have also heard cries, as of a man falling, that seem to come from the ceiling of the room.

When the hotel was being built, an Irish stonemason named Michael apparently was working on the high roof when he lost his balance and plummeted onto the open flooring of the second story far below. He landed in the exact spot where Room 218 would later be, and he died instantly.

Michael's spirit, it is thought, is the entity which spooks the visitors in that particular room. Michael is the most active of the hotel's ghosts, but he is by no means the only one.

A rather dapper gentleman has been known to haunt the bar area. Sporting a mustache and beard, and dressed in formal attire, the middle-aged gent from the Crescent's golden age seems quite at home there—and elsewhere in the hotel.

The same specter, dressed in a top hat, has been sighted on the main staircase leading down to the lobby, and in the grand ballroom as well. He is often seen on the stairs putting on an elegant pair of gloves—as if he were about to attend one of the balls that were held nightly in the Crystal Room during the 1880s. He also frequents the lobby itself.

Hotel employees have become used to his presence and have for years referred to him as the Victorian Gentleman. Recent research indicates that the description of the elegant gent seems to match that of Dr. Ellis, the hotel physician, who maintained an office in the Crescent during the late 1800s, in what is now Room 212. The good doctor evidently found the environment so congenial that he's never wanted to leave.

More tragic is the unnamed female ghost from the era when the hotel was used as a girls finishing school. It seems a young student fell—or was pushed—off a balcony and since her demise has been continually reliving her final moments at the hotel. When she appears to guests, she seems to be screaming as she falls backwards out of a window.

In 1987 a guest was walking down the corridor toward his upstairs room late one evening when he passed a woman, clad in a nurse's uniform, pushing a gurney down the hallway. This seemed a singular occurrence in itself; but the guest was shocked to see the nurse reach the wall at the end of the hall and walk right through it!

During the period the hotel was used as a cancer hospital, "Doctor" Baker gave orders that any of his cancer patients who died should not be removed from their rooms right away. The staff was to wait until after 11 P.M., when all the other patients were asleep, before taking the deceased to the morgue in the basement. Apparently the inventor-turned-physician didn't want his customers to know that his "miracle cure" was something less than miraculous.

The specter of the nurse with the gurney has also been seen by the hotel staff. Usually they spot her in the basement of the hotel, where Baker had set up his morgue. The autopsy table and walk-in freezer to store bodies are still there, adjacent to the laundry room. One janitor refused to go into the laundry ever again after seeing all the washing machines turn on by themselves in the middle of the night.

Some claim that Norman Baker himself haunts the Crescent. A man dressed in a purple shirt and a white linen suit has been sighted on several occasions in the lobby by staff and guests alike. The ghost wearing that unique color combination could only have been that of "Doctor" Baker.

Theodora was one of Baker's cancer patients. Now an active and quite vocal specter, she appears as a petite lady and is sometimes seen walking around in a robe. She makes her presence known invisibly as well, with the strong scent of her distinctive perfume. Theodora currently haunts Room 419, where guests on more than one occasion have returned to find their clothing strewn all about. Apparently, Theodora does not appreciate the company.

As part of a recent renovation, Room 419 was repainted in a new color scheme—green with star-shaped stenciling. A painter standing on a ladder while working on the stenciling heard a disembodied voice whisper in his ear, "I love what you're doing to my room."

Other rooms in the hotel can boast occasional encounters with the supernatural as well. One person recently photographed a ghost slouching in the closet of Room 202, for example. In fact, the Eureka Springs Ghost Tour, which now offers tours of the hotel and its supernatural inhabitants, even has a small library of ghost photos—many courtesy of Glenda Halpern—which depict gossamer-looking entities not only inside the Crescent but outside in its gardens as well.

Although the current owner, Elise Roenigk, protests that she is "not really into ghosts," even she has noticed that her Irish setter, Jazzy, behaves very oddly when in the hotel's north penthouse. Normally a very calm animal, he becomes extremely agitated in that space, refusing to be left alone in it. Could this be a sign of even more spectral residents?

Although the prospect of sharing a room with a ghost may seem daunting to some, to others, the elegance and Victorian charm of the Crescent Hotel are but secondary benefits to staying there. To those adventurous souls, traveling to Eureka Springs is often a pilgrimage in search of a supernatural encounter. And by staying in the much-vaunted, thoroughly haunted Crescent Hotel, they have a very good chance of attaining their heart's desire.

For information on booking reservations at the Crescent, you may call or write:

THE CRESCENT HOTEL
75 Prospect Avenue
Eureka Springs, AR 72632
(800) 342-9766
www.crescent-hotel.com

5

Fouke Lore

What a brave new world, to have such creatures in it.
—William Shakespeare, *The Tempest*

ARKANSAS, IT SEEMS, IS BLESSED with an abundance of odd and unusual creatures—only a few of which occupy political offices. There are the Growrow, the Highbehind, the White River Monster—and even a Wampus Cat or two; but certainly the most famous beast to stalk the hills and vales of Arkansas is the famed Fouke Monster.

Fouke is a small town in southwest Arkansas, just ten miles from Texarkana and a score or so miles north of the Louisiana border. It is a quiet farming area, located in a low-lying marshy part of the state.

This little whistle-stop of 615 souls attained national fame in May 1971, when some folks in Fouke had a terrifying run-in with a real life monster.

On the night of May 2 young Mrs. Ford was lying on a couch beneath a screened-in window, trying to catch an evening breeze and a little rest. Suddenly, her slumber was broken by a large, hairy hand thrusting through the screen.

The clawed hand was groping about, trying to grab the young woman. Mrs. Ford screamed in terror, arousing the attention of her husband, Bobby.

Rushing to his wife's assistance, Bobby Ford ran smack into a seven-foot-tall, red-eyed beast. As soon as he ran outside, Bobby was pulled to the ground. An unequal struggle ensued, and Bobby might easily have been fatally injured had he not managed to get free of the creature. Soon his brother Douglas came to his aid and drove off the creature.

The beast plunged into the undergrowth with the Ford brothers in pursuit. But the creature, whatever it was, gave them the slip.

Returning to the house, the Fords called the county sheriff, who soon arrived and began taking some notes. He also made a cast of some unusual footprints.

About an hour later, the creature returned to the Ford home. This time, the boys were ready and let loose with their squirrel guns at it. The creature high-tailed it into the undergrowth again—this time for good.

Later that night Bobby Ford was treated at the hospital in Texarkana for bruises, scratches, and symptoms of shock.

The incident at the Ford home created quite a stir in the local newspapers, but the monster mania really took off in Fouke when, a few weeks later, some other folks from Texarkana reported sighting a large, hairy beast in a soybean field on Highway 71, just outside of Fouke. Running across their line of sight, the travelers described it as being seven feet tall, stooped, and "able to run on two legs faster than a man." A plaster cast made of the strange footprints in the soybean field was said to be thirteen inches long. Other footprints found in the area were said to average some seventeen inches in length.

After this second run-in on May 23 with the Fouke Monster—as it was now called—reports of the creature started to mushroom. While the majority of the reports seem to have been genuine (if not always correct), at least one of them appears, judging by the evidence, to have been a case of some good ol' boys wanting to cash in on the phenomenon.

About a month later, in mid-June, three local residents reported another close encounter with the Monster. They had claw marks on their bodies, and there were three-toed footprints in a stand of trees where they supposedly encountered the beast.

But the sheriff began to smell a rat when he noticed the victims had traces of blood under their fingernails. Moreover, they reported the creature as being only four feet tall, a description that did not jibe with previous eyewitness reports.

The sheriff called in an anthropologist from Southern State College, Frank Schambach, to examine the new footprints. The fact that the footprints were three-toed should have been a dead giveaway from the start, since the creature was described as looking semi-human or gorilla-like.

After careful analysis, the anthropologist declared he was "ninety-nine percent sure" the footprints were a hoax. That was enough for Sheriff Leslie Greer. The three rustics were charged with filing a false report and were convicted and fined.

The Miller County sheriff and his deputies had been run ragged chasing down various reports of sightings for several weeks, and local farmers were now beginning to complain about trespassers tearing up their crops and doing other damage. To put a stop to such occurrences, Greer let it be known that he would arrest all would-be monster hunters he found.

However, despite the hoaxers and the skeptics, the Fouke Monster would not go so easily into that good night. All the sheriff's warning did was to discourage people from filing reports. The sightings continued, but the folks around Fouke simply kept mum about what they had seen.

One local businessman, however, decided the Fouke Monster would make a Jim-dandy subject for a movie. In January 1972 Charles Pierce of Texarkana announced he was producing a film on the monster. He recruited a cast of mostly local residents, and much of the film was shot on the locations where many of the events had taken place.

Pierce told the local newspaper that he would not be at all surprised if his magnum opus, budgeted at a whopping $160,000, was even nominated for an Academy Award or two. The resulting film—*The Legend of Boggy Creek*—did not win any awards, but it quickly became a mainstay of rural drive-ins throughout the South. It has even aired on television—albeit as a campy creature feature on the syndicated *Mystery Science Theater 3000*.

In 1973 the Right Honorable J. D. Larey, mayor of Fouke, expressed regret that folks there had not made the most of their brief fame. No one had opened a Fouke Monster Gift Shop or similar enterprise. Nevertheless, a few locals have made a dollar or two giving city slickers tours of the places in town connected with the incidents.

Today, about the only place in town a person can get a handle on the Fouke Monster phenomenon is at the Monster Mart, a local convenience store run by longtime resident Rickie Roberts.

Located along Highway 71, the Monster Mart boasts a large road sign with the Fouke Monster (with a serious overbite) astride the state's favorite mascot—a red razorback hog (also with a serious overbite). Roberts and his wife, Beverly, sell a range of monster memorabilia, and they can also update the curious on the creature's current doings.

Although the Fouke Monster is no longer a hot media item—or at least not so much as in the early seventies—that is not to say he hasn't been active.

In July 1977 a Miller County farmer's pig pen was raided by a large creature. Five hundred yards from the pen, the farmer found his animals mutilated, and tracks led back into the swamp. Also, two dogs belonging to neighbors were killed, and every bone in their bodies was broken. Although the swamp creature was not sighted, there was little doubt this was his handiwork.

In 1978 there was a spate of monster sightings in southwest Arkansas, although not specifically in Fouke. There were also encounters in Fouke during this period, but the incidents weren't reported until much later.

In 1979, for example, young Tracy Wilson saw the Fouke Monster while she was playing in her yard. The creature approached to within thirty yards of her, at which point Tracy carefully walked back into her house, locked the doors and windows, and waited till her mother returned.

Tracey's childhood encounter was hardly unique. Just about everyone in Miller County has a friend or relative who has sighted the creature at one time or another, if they haven't actually encountered it themselves.

In 1997 there were some forty sightings, according to unofficial Fouke Monster spokesman Roberts. Nowadays, however, most people in Fouke tend to keep such information to themselves.

While the local sheriff's office today may be less hostile to taking monster reports than it was in the early seventies, people are still reluctant to come forward with their stories, fearing public ridicule in the media. So long as the monster doesn't bother them or their livestock, the general attitude seems to be one of live and let live.

Experts, of course, have pronounced the Fouke Monster a hoax, insisting that no such creature roams the swamps and woodlands around Fouke, Arkansas. Everything that cannot be dismissed as fake, the scientific community has declared, is either a misidentification of a black bear, or a "popular delusion of the masses."

In support of the mainstream scientist's view is Professor Schambach's 1971 exposé of the pigmy monster cast as phony. However, that particular sighting was recognized from the beginning as suspect—which is why an anthropologist was called in. In fact, there was other, more trustworthy evidence of the creature's existence. One cast, stored at a local gas station, was destroyed in a fire; another cast, taken by the county sheriff, has been reported missing from his office. While these casts are lost to us now, there was nothing about them to suggest fakery.

Beyond this, however, is the fact that the Fouke Monster did not just appear out of blue sky in 1971. The first reports of sightings published in the media date back to the 1930s and forties. Over the last few years people in the small community of Fouke, people with a solid reputation for honesty and sobriety have seen the creature—often at close range—and for the most part their descriptions are consistent, not only from one witness to another but also in relation to reports of similar creatures emanating from other parts of the country.

A large, hairy creature, seven to ten feet tall, ape-like in appearance but with a human-looking face, making strange high-pitched sounds, and with an odor that would make a skunk wince—these are all characteristics of what is generally known as Bigfoot.

Over the years most Bigfoot sightings reported in the popular press have primarily come from the Pacific Northwest. But there have been many sightings of it (or him) throughout Dixie dating back as far as anyone can remember. For example, a colonist of Jamestown, Virginia, in the 1600s, citing reports of survivors of the "Lost Roanoke" colony, describes the inhabitants there as surviving on "wild turkeys *and mountain apes.*"

Traditionally, most reports of Bigfoot in the South—as in the Pacific Northwest—generally seem to come from upland regions. However, some encounters—as at Fouke—seem to cluster around low-lying swampy areas.

John Keel, legendary journalist of things weird and wonderful, describes this type of Bigfoot as an "Abominable Swamp Slob." From the swamps of Florida and Georgia to the Delta regions of Louisiana, various half-ape, half-human-looking creatures have been reported. The creature at Fouke is notable for the duration and frequency of the sightings linked to it. Elsewhere, such creatures mostly seem to avoid human contact, only venturing into human settlements when driven by hunger or, perhaps, lack of female companionship.

Aside from the more famous incidents of 1971, the majority of encounters with the Fouke Monster have been relatively pacific and thus have attracted little media attention outside the local area. But there have been encounters—and there still are.

Despite the abundant eyewitness confirmations of the Fouke creature's existence, anthropologists have long since dismissed the "monster" as a hoax. Often it is easier for scholars to ignore uncomfortable facts than to allow them to upset long-held, well-established academic dogma.

It is one of the pat assumptions of modern biology that there are no new living large-mammal species left to discover. That these animals may be better at avoiding contact with humans than scientists are willing to give them credit for is a possibility most scientists seem reluctant to consider.

Just a few years ago, a large four-footed animal—sporting a set of gills, no less—was captured in the jungles of Southeast Asia. Local tribes had had knowledge of this creature for years, yet scientists long ago dismissed it as a myth—"mere" folklore.

In Fouke, Arkansas, the local residents have more or less come to terms with the "monster" in their midst. Some folks thereabouts even take a certain pride that their community is the hometown of such a beast.

It can't be denied that, occasionally, some good ol' boys have taken advantage of Warren County's main claim to fame. But the fact that something strange dwells around the swamps of "Boggy Creek" is a truth which cannot be refuted—even if scientists still dismiss it as just so much Fouke lore.

There is not a heck of a lot to see in Warren County for travelers in search of the monster, and it is not advisable to go stomping about the countryside without permission of property owners. However, for the price of a sweet tea and a Little Debbie snack cake, I'll wager you are likely to get an earful about the Fouke Monster at:

PEAVEY'S MONSTER MART
104 North Monster Expressway (Highway 71)
Fouke, Arkansas, 71837
(870) 653-2497

(Fouke is 15 miles southeast of Texarkana.)

6

The Day the Devil
Came Down to Arkansas

NOWADAYS IT IS UNFASHIONABLE to believe in the Devil. Indeed, in some circles, you will find folks who scoff at the very notion of evil as a force in the world. A person is misunderstood, had a bad childhood, didn't know what he was doing—or maybe he just had a bad hair day. But no one is truly evil or commits evil acts.

There is something comforting in such disbelief; if there is no objective evil or good, then morality is just one's personal opinion and we do not have to worry at all about a malignant force seeking to ruin souls. But down in Arkansas, they know differently. For the Devil has been known to show himself in person there, and when he comes a-visiting, you'd best beware.

Vance Randolph, the sometimes humorist and folklorist, and an expert on the occult in the Ozarks, met a man back in the 1930s who had encountered the Devil. The old farmer had run into the demon while walking in the snow in northern Arkansas along the Missouri border.

The Devil outwardly looked just like any other good ol' country boy: bedecked in blue denim coveralls and an old slouch hat, with a thin face, long stringy hair, and a shotgun on his shoulder. But there was one telltale difference that the wise old farmer picked up on: the man cast no shadow, and after he passed, he left no footprints in the dirt. The Devil does not always wear horns or a tail.

The best-known visitation of His Satanic Majesty in Arkansas, however, happened many years ago, before statehood, when Arkansas was the edge of the frontier.

On May 25, 1784, two young men, John Chesselden and James Arkins, set out from the settlement of Kenfry to visit an old friend some twenty-five miles away. Kenfry was a small settlement in northeastern Arkansas, near to the Mississippi River. Their friend's home lay on the other side of a patch of forest called Varnum's Wood.

Leaving about eight in the morning, the two men hoped that if they kept a good pace, they might reach their friend's house before dark.

They had not gone far before Arkins started up a conversation about a strange incident that had occurred in Varnum's Wood a few months before. It seems a man named Isaac King claimed that while passing through the forest he had encountered a demon without a head or arms, and that King had barely escaped alive.

Arkins made light of the tale, saying that King ought to be driven out of civilized society for spouting such nonsense. Getting carried away with his own rhetoric, Arkins went on to brag that he *defied* the Devil to appear. Jim bragged that not all the devils inhabiting the inner regions of hell could intimidate him.

Arkins's talk made Chesselden nervous, and John upbraided his friend. Even though King may have imagined the whole affair, he said, he nevertheless believed that it was indeed possible for the Devil to appear to mortal men.

Arkins, however, was on a roll. He bragged that "if there ever appeared a devil or any spirit unto men while on earth, I desire that I might, in passing this wood, have one of them for a guest."

There's an old saying that if you speak of the Devil, he will soon appear. Another old saw warns, be careful what you wish for; you just may get it. Apparently Jim had never heard either.

The two young men had not gone more than two miles when they forded a shallow stream, at which point they decided to take a break. As they were resting, they noticed a commotion in the bushes ahead.

They supposed it to be porcupines or some other woodland animal rustling the leaves. They sat a while to see what would emerge from the brush, but when nothing was forthcoming, John and James walked on ahead to meet it.

A quarter of a mile farther on, the two came to a small rise from which they could see a large clump of bushes from which the rustling seemed to come.

They were almost on top of the bushes when there suddenly issued forth a cloud of smoke, "as large as that from the mouth of a cannon," and a beast appeared. It was as large as a moose but "with the most tremendous and hideous aspect," almost like a lion.

Its eyes appeared to be living fire, while its mouth belched forth smoke. The apparition reared up to its full height in front of the terrified duo, and as it did it changed form.

The two men sank to the ground, insensible with fear. When Chesselden came around, the monster was scarcely three yards away, floating horizontally about eight feet above the ground. By now the demon had assumed human shape—but lacked head and hands.

Arkins, recovering, sprang up and called on God to preserve them from harm. At this, the demon moved to confront Arkins directly. The being began a series of maneuvers to harass John and James, who were too terrified to move from the spot.

This went on until early afternoon, at which time the pair realized that darkness would soon be falling, and they feared what would happen to them after dark. John and James resolved to make their escape and would try to return to their settlement, only a few miles distant.

When they moved to escape, the demon—which now had a head and hands and was dressed in the most dazzling of garments—proceeded to follow them. The being now adopted a more conciliatory attitude, asking in pleasant tones, "Why do you hurry yourselves, friends? I will shortly be your companion and will attend you where you please."

Then the demon bade them to "come young friends, walk as I do," and upon saying that, he proceeded to walk three feet above the surface of the stream, accompanying them as they made their way closer to home.

When they were almost home the Devil told the two they "got to go a little way" with him, adding that he would show them several cities, elegantly adorned, and "many pleasant dwelling places" where he thought they would want to live *permanently*.

Chesselden tried to beg off diplomatically, saying, "My business being of such a nature, it renders it impossible for me to attend you to this delightsome dwelling place."

At this, however, the demon became violent, grabbing Arkins by the hair and yanking half of it out by the roots and wounding him in various parts of his body. They were still four miles from home, and night was fast approaching. Arkins was badly wounded, and Chesselden despaired that they would ever be able to escape the demon's clutches. Not knowing what else to do, he fell to his knees and began praying to heaven for relief—and the Devil then disappeared. Not waiting for the demon to return, John picked up his friend, put him on his back, and returned to Kenfry by about eight o'clock that night.

The next morning the two related to the good folk of Kenfry all that had happened. Their friends spread the word about their encounter, and soon a crowd numbering nearly two hundred assembled. While many townspeople were disposed to believe the two young men, some were still dubious. So, John and James led a deputation four miles out of town, where the demon had moved a giant boulder at least twelve feet—something no two men could have done on their own, Then, too, there was James Arkins's bruised and bloody countenance as visible proof.

There were, of course, those who thought the whole thing had been made up—that the boys had gotten hold of some bad whiskey and had hallucinated it all. But the physical evidence was real enough. James Arkins, whose bragging had brought forth the demon, repented his ways, and John Chesselden did, too.

To this day the tale of the day the Devil visited Arkansas is still told. And as they used to say around the courthouse square, if that isn't the gospel truth, then God bless the Devil!

If you go ...

More haints and haunts of Dixie to see in Arkansas:

ARKADELPHIA
HENDERSON STATE UNIVERSITY
1100 Henderson Street
Arkadelphia, AR 171999-0881
(870) 230-5000
www.hsu.edu

A "Lady in Black" haunts the campus, most often seen during homecoming week.

HOT SPRINGS
THE MALCO THEATRE
817 Central Avenue
Hot Springs, AR 71901
(501) 623-6200

In 1888, a woman disappeared on stage during a stage magician's performance and was never seen again. Since then, a female ghost has haunted the basement and objects have been seen to move on their own.

LITTLE ROCK
THE OLD STATE HOUSE
300 West Markham Street
Little Rock, AR,72201
(501) 324-9685
www.oldstatehouse.com

Now a history museum, in the nineteenth century an irate legislator stabbed a fellow politician to death; the murderer's ghost regularly returns to the scene of the crime.

Arkansas Ghost Tours

EUREKA SPRINGS
EUREKA SPRINGS GHOST TOURS
P.O. Box 189
Eureka Springs, AR 72632
(479) 253-6800

HOT SPRINGS
HOT SPRINGS GHOST TOUR
Nightly
(501) 538-4535
www.hotspringsghosttour.com

7

The Barnsley Curse

N O ONE IS QUITE SURE how it all started. Perhaps it began when God-frey Barnsley chose to build a mansion for his family atop an ancient Indian burial mound. The mound, it was rumored, contained the remains of a powerful medicine man.

Godfrey, with nearly four thousand acres of land to chose from, picked a scenic knoll on which to build his home. In so doing, he ignored the local tradition that the Cherokee held the mound sacred—that the spirits entombed there would wreak vengeance on any who dared defile the taboo tumulus.

In many ways, Godfrey Barnsley had led a charmed life in the years before he moved to north Georgia. Coming to America from Britain at the age of eighteen without a penny to his name, Godfrey became involved in the cotton business and within a few short years had amassed a fortune.

It was the heyday of King Cotton, and Godfrey Barnsley's astute business sense and knowledge of the British textile market were amply rewarded. The textile mills of England were hungry for raw material, and the sprawling plantations of the deep South were eager to open new markets for the white gold they grew. As a cotton factor, Barnsley bought, sold, and shipped cotton, connecting sellers with buyers all over the world.

Godfrey's English accent and courtly manners also went over well in polite society. This, combined with his enterprise and business acumen, gave Godfrey entrée into the upper echelons of Savannah society in the 1820s—something no amount of money or ability could have bought him in the rigid class structure of aristocratic England.

Godfrey Barnsley's star was on the rise when he met Julia Henrietta Scarborough. She was the daughter of a wealthy Savannah shipping magnate, beautiful, charming, and elegant. If there is such a thing as love at first sight, then surely the romance between Julia and Godfrey was it.

Julia and Godfrey's whirlwind courtship and marriage were the talk of Savannah's social season in 1828. Not even her domineering mother could dampen the ardor of Julia's love for Godfrey, and in the end all her parents could do was bow to the inevitable. Her father, at least, might console himself with the knowledge that he was not so much losing a daughter as gaining a successful cotton broker.

For the first two years of their marriage the couple lived abroad in England, where Godfrey kept busy building his cotton business. But the damp climate didn't agree with Julia, and in 1830 they returned to Savannah.

Renewing his contacts in that thriving port, Godfrey's enterprise flourished as never before. Even though a financial "panic" hurt Barnsley's business, with Julia's love and encouragement he rebuilt his fortune bigger than before.

Seeking a healthier climate for his wife and growing family, as well as wishing to create a proper showcase to display his wealth, Godfrey purchased a huge tract of land in the Appalachian foothills of north Georgia. It was still largely wilderness, only lately vacated—at gunpoint—by the Cherokee.

Godfrey wanted to create a plantation in this wilderness along the lines of the great manors of the British aristocracy. He resolved to spare no effort to provide an earthly garden of delights for his wife and their burgeoning family.

This was the very heart of the ancestral Cherokee homeland, and as such it was venerated by the entire Cherokee nation. Family tradition holds that when Godfrey first visited the area in 1838, he encountered an old Cherokee medicine man still residing on the property. Somehow, the ancient one had evaded the sweeps by Federal soldiers who had already rounded up all the others of his clan and sent them west.

Godfrey, taking pity on the old man, took him on as caretaker so he could continue to reside on the land of his forefathers. The white-haired old native, however, warned Barnsley that the site was hallowed ground and ought never be desecrated.

Godfrey thought nothing of the warning. In 1841, however, as work on the mansion began, the wizened native, having learned that Godfrey was about to build atop the old acorn-shaped mound on the grounds, grew greatly agitated.

The mound was sacred ground, the old man declared—a holy place held sacred by the Great Spirit. Barnsley must inevitably incur the wrath of the Cherokee ancestors and the Great Spirit if he persisted in building there, the medicine man warned.

Barnsley had humored the old man in many things, but in this matter Godfrey remained firm. The Englishman had plans for his estate, and the mound was the ideal spot for Godfrey to build his family's new home.

The old Indian, livid with rage at Barnsley's attitude, laid a curse on Godfrey and his family. Whosoever resided in the house built over holy ground would know nothing but tragedy and loss, he intoned.

The next day, the old native disappeared without a trace, never to be seen or heard from again.

In light of what would later befall the Barnsley family, it may well be that the old Cherokee was not quite what he seemed. He was old, to be sure; his copper skin was creased with a thousand wrinkles, and his bones were stiff and his body infirm. But the power of a medicine man is limited by neither age nor physical state. The old medicine man may well have remained behind to guard a place sacred to his ancestors.

Godfrey, a believer in progress and modern ideas, did not take the man's words seriously. Moreover, between managing his thriving cotton business and overseeing the construction of his opulent manor, Godfrey's hands were full with more practical affairs and he quickly put the incident out of his mind.

So Godfrey and Julia watched with pride and anticipation as the thick brick walls of their Italianate villa rose higher and higher atop the acorn-shaped knoll, majestic with its grand panorama of the Georgia hill country.

Godfrey had planned every aspect of the house, from indoor plumbing with hot and cold running water (virtually unheard of at the time) to a thermally powered rotisserie oven. Imported woods and tiles, antique furniture, and custom-made appliances also graced the interior. Godfrey spared no expense to make it the grandest showplace in the South.

But it was to the gardens surrounding the house that Julia devoted most of her care and attention, and Godfrey was eager to indulge her every desire.

Every known variety of rose was planted in the rose garden, and exotic foliage from around the world was imported to decorate the grounds. Along the circular drive leading to the main entrance a formal boxwood garden was laid out in elaborate geometric designs. There was also a rock garden, croquet grounds, a sunken garden, a pond stocked with oriental fish, and even a deer park. Godfrey spared no expense to transform the north Georgia wilderness into a Garden of Eden for his beloved Julia.

As he had hoped, the fresh mountain air of the region was a great improvement over Savannah's muggy malarial summers. But Woodland Manor was far from Barnsley's business interests, and he was often absent for long periods of time. While the summers were milder, the winters were both cold and rainy there, aggravating Julia's delicate constitution.

Then, in the fall of 1844, Julia fell ill—seriously ill. Godfrey was away on a long business trip, and Julia had to be moved to Savannah where physicians and family could care for her. Despite constant care, Julia's condition worsened, and she lingered until February 1845.

Godfrey was stunned and heartbroken—doubly so because he had not been able to be by her side. His grief was compounded when their newborn child also died.

Barnsley's mansion and gardens were still unfinished at the time of Julia's death, and for a time Godfrey abandoned all work on the estate. Inconsolable, all he could think to do was immerse himself into his far-flung business enterprises.

Then, on a visit to Mobile, Alabama, out of idle curiosity, Godfrey attended a séance. The occult ritual had been devised by three sisters from upstate New York in the early 1840s as a way to communicate with a restless spirit haunting their home. The séance became a popular pastime and was soon a widespread form of parlor entertainment in America. However, for those who had lost a loved one—like Godfrey—the séance seemed a way to assuage their grief and maintain contact with the departed. To Barnsley, it seemed a godsend.

The medium in Mobile convinced Godfrey that he could put the wealthy merchant in touch with his lost love. Barnsley, united with Julia once again—if only in spirit—had found a reason to continue living.

Julia's spirit indicated to Godfrey in one séance that she wished to see their home and gardens finished. Completing Woodlands soon became an obsession with Godfrey—an obsession which his children would also come to share. Whenever his duties would allow, Godfrey returned home to oversee every little detail of the construction.

When she was alive, Julia had put her heart and soul into landscaping the elaborate gardens. Here, in these same gardens, Godfrey now felt closest to his dead wife. He would often sit in the boxwood garden, surrounded by the flowers Julia had loved so much, meditating and remembering.

While in this garden so fragrant with memories, Barnsley soon found that he had no need for mediums or séances to contact his dead wife. One night in 1846, as Godfrey walked through the boxwood garden, he found he was no longer alone. Julia appeared to him. More than that, she conversed with him, the two talking together in the garden much as they had done when she was alive.

Julia's apparition soon became a regular visitor. Almost every night Godfrey would walk with her in the boxwood garden, talking with her about the day's events.

Oftentimes, Godfrey gave workmen building his home instructions based on what his wife had told him the night before. Barnsley even claimed that he received a ghostly letter through the mail from Julia.

If Godfrey's passing on directions from his dead wife seemed a trifle odd, the locals could chalk it up to the peculiarities of an eccentric Englishman. But when Barnsley's second daughter, Adelaide, died just a year after marrying, gossip about an Indian curse on the family and estate was revived.

As the Civil War approached, Woodlands Manor was almost complete. The dream Godfrey and Julia had shared so many years before was nearly a reality.

Indeed, at its height Woodlands was a breathtaking sight to behold. Godfrey had gradually acquired surrounding property, until the plantation encompassed nearly ten thousand acres. The estate—commonly referred to by locals now as simply Barnsley's Gardens—became renowned throughout Georgia and the South for its beauty and elegance. Even into the twentieth century, long after its prime, its fame was such that when Margaret Mitchell wrote her epic novel *Gone With the Wind*, she modeled the fictional Tara on Woodlands Manor. Her dashing leading man, Rhett Butler, she patterned after the passionate but cultured Godfrey Barnsley.

But even as Barnsley's long sought-after earthly fulfillment seemed to be within his grasp, fate once again intruded to shatter his dreams.

First, his oldest son, Howard, was murdered by pirates as he was returning aboard a China clipper from an overseas business trip on behalf of his father.

The Civil War was under way when the news of Howard's death reached Barnsley. Although he opposed secession, Godfrey was loyal to his adopted land. He bought Confederate war bonds and donated his merchant fleet to the Confederate Navy, even as his cotton exporting business began to shrivel up and die due to the Yankee naval blockade.

In 1864, when General Sherman began his infamous March to the Sea, Barnsley's estate lay directly in the path of the marauding invaders. Godfrey raised the Union Jack over his estate and claimed neutrality; but someone betrayed him to the Yankees, telling them of Barnsley's two sons in the secessionist army and his large contributions to the Rebel cause. Even though Union General McPherson gave orders not to pillage the estate, foraging troops that followed in his wake showed no respect for private property or civil rights.

Yankee troops looted the Barnsley estate at will, stripping it of nearly everything of value. And what they did not steal they vandalized or destroyed, going so far as to trample the imported roses in the rose garden and smash rare crystal and china.

About this time a close friend of the family, Colonel Earle, was killed near the house in a skirmish with Union troops. His body, riddled with bullets, was buried on the terrace behind the house, beneath one of its windows. Some say he, too, was a victim of the Barnsley Curse.

While the end of the war saw an end to the pillaging of Woodland Manor and the partial destruction of Barnsley Gardens, it also spelled the end of the Barnsley fortune. Godfrey Barnsley tried desperately to revive his cotton business, but the carpetbaggers who descended on the South after the war like a plague of locusts made honest enterprise almost impossible. In 1873 Godfrey Barnsley died in poverty, still clinging to dreams of restoring his beloved estate to its former glory.

Even in death, however, the Barnsley Curse still worked against Godfrey. One dark night Godfrey's grave was dug up and his corpse was mutilated.

Godfrey and Julia Barnsley's surviving children not only inherited Woodlands, they also inherited Godfrey's obsession with the plantation. The Barnsley children also inherited the Barnsley Curse and an ever-growing number of ghosts.

In 1906 the main part of the mansion was devastated by a tornado which tore off its roof. Members of the family still residing there were forced to move into the surviving wing, and the main building remained an empty shell. Woodlands mansion—like the Barnsley fortune—was literally gone with the wind.

One of Godfrey Barnsley's granddaughters, Adelaide, married a man named Saylor. As with other family members, however, Addie was fated to experience sorrow and loss. Her husband died after just a few years of marriage, leaving her a widow with two young boys to raise.

The sons, Harry and Preston, were raised on the Barnsley estate and cut their teeth on tales of the Woodlands' former glory. And as they grew into manhood, they in turn became filled with the family ambition of restoring the gardens and mansion.

Preston Saylor gained renown as a heavyweight boxer, fighting under the name K. O. Dugan. Preston dreamed of using his winnings to finally restore Barnsley Gardens and the mansion.

However, once again fate played a cruel trick on the family. The blows Preston received in the ring began to cause brain damage. His injuries not only put an early end to his prizefighting career, they also caused Preston to be put away in a mental asylum in Milledgeville, Georgia.

In his dementia, Preston developed the delusion that his brother Harry was trying to steal his portion of the Barnsley estate. Slipping away from the asylum one night, Preston returned to Barnsley Gardens and, gun in hand, began shooting wildly at his brother.

Although Harry tried to flee, the hail of bullets found its mark. By the time Preston was restrained, it was already too late. Harry died in his mother Addie's arms. One more spirit was added to the roster residing at Barnsley Gardens.

Like her grandfather, Addie often caught sight of grandmother Julia in the boxwood garden. But Addie was also aware of her grandfather's presence at the estate.

Addie frequently heard sounds coming from the library—as if Godfrey were still at work. She recognized the scraping sound of her grandfather's chair pushing away from his large writing desk—a familiar sound from childhood. Addie could also hear the ghostly laughter of deceased Barnsley children playing in the now ruined main wing of the mansion.

Out behind the house, Addie on occasion heard the sounds of hoofbeats and of men cursing and shouting, as if in battle. Colonel Earle's ghost was also a permanent resident of Barnsley Gardens.

After his death in 1935 Addie's son Harry remained on the estate in spectral form. Adelaide claimed Harry's ghost came to her regularly and they held long conversations together, much as her grandfather had done with grandmother's ghost.

Some regarded Addie as an eccentric, to be sure. But there are substantial indications that these spectral doings at Barnsley Gardens were considerably more than just widow Saylor's imagination.

In late November 1941, for example, Addie told an Atlanta columnist that the spirit of her son had warned her of an imminent attack on the American Pacific Fleet. The syndicated column reporting this prediction ran nationally on November 30, 1941. However, most newspaper editors deleted that part of Colonel Spencer's column containing Harry Saylor's ghostly warning. The newspapers considered Harry's prophecy too scurrilous for any respectable newspaper to print. The next week the Japanese bombed the Pacific Fleet at Pearl Harbor.

Over the years, the Barnsley family was forced to sell off various parcels of their 10,000-acre estate, just to maintain themselves on the remaining property. But Adelaide stubbornly held onto the remaining gardens and ruined mansion. When Addie died, however, her heirs

were forced to auction off the estate and with it the last of the Barnsley heirlooms and other possessions. And so Barnsley Gardens passed
at last out of the family.

For the next two score years and more, the Barnsley property was
used solely for commercial agriculture by area farmers. The old manor
house and gardens succumbed to neglect and became overgrown with
brambles and vines. The empty brick shell of Woodlands mansion
took on the aspect of a medieval ruin and was in fact commonly
referred to as "the Castle" by locals.

As in a fairy tale, Barnsley Gardens seemed to have fallen under an
enchantment, its only residents the ghosts of ages past. The old Indian
curse had triumphed at last over the hopes and dreams of generations
of the Barnsley clan. At least so it seemed.

However, like the enchanted castle of Sleeping Beauty, after lying in
a state of disrepair for many years the dormant Barnsley Gardens was
brought back to life when a prince arrived to break the spell.

By 1988 little was left of Godfrey and Julia's dream. Somehow,
though, Prince Hubertus Fugger Babenhausen saw beyond the decaying eaves and weed-choked gardens, instead envisioning what Godfrey Barnsley had once seen. Prince Fugger bought Woodlands, resolv-
ing to not only restore Barnsley Gardens to its former glory but also to
finish Godfrey's master plan—and perhaps even add to it.

Using Godfrey's own notes, drawings, and other records, Prince
Fugger brought the estate back from the edge of oblivion. By 1992
Barnsley Gardens was opened to the public so that all might enjoy its
beauty and enchantment.

Prince Fugger spared no expense in his efforts and even imported
180 varieties of heirloom roses, as Godfrey had done. The surviving
right wing of the old mansion was restored and converted into a
museum, while the gutted brick tower was stabilized and preserved.
Greenways and footpaths were created throughout the grounds, show-
casing scores of exotic plants and trees that Godfrey—and the
Prince—had brought from all over the world.

In addition, a golf course, spa, riding stables, restaurants, and Vic-
torian-style guest cottages were built on the sprawling estate. As a nod
to the Prince's homeland, a Bavarian beer garden was added—and
more improvements were planned. All this was well and good, one
may say; but what of the Barnsley Curse?

Although Prince Fugger was obviously a practical businessman as well as a lover of beauty, he was also wise enough not to tempt fate. Bavaria, too, has its fair share of haunted castles and hereditary curses; thus, armed with knowledge of the Barnsley Curse, Prince Fugger chose the better part of valor before embarking on his extensive restoration of Barnsley Gardens.

The prince engaged the services of two Cherokee medicine men to remove the ancient curse from the estate. One medicine man was of the Eastern Band of the Cherokee, now residing in North Carolina; the other came from the western branch, now living in Oklahoma. As the two shamans performed the Eagle Dance, they petitioned the Great Spirit to bring peace and harmony to Barnsley Gardens and all who reside there, and to lift any curse that may have been laid upon that land.

Since the visit of the Cherokee shamans, the shadow over Barnsley Gardens seems to have disappeared for good. But while the curse may be gone, the ghosts remain, for nothing—not even death—can separate Julia and Godfrey from their earthly paradise.

BARNSLEY GARDENS RESORT
597 Barnsley Gardens Road
Adairsville, GA 30103
(877) 773-2447
www.barnsleyresort.com

The old manor house is now known as "The Ruin" and what's left operates as a museum. The resort offers a "garden tour" of the haunted mansion grounds.

8

Savannah Specters

SINCE THE FOUNDING OF GEORGIA in Oglethorpe's day, the port of Savannah has served as a meeting of the ways, a place where people from different worlds could mingle. It is a place where Native Americans met Englishmen; where sailors from the world over gained their first glimpse of Dixie, and also where notorious pirates met respected merchants to conspire. Today, sedate and civilized Savannah is still a meeting place—one where the mortal and supernatural realms meet. In truth, this distinctive Southern city is one of the most haunted cities in the world.

A favorite haunt during buccaneer days was the aptly named Pirate's House Inn. Once the abode of cutthroats, smugglers, and scoundrels, the inn today caters to a more refined clientele.

The Pirate's House may be the oldest surviving building in the entire state of Georgia. Parts of it date back to 1734, scarcely a year after the colony was founded—although it has been expanded over the centuries.

If local tradition is to be believed, the list of the inn's former guests reads like a who's who of the pirate world. Jean Lafitte was reputed to have lived there for a spell, and the infamous Blackbeard may have paid a visit or two to the old tavern as well. But the scoundrel with the closest connection to Pirate's House is the storied pirate Captain Flint.

It's said that the grizzled old buccaneer passed his last days at Pirate's House. Supposedly, as Flint lay near death he bellowed to his first mate, "Get me one more cup of rum, Mr. McGraw!" The inn's Captain's Room was named after him. Apparently Robert Louis Stevenson heard stories about the tavern and Captain Flint, and used them as the basis for his fictional English tavern in *Treasure Island*. But Captain Flint and the tavern were real enough—and so are the ghosts that inhabit the Pirate's House.

Waiters and other restaurant staff say they frequently hear phantom voices throughout the old inn. The Captain's Room seems a particularly active area for supernatural phenomena.

Voices are also often heard wafting up from an old smuggler's tunnel beneath the Captain's Room. One venturesome visitor who went into the tunnel even claimed to have encountered the shades of Flint and his cutthroat crew.

Other spots in the rambling building—such as the attic and "Hideaway No. 4"—are also said to be rife with ghosts.

Another phantom closely connected with the sea, but of a far more benign nature, is "the Waving Girl."

For many years, the Elba Island Lighthouse at the entrance to Savannah harbor guided ships to a safe anchorage. And for almost forty-four years, during the late-nineteenth and early twentieth centuries, Florence Martus was as familiar a sight to sailors returning to port as was the great light kept by her brother.

For nearly four and a half decades Florence greeted each passing ship by waving her white apron in welcome to sailors returning home from the sea. At night she would wave a lantern at the passing vessels. For lonely sailors returning to port after a long voyage, Florence's greeting was a welcome sight, and it earned her the title "Sweetheart of Mankind."

But behind Florence's friendly greeting lay a tragic love affair. When she was younger, Florence had fallen in love with a sailor who sailed into port one day and during a whirlwind romance promised her the sun, the moon, and the stars if only she would be his wife. He vowed they would wed when next he returned from the sea, and she promised to wait for him.

Florence anxiously awaited his return, and since she did not know upon which ship he would be sailing, she would greet every vessel that passed the lighthouse, hoping that it would be the one bringing her true love back to her.

But her fiancé never returned. Whether he was lost at sea or married someone else is not known. But Florence, faithful to her parting promise to him, continued to wave at every ship. She kept her vigil until the day in 1931 that her brother retired as keeper of the Elba Lighthouse. Florence and her brother then moved to town, and she lived a quiet life in Savannah—well loved—until her death in 1943.

But a curious thing happened after they laid Florence Martus to rest. Sailors passing the lighthouse claimed the "Waving Girl" still greeted them as she had done for so many years. Many said they could see Florence, clad in a calico dress and waving her white apron in welcome, her faithful dog by her side.

At first people in town did not believe the sailors' stories, but soon local yachtsmen began to see her as well. Others said there were nights when they could see a light like that of a lantern signaling from the now-deserted island.

A statue depicting Florence greeting the ships was erected by the city along Savannah's riverfront in 1971. But there really was no need to build a reminder of Florence—for her ghost continues to greet wayfarers returning home from the sea.

Not all of Savannah's ghosts look toward the sea. Juliette Gordon Low, founder of the Girl Scouts, was born in Savannah, and her birthplace is now a historical site open to the public. It is also certified as a haunted house.

The house, built in 1819 for a Supreme Court justice, is comfortable and capacious. Sarah Gordon, Juliette Low's grandmother, lived there for a number of years with her son and daughter-in-law, William Washington Gordon II and Ellie Kinzie Gordon.

The two ladies apparently got along famously, and the spacious Gordon house at 142 Bull Street suited all three quite well—so well, in fact, that the two women have never really left.

Ellie and Sarah, it seems, tend to fuss over various items around the house, going so far as to sometimes rearrange furniture to suit their fancy. At other times, one of the two spectral ladies plays the piano.

There are also reports of a ghost sliding down the stairway banister after the house museum closed to the public for the day. Visitors have even seen Sarah Gordon, dressed up in elegant Victorian clothing, gliding about the house.

The apparition has become so popular that Girl Scouts whose troops visit the Juliette Gordon Low House can even get a patch that states, "I survived the Hauntings Tour!"

Savannah has long had a reputation for its rather special relationship with its spectral residents; but it was a scandalous murder case that put the city on the map. The best-selling book and movie *Midnight in the Garden of Good and Evil* focused on the murder of Danny Hansford—believed to have been committed by his lover, prosperous antiques dealer Jim Williams—and its aftermath.

On the surface the Hansford case was a routine—if sordid—incident. But there were a number of supernatural overtones to the affair that did not receive full attention at the time.

Jim Williams had to undergo three protracted trials before finally beating the murder charges and being acquitted. However, not long after that, Jim died of a heart attack in his home, the Mercer House on Monterey Square. But there was one curious aspect to Williams's "natural" death: the spot where his body was found was exactly where it would have lain had Danny Hansford succeeded in killing him (as Williams claimed he tried to do) several years before.

Minerva, the hoodoo "conjure doctor" whom Williams had hired to help him with his murder trial, had warned Williams that Hansford's spirit was out for revenge and needed to be placated. Some paranormal investigators feel Williams did not do enough to satisfy the dead man's vengeful spirit. Another interpretation is possible, however.

Some years before he came to reside in the Mercer House, Jim Williams had lived in the Hampton-Lillibridge House in Savannah. The Hampton-Lillibridge House is, by common agreement, the most haunted home in Savannah, and at least one paranormal investigation has even labeled it "the most psychically possessed house in the nation." Moreover, by all accounts, the spirit that possessed Hampton-Lillibridge is quite malevolent.

In 1963 Jim Williams purchased the house with this idea of restoring the 1796 home and reselling it for a profit. Toward that end, he moved the building four blocks to a lot he owned and then hired contractors to begin work on the structure.

Soon, however, Williams begin to have trouble. Brick masons working on the foundation walked off the job, saying the house was full of "people" who weren't visible.

Williams himself heard loud crashes—like furniture being tossed about—and there were reports of footsteps running across the floors upstairs and kicking over heavy objects. Yet neither Williams nor the bricklayers could find any living soul inside the house.

The next day the construction crew returned to the Hampton-Lillibridge House. But again the bricklayers became spooked—this time they said they heard whispers and laughter. Many of the masons walked off the job for good, and those construction workers who remained were too shaken to get much work done.

In desperation Williams convinced an Episcopal bishop to perform an exorcism. The workers watched as the cleric blessed the house and called upon whatever spirits were there to leave. This seemed to calm both the workers and the ghosts.

After that, the restoration seemed to go smoothly until it came time to do the woodwork. The contractor in charge of refinishing the floors inside the house called Williams to ask if he'd been in the house the night before. Surprised, Jim answered no. Evidently, the contractor had varnished the floors the night before, and when he heard footsteps in the house he became upset that someone might be ruining his fresh work.

Taking a flashlight, he went upstairs to investigate. Shining a flashlight on the area, he found that not only was no one there but there were no footprints either.

Williams moved into the restored home in May 1964 and had not been living there very long before he was awakened one night by a raucous racket. He heard what sounded like people in heavy shoes or boots shuffling up the stairs en route to the top floor. Then the commotion began to sound like someone having a wild party: loud voices, dancing, and screaming.

The ghostly bacchanal continued off and on for as long as Williams lived in the house. He kept a German Luger by his bedside for protection against intruders, but Jim soon found it was useless against spectral revelers.

One time a dark figure entered his bedroom, then vanished. This sinister entity may also have been responsible for an incident involving some houseguests of Williams.

When Jim was still at work one night, three visitors to his home heard a commotion upstairs, and one of their number went to investigate. When he didn't return after a while, his two friends went looking for him. They found him lying on the floor, white as a sheet. The houseguest said that as soon as he had stepped into the upstairs room he felt something very clammy and then had the sensation that he was being pulled toward a thirty-foot chimney shaft at one end of the room. He threw himself down on the floor to avoid being hurled down the shaft.

Visitors to the house have also reported sighting a man in formal attire and bow tie in the third-floor window; others have heard the sound of a woman screaming in terror. Psychic researchers who have gone through the house have confirmed the presence of very strong psychic activity there.

Curiously, previous owners of the house reported no psychic activity when they lived there. It was only when Williams moved it to its present location at 502 East Julian Street that the hauntings began. Interestingly, the house's next owner also did not experience the level of psychic activity that Williams did.

There had been an empty crypt on the property before the house was moved there, so perhaps the land itself was possessed. Then too, the very act of moving the house may have dislocated something that didn't wish to be disturbed. It is also possible that the antique building materials drawn from an old house in middle Georgia may have carried with them something more than red clay.

Yet whatever was in that house and however it got there, at least one of the spirits was homicidal in nature. Could this malevolence have somehow followed Williams when he finally moved to the house on Monterey Square? Could it have subconsciously affected the behavior of both Williams and Danny Hansford to the point that a deadly confrontation ensued?

It may seem far-fetched, but an entity that can physically drag a strong man toward an open shaft may also be capable of more subtle— but equally deadly—actions.

In Savannah, not even the resting place of the dead is immune to restless spirits. Bonaventure Cemetery has become famous in recent years because of the haunting image of the "Bird Girl" that was featured on the cover of *Midnight in the Garden of Good and Evil*—but that is hardly the cemetery's only claim to fame.

The life-size statue of Gracie Watkins, the "bird girl" who died at a young age, has long had a supernatural reputation. People who visit the cemetery often leave little offerings of money or trinkets in her outstretched hands. It is said that one can hear her crying out at night. Moreover, if someone removes the offerings from her hands, she will weep tears of blood.

Elsewhere in the graveyard, a pack of phantom hounds is known to roam. You can hear the baying of the dogs and may even feel their breath on your neck as you run from them—but no mortal animal has ever been seen.

The most celebrated ghosts of Bonaventure Cemetery, however, are those of Col. Joseph Tatnall and friends.

In the early 1800s the grounds of the modern cemetery were part of the Tatnall estate. Josiah Tatnall was renowned for the dinner parties he threw at Bonaventure, and the most elaborate of these celebrations was the banquet he held on Thanksgiving Day. This annual feast was always the talk of the town.

During one such fête, however, the house caught fire. Rather than ruin the party, Tatnall ordered his servants to take the tables, chairs, and food outside. As the mansion burned to the ground, Tatnall entertained his guests on the lawn, the flames of the mansion illuminating the party. It is said that Tatnall offered this toast: "May the memory of this joyful occasion never end." With that, the guests drained their wine glasses and smashed them against an ancient oak tree.

Today, the gnarled old oak still stands, although the mansion is long gone. Bonaventure was never rebuilt, and the estate eventually became a cemetery. But the memory of that joyful occasion apparently has lingered.

On a number of occasions, persons walking by the cemetery in late November have heard the sounds of people laughing and talking, and the sound of crystal glasses shattering, one after another. People have even claimed to see figures dressed in period clothing celebrating there.

The paths of glory, they say, lead but to the grave. But if Bonaventure Cemetery is any gauge, it is not a one-way trip.

In a sense, however, Bonaventure Cemetery in many ways reflects the city of Savannah as a whole. It remains a beautiful antique garden, brimming with memories of the past—and filled with the spirits of the dead.

THE PIRATE'S HOUSE INN
20 East Broad Street
Savannah, GA 31401
(912) 233-5757
www.thepirateshouse.com

JULIETTE GORDON LOWE BIRTHPLACE
10 East Oglethorpe Avenue
Savannah, GA 31401
(912) 233-4501

BONAVENTURE CEMETERY
310 Bonaventure Road

The old plantation turned cemetery is seven miles from downtown. It is open daily to the public but the gates are locked promptly at 5 p.m. The famed "Bird Girl" statue is no longer in the cemetery; to prevent vandalism—and "fetish doings"— the original bronze statue was removed to the Telfair Museum downtown.

9

The Haunted Pillar

IN THE HEART OF DOWNTOWN AUGUSTA stands an old pillar of brick and concrete. Ten feet tall, the pillar is devoid of any special markings or decoration, or of anything that would identify its origin or purpose.

The pillar juts out of the sidewalk where Broad Street and Fifth meet, and seems oddly out of place there. But despite the hustle and bustle of downtown life, native Augustans are careful to avoid bumping into the strange column, or even brushing against it. For you see, the pillar is cursed.

Some years back, city officials decided to do away with the old pillar. It was out of place on a modern city sidewalk and was impeding pedestrian traffic—or so they said.

However, each time the city hired a contractor to demolish the pillar, the individual in charge of the project would die unexpectedly. The deaths were always attributed to natural causes; nevertheless, the relationship between being hired to destroy the pillar and a sudden shortening of one's life-span became obvious. After a while, no one could be found who was willing to oversee the demolition.

On another occasion, when Broad Street was being widened, two men were hired to simply move the pillar out of harm's way. As they went about their task, both men were suddenly struck by lightning that came from out of the blue.

More recently, a man lost control of his car and careened into the pillar. It was just a minor traffic accident; and by rights no serious injury should have resulted. When the police arrived on the scene, however, they found the driver dead behind the wheel.

Again, common sense would explain the incident as just a fluke— a freakish accident. But many citizens of Augusta, Georgia, said the "Haunted Pillar" had claimed another victim.

What is it about this antique architectural artifact that should cause it to possess so ill-starred a reputation?

The cause of the pillar's infamy—and its preservation in downtown Augusta—has been ascribed to different causes, yet all have a supernatural cast to them.

At one time, the pillar was part of the old Farmer's Market. Built around 1830, the market was the central place of commerce for the city, and a wide variety of commodities were bought and sold there daily. The Farmer's Market used to be located at the intersection of Broad and Center (now Fifth) Streets, just a few blocks from the riverboat landing on the Savannah River, and it served as the city's business hub until 1878.

According to the official version of the story (the one the City Council would prefer), an itinerant preacher showed up in town one day, wishing to preach his fire-and-brimstone sermons in the middle of the marketplace. Local merchants, it is said, felt that would be bad for business and pressured the city to prohibit the preacher from evangelizing there.

The traveling preacher was exceedingly wroth that his divine mission was being curtailed. And so, standing in the middle of the market, he threatened that a great wind would come and smite the wicked citizens of Augusta. Nothing would be left of this temple of Mammon, he declared—nothing except for a lone pillar.

The pillar, the preacher prophesied, would be left as a reminder to the city never to trifle with a messenger of God again. And whosoever would dare to move this pillar, try to destroy it, or even just touch it would be struck down by the sword of the Lord.

At 1 A.M. on February 7, 1878, the tolling of the market's bell was heard for the last time. Just minutes later, a freakish winter tornado roared through downtown Augusta. It barely missed a local school, Richmond Academy, and came down squarely on top of the Farmer's Market.

When the winds subsided and the dust cleared, the only thing remaining was the solitary pillar. The traveling preacher's curse was fulfilled.

There are those, however, who claim the pillar was haunted long before the market's destruction. The curse, they claim, dates to long before the Civil War.

The large pillar, according to this account, was indeed part of the old market, but it was also a place where human beings were sold along with livestock, produce, and cotton.

One day a slave was chained to the pillar while a slave-trader sought to sell him to the highest bidder. The slave, apparently possessed of occult abilities, laid a curse on the pillar, the symbol of his bondage—and on all who might come in contact with it.

Whatever the precise cause of the curse, generations of Augustans have learned to shun the pillar. And if on occasion some have come away unscathed from a close encounter with the Haunted Pillar, that is not to say it still will not fulfill its mission on others.

If you go ...
More haints and haunts of Dixie to see in Georgia:

ATLANTA
The Wren's Nest
1050 Ralph D. Abernathy Blvd. SW
Atlanta, GA 30310
(404) 763-7735 • fax (404) 753-8535
www.wrensnestonline.com

The home of Joel Chandler Harris of "Uncle Remus" fame is believed to be haunted by at least one his children who died young.

AUGUSTA
AUGUSTA STATE UNIVERSITY
2500 Walton Way
Augusta, GA 30904
(706) 737-1400
www.aug.edu

Several Civil War ghosts have been reported around the area of the old arsenal on campus and the nearby cemetery.

1797 EZEKIEL HARRIS HOUSE
1822 Broad Street
Augusta, GA 30904
(706) 722-8454
www.augustamuseum.org

Sometimes mistaken for the McKay Trading House, where Tories tortured and massacred dozens of Patriots in 1780; this house is definitely not haunted by martyred Revolutionary War soldiers. However, an unidentified female ghost has been reported haunting the second floor.

FORT OGLETHORPE
CHICKAMAUGA NATIONAL
MILITARY PARK
P.O. Box 2128
Fort Oglethorpe, GA 30742
(706) 866-9241

This battlefield on the border with Tennessee is the haunt of a number of Civil War ghosts as well as a monster referred to by locals as "Old Green Eyes".

SAVANNAH
THE OLDE PINK HOUSE (1771)
23 Abercorn Street
Savannah, GA 41401
(912) 232-4286

Adjacent to The Planter's Inn (also haunted) this restaurant and tavern has had multiple reports of spirits (in addition to the alcoholic kind) inhabiting the old building; they seem most active between October and March.

Georgia Ghost Tours

ATLANTA
GHOSTS AND LEGENDS TOUR
(A City Segway Tour)
Ages 12 and older
(877) 734-8687 • (404) 588-2274
E-mail: Atlanta@CitySegway
Tours.com

AUGUSTA
AUGUSTA GHOST WALKS
Candlelight tour
(706) 364-0910
www.augustaghostwalks.com

DALTON
DALTON GHOST TOURS
(706) 313-8724
www.daltonghosttours.com

ROSWELL
ROSWELL GHOST TOUR
Trolley tour also available for groups
(770) 649-9922
www.roswellghosttour.com

SAVANNAH
*Midnight in the Garden
of Ghost Tours*

BUMP IN THE NIGHT
BORDELLO TOUR
Haunted Bordello History Tour
(912) 238-3843
www.savannahtours.com

COBBLESTONE TOURS
*Haunted Pub Crawl (adults only)
Savannah Haunted History Tour*
(912) 604-3007
www.ghostsavannah.com

GHOSTS AND LEGENDS TOUR
OF SAVANNAH
(America by Foot)
(912) 236-4467
www.theghostsofsavannah.com

GHOSTS AND GRAVESTONES TOUR
OF SAVANNAH
Aboard "the trolley of the dead"
Historic Tours of Savannah
(800) 213-2474
www.ghostandgravestones.com

GHOST TALK GHOST WALK TOURS
Walking tour
(912) 233-3896 • (800) 563-3896
www.savannahgeorgia.com/ghosttalk/

HAUNTED PUB TOUR
OF SAVANNAH
"Creepy Crawl"
(912) 238-3843

HAUNTINGS TOUR SAVANNAH
(912) 234-3571
www.hauntingstour.com

HAUNTED TROLLEY TOURS
(Oglethorpe Tours)
(912) 233-8380
www.oglethorpetours.com
HEARSE GHOST RIDE TOUR
*Savannah Ghost Tour
"Ghost Savannah"*
(912) 695-1578
www.hearseghosttours.com

SAVANNAH GHOST TOURS/
EAST RIVER STREET
(Old Town Trolley Tours)
(912) 233-0083
www.trolleytours.com/Savannah
/river-ghost-tours.asp

SAVANNAH HAUNTINGS TOUR
87-Savannah

SIXTH SENSE SAVANNAH
GHOST TOUR
(866) 666-3323
www.sixthsensesavannah.com

ST. SIMON ISLAND
ST. SIMON'S GHOST TOUR
(912) 638-1501

ST. SIMON'S GHOST WALK
(912) 638-2756

10

Mysteries of Mammoth Cave

BENEATH THE SUNLIT WORLD IN WHICH WE DWELL lies a darker realm—a realm whose mysteries we but dimly grasp. Though this kingdom of shadow lies just beneath our feet, its innermost recesses have yet to be plumbed.

Since time before remembering, this underworld has held a fatal fascination for man. From Orpheus to Floyd Collins, a silent siren's call has lured men into the bowels of the earth, at times never to return. Yet men continue to go, questing ever deeper into this other realm in search of its hidden secrets. Certainly no part of this kingdom of eternal night has ever held greater fascination—or danger—than Mammoth Cave.

Mammoth Cave is well named, for with over three hundred miles of known passageways, and countless more still unexplored, Mammoth is the largest cave in the world. Located in the heart of what is called a Karsk region, it is but one of many caves riddling the bedrock of south-central Kentucky. Some theorize that many of these lesser caves ultimately connect with Mammoth.

According to tradition, Mammoth Cave was originally discovered in 1809 by a hunter tracking a wounded bear. In truth, however, long before its discovery by whites, Native Americans had known and used the cave for centuries uncounted. Traces of Indian activity have been found even in the deepest recesses of the caverns.

In the nineteenth century reports surfaced of prehistoric mummies—some reportedly with red hair—being found in the cave. How a pre-Columbian mummy could have red hair was never explained. Nor was any scientific explanation forthcoming for the mummies of short stature found there, mummies which gave credence to old legends of an ancient race of pygmies who had once inhabited the South.

While the significance of these mummies remains moot, what is not in dispute is that generations of Native Americans ventured deep into Mammoth's heart of darkness. What they were seeking, no one knows. Some say these natives were no ordinary Indians but instead were powerful shamans—medicine men—who ventured deep into the caverns in search of power. By seeking encounters with the many spirits they believed to inhabit those awesome caverns, these native wizards hoped to increase their magical abilities. If this was so, then they were certainly looking in the right place.

Mammoth Cave is one of the great natural wonders of the world, and it ranks as one of the great supernatural wonders as well. As one descends through its cathedral-like galleries and spectacular rock formations, it is easy enough to accept all the stories told about the caves as gospel.

In a section of the cave called Echo River, for example, visitors and guides alike have heard strange sounds. Sometimes, it is the sound of a woman coughing; at other times there is the distinct but plaintive sound of a woman calling out, as if she is searching for someone. These weird noises are usually attributed to a spirit named "Melissa."

By all accounts, Melissa was a beautiful young Southern belle who lived in the area in the 1800s. As the daughter of a well-to-do family, her father could well afford a private tutor to educate her. The tutor, it turned out, was a handsome young man named Beverleigh. He was fair of face and manners, and his only fault lay in the fact that he was a Yankee.

The problems began when Melissa, smitten with the tall and attractive Northerner, wished to give her tutor some lessons that were not in his schoolbooks—lessons in love. Hell hath no fury like a woman scorned, as the saying goes, and when Beverleigh rebuffed Melissa's advances, she resolved to teach him a lesson he would never forget.

On the pretext that she would show him something unique, Melissa took Beverleigh to Mammoth Cave. She led him deep within the bowels of the cave, to a spot on the Echo River called Purgatory Point. There, Melissa deserted her unaffectionate lover, leaving Beverleigh to find his own way out.

Her prank backfired, however; the greenhorn Yankee, unfamiliar with the endless labyrinth of passages, became disoriented in the dark and never made it back to the surface. His body was never found. Perhaps Beverleigh stumbled off a high cliff in the dark, or perhaps he simply wandered throughout the maze of caverns until he collapsed of exhaustion, some sunless subterranean passage becoming his sepulcher.

In any case, Melissa never forgave herself for his death. She made repeated searches along the river, calling out his name again and again in vain. Only the sad sound of her own voice resounding off the cavern walls ever answered her plaintive cries.

For the remainder of her life, Melissa lived with her guilt. Some say she later contracted consumption—her declining health was brought on by mourning and guilt, it was said—and Melissa's chronic cough became a familiar sound during her many fruitless searches underground.

So it is that to this day, visitors may still hear Melissa calling out for her lost love, her doleful refrain and her coughing telltale signs that her restless spirit roams the caverns still.

Although the tragic tale of Melissa and her lost love is a haunting one, the person most closely connected with Mammoth Cave and its history is a man named Stephen Bishop. While living in the cave region in the early nineteenth century, Bishop developed a fascination with Mammoth Cave and became one of its earliest and greatest explorers.

Stephen first explored the cave as a boy, and by the time he was fully grown he had become the leading explorer of Mammoth, discovering dozens of new passages and galleries and guiding others through the hidden wonders of the underworld. Indeed, Bishop's skill as a guide was legendary, and it was said that no visitors under his supervision ever came to harm. For decades, Stephen Bishop led tourists through the labyrinths of Mammoth, and it seemed to many that Bishop had been born to be a guide, so great was his affinity for the place.

Ironically, on the sunlit surface, Stephen Bishop was a slave, a mere piece of chattel. Whenever he entered the portals of Mammoth Cave, however, he was transformed into a king, one whose domain was the inky blackness of the underworld. Despite Bishop's lowly status, his extraordinary aptitude for the underworld and his ability as a guide earned him the respect of many whites. Many scores put their lives in his hands and never was their trust in him misplaced.

At one point, realizing the injustice of keeping a man as talented as Bishop in bondage, Stephen's master offered to set him free. But Stephen refused the offer of manumission, for under the old slave laws he would have been required to leave the state immediately, and the freedom he felt roaming Mammoth Cave was more precious to him than roaming the surface world as a free man.

Given Bishop's great affinity for the caves, and their repute as the abode of the spirits, it comes as little surprise to find that Stephen Bishop's ghost also is believed to roam Mammoth's sprawling caverns. If his spirit does abide in the caves he knew so well, then his presence is unquestionably a benign and helpful one.

On one occasion, a National Park Service guide sighted the apparition of a black man accompanying a woman and two children. The man was dressed in white pants and vest, a dark-colored shirt, and a Panama hat—a description which exactly matches that of Bishop. Often visitors will ask, "Who is that over there?" but when others look toward the area indicated, no one can be seen. At other times, folks have simply felt an abiding presence that guiding them safely through dangerous passages, and many credit Bishop for his invisible aid.

Far and away the best-known personality connected with the region's caves, however, is that of Floyd Collins, and his spirit, more than any other, has reason to be restless.

By the 1920s tourism had become a big industry in Kentucky's cave country, and anyone who could find a new entrance to Mammoth could become rich off the admission fees he charged to see the cave. In January 1925 Floyd had set out to explore other caves in the area in hopes of finding a new and more accessible entrance to Mammoth Cave. Floyd already owned Crystal Cave and felt sure that if he could locate a new entrance to Mammoth, his fortune would be made.

However, while exploring nearby Sand Cave, Floyd's ankle became wedged between boulders. He was stuck tight, but there was every reason to believe a rescue party would soon be able to find and free him.

Although rescuers got close enough to talk to Floyd and bring him food, little was done to extricate him. In fact, the rescuers seemed more intent on generating stories for the newspapers and radio than on freeing poor Collins.

For sixteen days, Floyd Collins lay there in the darkness, helpless and injured, while a virtual media circus took place above him. When rescuers finally broke through the roof of the cave to get him out, Collins was dead.

Collins was buried in his family cemetery, but his corpse was not left to rest in peace. In 1926 tourism promoters dug up Floyd's body and put it on display in a glass coffin, charging admission to visitors for the privilege of gawking at the famed caver's corpse. The gruesome exhibit was a good moneymaker until someone stole the body. Although Collins's corpse was recovered, strangely, when it was returned it was missing a leg.

Floyd Collins's body lay on display just inside the entrance to Crystal Cave well into the 1960s. The tragic circumstances of his death, the bizarre treatment of his corpse after burial, the matter of his unresolved quest for a new cave entrance—all these factors may have had something to do with the many reported hauntings in the area.

There is, for example, the sighting of a pair of disembodied legs running around in broad daylight near the park's visitors center. The legs were said to be dressed in denim pants and work shoes, very similar to the clothes Floyd wore when he was trapped below.

Once on a private tour of Crystal Cave by park employees, someone noticed an old whiskey bottle still *in situ* where Floyd had left it. On their way out, two of the park guides heard a sound like someone flicking a finger against the bottle and then watched in awe as the bottle flew across the passageway and fell to the ground, apparently hurled by an invisible force.

In 1976 two hydrologists surveying groundwater resources in the area were checking the spring near Floyd Collins's old house, when one of them heard the faint but distinct sound of a man calling for help. "I'm trapped, help me" was the refrain the man thought he heard repeated over and over—and the pleas were coming from the direction of Crystal Cave.

Members of the Cave Research Foundation have had many uncanny encounters that they often attribute to the ghost of Floyd

Collins. Members frequently have reported hearing strange sounds in Mammoth Cave, and while some dismiss them as just the garbled sounds of a distant waterfall, others insist they are human voices. On one occasion a former president of the foundation heard someone call out to him and his party, telling them to wait. After stopping for some time but not seeing anyone coming, they moved on. When they checked the caving log for that area of the caverns, they found that no one had been there. This, it seems, has happened to several other spelunkers visiting the same area.

At nearby Crystal Cave, where Floyd's body lay for so many years and where his house still stands, CRF researchers and park personnel alike have had numerous strange encounters. In one case a ranger walked right past a man dressed in 1920s-style coveralls. At other times candles have been known to flicker wildly in one certain passage of the cave—as if Floyd was telling visitors it was time to go.

Located directly above Crystal Cave is Floyd Collins's house and associated buildings, which are now used to house visiting researchers. Caretakers there have reported hearing the sound of footsteps coming up to the door, and on occasion have even found a set of footprints leading up to the bolted door—and ending there without any trace of steps leading away.

The lights in a nearby shack once used as a ticket office for the cave have been observed going on at night for no apparent reason. On one occasion, a park ranger at CRF headquarters was listening to his radio only to be startled to hear what sounded like a "live" broadcast of the attempts to rescue Floyd Collins. But upon checking, the ranger found that no such rebroadcast of those events had been done by any of the local stations.

It would be a mistake to assume that Floyd, Stephen, and Melissa are the only spirits that roam the dark vastness of Mammoth Cave. Other equally bizarre sightings and encounters have been reported which cannot be traced to a known individual. With some 150 reported sightings there over the last several years, Mammoth Cave has well earned its accolade as "one of the nation's most haunted locations."

To be sure, most visitors to Mammoth Cave National Park probably will never have any paranormal encounters while there. And perhaps the breezeless flickering of candles in the passages, the shadowy movements caught out of the corner of the eye, and the brush of something against one's flesh in the dark may all just be coincidences, as skeptics contend.

Still, if you tour the caverns, by all means stay with your guide—and under no circumstances follow a pale young lady with a chronic cough, especially if she beckons you to follow her to Purgatory Point.

MAMMOTH CAVE NATIONAL PARK
Mammoth Cave, KY 42255
(502) 758-2328

(Take Highway70 off I-65 interstate exit; the entrance is well marked.)

11

The Happy Hollow Horror

GHOSTS COME IN DIFFERENT VARIETIES; they may be protective, vengeful, reflective, and the like. Some ghosts haunt a particular spot for decades, even centuries, reliving past events; other spirits seem to appear only for specific reasons. And a few apparitions materialize but once, deliver a specific message, and then vanish.

In 1932 a bizarre incident occurred in southern Kentucky that is still talked about to this day—although what exactly happened, and why, is still a mystery. While it remains a curiosity to us today, for those who experienced it, the shock and horror were all too real.

Happy Hollow is a small rural community, a mile or so southeast of Greensburg, the Green County seat. A quiet community both now and then, with little crime and fewer worries, it was hardly a place known for troubles—or ghosts.

One morning in August 1932 the Ragland family was sitting down to breakfast. Mrs. Ragland had been up before dawn, busy in the kitchen fixing a hearty country breakfast: thick sliced bacon, eggs, cornbread hot from the oven, and fresh-brewed coffee. After calling her husband and three children down from the upstairs bedroom, Mrs. Ragland and her family sat down to eat.

They were just digging into the hearty repast when they heard a commotion coming from the front of the house.

At first they thought it might be a neighbor at the front door, perhaps stopping by to borrow a tool or two.

Suddenly, the family heard the front door burst open with a bang, followed by the sound of footsteps echoing down the hallway. It sounded as if several persons were walking in measured footsteps on the hardwood floors, and the tramping grew louder and louder as it seemed to approach the rear of the house, where the kitchen was.

The Raglands were perplexed at first, for most neighbors knew enough to come around to the kitchen door at this time of the morning. If the visitors were strangers, who could they be and what did they want?

As the footsteps drew nearer, the Raglands saw that the sounds were being made by six men dressed in black who bore a large black object on their shoulders. It was a coffin, and stranger still, atop the coffin was a lamb.

The lamb was snowy white, but its head had been severed at the neck, and the headless corpse was bleeding from the gory wound. The six men in black stared straight ahead as they marched solemnly down the hallway and then right past the Raglands, who were frozen with fear at the awful sight.

Then the rear door swung open of its own accord, and the spectral procession passed over the threshold and entered the yard beyond.

When the Raglands looked out the back window to see where the men were headed, there was no one there.

In a panic, Mr. Ragland bundled his wife and children into the car and drove to nearby Greensburg to fetch the county sheriff.

It had been a quiet morning at the courthouse—most mornings were in Green County—and Sheriff J. W. Thomas was getting caught up on some paperwork when he heard a commotion in the other room.

The Raglands had burst into the office all in a dither and were excitedly telling his deputy Sam about some strange happening out at their place. The Raglands, he recalled, had been leasing the old Blakeman place, just a mile or so southeast of town. After calming the family down and getting the straight story from Mr. Ragland, J. W. promised to investigate the matter.

In due course, Sheriff Thomas and Sam, his deputy, arrived at the Blakeman place and checked the grounds thoroughly. They found no sign of anyone fitting the description Mr. Ragland had given them— much less six such fellows. J. W. and Sam also checked out the front of the house for footprints or signs of forced entry but again found nothing. Likewise, when they went around back, the only marks in the dirt they could find were those the Raglands had left when they piled into the fliver to go to town.

Checking with neighbors also proved a dead end. No one fitting that description had been seen in the neighborhood, and in Happy Hollow everybody knew everybody—strangers would have been noticed mighty fast, especially strangers carrying a coffin around on their shoulders.

If the strange visitation had been a prank or practical joke, the joke-sters had disappeared into thin air, and someone in the community would have been wise to it. On the other hand, there was no doubt that the Raglands were sincere and were telling the truth about what they'd seen. All the sheriff could do was write a report on the incident.

But what could Sheriff Thomas put down? Six men dressed like pallbearers broke into a family's home in broad daylight, walked through their house, and terrorized them at breakfast?

It sounded absurd.

If the sheriff even took the time to write up a trespassing complaint, he buried it deep in the files where no one would ever read it.

For a time, the incident was widely talked about in the community. Folks would drive over to see the house where it happened, often tramping through the house to see for themselves where the bizarre incident happened. At night, local teenagers would drive out and park around the side of the house, waiting for the apparitions to appear again.

Some claimed to see things in the shadows. But the phantom pall-bearers never appeared again, so far as is known.

The Raglands, needless to say, moved out of the house at the first opportunity. The landlord had a hard time leasing the Blakeman place after that, and the house gradually fell into decay and came to be regarded as haunted.

It was truly a bizarre incident; a seemingly unique event. Other than the house becoming a nighttime hangout for teenagers, and the incident becoming a nugget of local lore, life more or less returned to normal in Green County. After all, nobody had been injured or killed—or had they?

In the annals of the supernatural, it is not unusual to hear of an encounter with an apparition that is on a mission and seems to be trying to communicate with the living.

In some cases such a ghost may be trying to deliver a warning. "The Gray Man" of Pawley's Island, South Carolina, is a classic example of this sort of spirit. Other ghosts are guarding a secret—be it a buried treasure or even hidden documents of some value. The famed Memphis haunting by Lizzie Davidson's ghost in the 1870s is one of the better-known examples of this kind. Lizzie could not rest until she had revealed the location of some hidden valuables to an adolescent schoolgirl.

Finally, there are those specters that clearly seem to be trying to inform the mortal plane about some past event or crime. There was a case in West Virginia, for example, where a woman's ghost came back to testify to police against the man who had murdered her. As bizarre as the Happy Hollow haunting may seem at first glance, it is clear that the apparitions which materialized in front of the Raglands were trying to communicate some message, albeit on a symbolic level.

The phantom funeral procession through the home obviously indicated some unrecognized death—either in the local community or in the house itself. More telling, however, is the white lamb atop the coffin.

Not all apparitions appear in human form. Some persons who have led wicked lives, for example, have been known to be transformed into the shape of a black dog—a "devil dog"—symbolic of their dog-like devotion to evil. By contrast, the white lamb is symbolic of both purity and innocence. An apparition in the form of a white lamb is usually indicative of a child who died prematurely. So perhaps a young child had died in or near the Raglands' house.

The gory and gruesome aspect of that lamb also tells us something about the manner of the child's death. The lamb with a severed head, bleeding profusely, can have but one meaning: a slaughtered innocent. A young child had been brutalized and murdered, and its death had been hidden from the world at large.

Sheriff Thomas and the folks of Green County could make no sense of this strange haunting at the time, although no one doubted that it actually occurred. While the Happy Hollow Horror became a local legend, there is no indication that anyone ever tied the unearthly visitation to any missing-person report, or even to an adult suddenly leaving the area unexpectedly.

The house the Raglands lived in at the time of the event had been leased to several other people before them—both Blakeman and someone named Edwards are mentioned as previous residents. Therefore, more than one individual or family was connected with this particular house.

The Raglands were as baffled by the incident as they were horrified by it, and they were not alone in those feelings. But if the Raglands and the residents of Happy Hollow were at a loss to explain their experience, there was likely one individual who fully understood its meaning—and knew exactly who the slaughtered innocent was.

If we read the signs correctly, a heinous crime was committed in the peaceful community of Happy Hollow in the 1930s. The truth about that evil act and the identity of the murderer have yet to see the light of day—and that is the true horror in Happy Hollow.

12

The Late Mrs. Varick:
The Gray Ghost of Liberty Hall

ONE OF THE MOST DISTINGUISHED HOMES in Frankfort, Kentucky, is Liberty Hall. Notable as the home of Kentucky's first U.S. senator, the Honorable John Brown, it is also recognized as home to one of Kentucky's most famous ghosts—"the Gray Lady."

John Brown was a leading citizen of the state during the frontier era, and even a partial list of visitors to Liberty Hall reads like a who's who of early America. No fewer than three presidents visited Liberty Hall: James Monroe, Andrew Jackson, and Zachary Taylor. John Brown and his wife, Margaretta, also played host to the Marquis de Lafayette when he toured the United States in 1825.

When it was built in 1796, the three-story Georgian brick mansion was considered the most luxurious home west of the Appalachians. Moreover, when John married the sophisticated New York socialite Margaretta Mason a few years later, he spared no expense stocking the dwelling with as many of the refinements and amenities that his wife was used to back east. Massive brass locks imported from England were set in "witch doors," designed to ward off evil spirits.

Margaretta was the daughter of Rev. John Mason, who had served on George Washington's staff during the Revolution. Her mother had died when Margaretta was still young, and with her father away at war, she was raised by an aunt, Mrs. Margaret Varick. Mrs. Varick was greatly attached to Margaretta and doted on her constantly.

Therefore, when word arrived back east in 1817 that Margaretta had lost a child, Mrs. Varick did not hesitate for a moment to pack her bags and go to her niece's assistance.

In those days the trip from New York to Kentucky was a long and arduous one—all the more so for a woman of sixty-five unused to extreme physical exertion. For Aunt Margaret, however, no mountains were too high nor forests too deep to keep her from coming to the aid of her favorite niece. Travelling by carriage, stagecoach, and horseback, Mrs. Varick made her way west, at last arriving on the other side of the mountains at Frankfort. Sadly, though, the rigors of more than eight hundred miles journeying proved too much for the elderly woman's condition.

Within three days of arriving at Liberty Hall, Mrs. Varick, Margaretta's doting aunt, died of a heart attack in one of the upstairs bedrooms. She had come to comfort the bereaved Mrs. Brown and to assist around the house, but Mrs. Varick herself became a further cause of bereavement.

The late Mrs. Varick was laid to rest in a small family plot laid out beside the elaborate formal gardens that Margaretta had planted. A few years later the family plot was moved to a larger public cemetery. However, by that time the exact location of Mrs. Varick's grave apparently had been forgotten, and her body was not re-interred with the rest of the family. As it turned out, Mrs. Varick was fated to remain at Liberty Hall in more ways than one.

The first inkling that the late Mrs. Varick had not left occurred just a few years after her death. In 1820 Senator Brown's grandson, Benjamin Gratz Brown (later a governor of Missouri), was getting married, and his bride to be was given an upstairs guest bedroom. The bedroom was in the southwest corner of the house and featured a scenic view of the garden. It was the room where Mrs. Varick had died.

As the bride stood there, she saw Aunt Margaret walk right across the room in front of her, clad in a plain gray housedress. The startled bride could scarcely believe her eyes.

Benjamin's half-sister, Margaretta (Mrs. W. F. Barrett), was the next to meet the late Mrs. Varick. Margaretta encountered her great-great-aunt's ghost descending the house's grand staircase, again dressed in gray, which earned her apparition the appellation of "the Gray Lady."

Not long after, Rebecca Averill of Frankfort was also guest in the house. Rebecca had already turned in for the night, when she saw Aunt Margaret, clear as daylight, standing next to the fireplace in the guest bedroom. Mrs. Varick made no movement toward Rebecca, nor did Miss Averill have any desire to exchange words with the ghost. Instead, Rebecca pulled the bed sheet over her head and prayed that Mrs. Varick would disappear. When she finally worked up the courage to peek out from under the covers, the late Mrs. Varick was gone.

Over the following years, Mrs. Varick continued to be sighted by family members and houseguests, and while her unexpected appearances could be very disconcerting to the uninitiated, it was soon realized that the Gray Lady was a benign presence in the house.

The late Mrs. Varick has not confined herself solely to the bedroom, however; her presence has been felt or seen throughout the house. Overnight guests would sometimes awaken to find themselves being tucked in by a smiling, matronly ghost. At other times, members of the household would find blankets neatly folded in the morning, and even clothes in need of mending often would even be found neatly sewn—all of which was attributed to the unseen hands of kindly Aunt Margaret.

The last member of the family to reside in Liberty Hall was Mary Mason Scott, the niece of Benjamin Gratz Brown. Although she is said to have greatly resembled her great-great-aunt, she had been unaware that her ancestor was still haunting Liberty Hall. Then, returning home one weekend from college, Mary was given Mrs. Varick's old room to sleep in. On her first night back, Mary awoke in the middle of the night to find Aunt Margaret standing next to the bed.

The Gray Lady apparently took a liking to her great-great-niece. In the 1920s, when Mary in turn was mistress of Liberty Hall, Mrs. Varick began to communicate directly with her, using Mary as a medium. Apparently one reason for the Gray Lady's continued presence in the house was the failure to locate her grave and relocate her body to be with the rest of the family. Efforts were made to find the gravesite but without success. So, to this day, the Gray Lady continues to dwell in the mansion.

The last of the Brown family to own the property wished to sell Liberty Hall; fortunately, the Colonial Dames of America wished to acquire the house to preserve it in the public interest. In 1937 Liberty Hall passed to the Colonial Dames, who restored it and converted it into a history museum. Although the Brown clan had ceased to reside there, nobody seems to have notified Mrs. Varick, and the Gray Lady has continued to appear to volunteers and staff.

In the process of restoring Liberty Hall, one of the house's curators took photographs to document the restoration process. One photo she took of the grand staircase, when developed, showed the faint but unmistakable image of a woman descending the staircase. She was sure no one had been on the stairs at the time and was positive the film had not been previously exposed.

On another occasion, the same curator found a group of three gold bracelets on a nightstand in the "ghost" bedroom. A thorough search of the house's inventory turned up no such jewelry in the museum collection. An expert declared the bracelets' workmanship to date to the era of Mrs. Varick. Perhaps it was the Gray Lady's way of saying "thank you" for restoring the mansion.

On a number of occasions passersby have claimed to see Mrs. Varick staring out a window in the mansion. A college professor theorized that the sightings were nothing more than moonlight reflecting off the windows. So the professor stayed at Liberty Hall for six weeks, through an entire cycle of the moon's phases, to prove his theory.

Throughout his stay the professor detected no unusual reflection in the windowpane, and he checked it under every different condition. However, on one of his last nights in the mansion, he was awakened by a gentle touch, and when he opened his eyes, he saw Mrs. Varick smiling down at him. Perhaps Aunt Margaret didn't want him to go away disappointed.

At times, the Gray Lady has even been known to anticipate the staff's wishes. During the 1980s, a resident caretaker of the Colonial Dames was taking a bath in her apartment over the kitchen, when she realized she had left the bathroom doors open. She thought to herself, "I wish I'd closed that," and no sooner had she done so, than the heavy wooden doors to the bathroom closed all by themselves.

On another occasion, the resident docent was musing about an old boyfriend, when suddenly her music box—which hadn't played in hospitality. It's doubtful, however, that the Hon. John Brown ever imagined that Liberty Hall would play host to one houseguest for some 180 years!

Still, one can't deny that Aunt Margaret has made herself useful around the house for all that time. One would even wager that there are more than a few householders who wish they had a resident relative—living or dead—who was half as helpful as the late Mrs. Varick.

Liberty Hall is now a historic house museum operated by the Colonial Dames of America. It is open daily to the public. For further information on visiting, contact:

LIBERTY HALL HISTORIC SITE
218 Wilkinson Street
Frankfort, KY 40501
(502) 227-2560 • (888) 516-5101
www.libertyhall.org • E-mail: libhall@dcr.net

years—began playing its tune, with the lid closed and without an winding. Apparently, the Gray Lady has her sentimental side as well

While the Gray Lady is certainly the most famous phantom of Lil erty Hall, she is not the only one.

Around 1805 the Browns, seeking to bring some refinement an culture to Kentucky, invited a Spanish opera singer from New Orlea to perform in Frankfort. While she was there, the Browns invited h to stay with them and held a party in honor.

During the party, the beautiful Creole soprano took a stroll in tl garden behind the mansion. She was last seen walking down the ga den path toward the river, which bordered the back of the proper She never returned and her fate is still unknown.

Although a search was made for the missing diva, no trace of h was ever found. Some speculate that she was kidnapped and killed Indians; but this is highly unlikely, as the Southern tribes were peac ful by that time. She may simply have fallen in the river by accide and drowned. More likely, however, the opera singer ran afoul of sor white savages, for in those days the highways and rivers were st infested with road agents and "land pirates." And they may well ha been skulking around the grounds hoping to waylay a wealthy gue:

The mystery of the missing diva remained unsolved. Howev since she vanished, from time to time a dark-haired woman has be seen in the garden, especially on sultry summer nights. Some wl have seen her claim she is running from someone, and that her mou is open and she is wide-eyed with terror. Her appearance in the forn gardens is infrequent but disconcerting.

A third ghost, rarely sighted, is supposed to haunt the grounds the mansion as well. During the War of 1812 a young soldier met ar fell in love with a young and beautiful cousin of the Browns who w visiting the family. Apparently the Browns did not approve of l romantic overtures, and the soldier was sent away brokenhearted.

He may have died in the war—or perhaps he died of a broken hea At any rate, still longing for his sweetheart, the young soldier's ghc can be seen on rare occasions, standing outside a ground-floor wi dow. The soldier is said to peer in, look wistfully at the scene insic and then sadly turn and walk off into the ether.

The Browns of Kentucky were a distinguished clan, renowned f their service in peace and war, and even more renowned for the

If you go ...
More haints and haunts of Dixie to see in Kentucky

BARDSTOWN
FEDERAL HILL (1818)
My Old Kentucky Home State Park
501 East Stephen Foster Avenue
Bardstown, KY 40004
(800) 323-7803

Home of Judge John Rowan, where Stephen Foster was inspired to write his most famous song, is haunted by family ghosts—as is the nearby cemetery where the judge is buried.

LEXINGTON
ASHLAND
120 Sycamore Road
Lexington, KY 40502
(859) 266-8581
www.henryclay.org

This house was the residence of Henry Clay, famous antebellum statesman and senator. Although he died in 1852, Clay's spirit abides in the house still.

LOUISVILLE
THE BRENNAN HOUSE (1888)
631 South Fifth Street
Louisville, KY 40202
(502) 540-5145
www.thebrennanhouse.org

A historic house that now serves as a museum, the building was home to generations of the same family, several of whom have apparently chosen to remain after death.

RICHMOND
WHITE HALL
500 White Hall Shrine Road
Richmond, KY 40475
(859) 266-8581

The home of Cassius Clay, prominent Civil War era politician, is now a state historic site. Open to the public from April through October; they offer a "ghost walk" in late October. The ghost of Clay, described as "an old man in dark clothing", and a child ghost have been reported haunting the building.

Kentucky Ghost Tours

BARDSTOWN
BARDSTOWN GHOST TREK
June–November, Saturdays
(859) 576-5517
www.GhostHunter.com

LOUISVILLE
GHOST TOURS OF OLD LOUISVILLE
February–December
(502) 637-2922
www.tourlouisville.com

OWENSBORO
HAUNTS OF OWENSBORO GHOST TOUR
Friday and Saturday
(270) 313-5596
www.hauntsofowensboro.com

13

The 'Most Haunted' Myrtles

ALONG THE TWINING BYWAYS OF DIXIE lie many, many haunted homes. Yet of all these, the Myrtles is one of the few that can truly lay claim to the title "the Most Haunted House in America."

The Myrtles has earned that epithet, in part, by possessing no fewer than fourteen ghosts. But even without so great a gathering of specters, the Myrtles' often bloody history and its lingering aura of mystery would still make it a fascinating destination.

The spectral presence at the Myrtles had an early start. Gen. Daniel Bradford, founder of the plantation, chose to build his house on the high point of the estate. What he did not realize, however, was that the spot, though scenic, was also the site of an ancient burial ground of the Tunica Indians.

Bradford, a hero of the American Revolution, had run afoul of the federal government when he and his fellow frontiersmen raised a ruckus over the taxing of the whiskey they were distilling. When George Washington sent troops to suppress the so-called Whiskey Rebellion, Bradford hightailed it to sunnier climes—and out of the government's reach.

In the 1790s Louisiana was still Spanish territory, and Bradford set-tled there on 650 acres of land near St. Francisville, a small bayou town not far from Baton Rouge. According to tradition, before the Myrtles was built, General Bradford saw an apparition of a nude Indian maiden, standing in the backyard near where the modern gazebo now stands. In retrospect, it seems clear that the apparition appeared to warn Bradford against building on sacred ground. It was a warning Bradford chose not to heed.

After his death, the plantation and house passed to Bradford's daughter, Sarah. Sarah Bradford married an ambitious lawyer, Clarke Woodruff. It was a seemingly happy marriage; Sarah bore her husband three children, and the hard-working attorney was rewarded for his earnest efforts with a judgeship.

But life was not all moonlight and magnolias in the Woodruff house-hold. Judge Woodruff had taken as his mistress his children's gov-erness, a mulatto slave named Chloe. After a time, however, the judge tired of Chloe and took up with another slave girl. He threatened to put Chloe back in the fields if she breathed a word of the illicit affair.

Chloe was both jealous and fearful of being sent away. Anxious for information concerning her fate, she began listening at keyholes to the judge's private conversations. One day the judge caught Chloe listen-ing at the door to his library.

In a violent rage, Woodruff cut off the ear Chloe had been eaves-dropping with. Chloe survived the attack but forever after wore a green turban on her head to hide the missing ear. She also sported an earring dangling from the turban where her ear should have been.

According to Hester Eby, who manages the tours at the Myrtles nowadays, Chloe still loved the judge, despite his cruelty. To win back his affection, she took the occasion of a family birthday to bake a cake—a very special cake.

Chloe laced the birthday cake with oleander, a poisonous shrub. Miss Hester feels that Chloe only intended to make the family ill, thinking that she would then step in and nurse them back to health—thereby proving how essential she was. In that manner, Chloe thought, she would win back her master's affections. But if indeed those were her plans, they went seriously awry.

Woodruff's wife and two of his children fell ill from the poisoned cake, as planned. But instead of simply becoming sick, Sarah and her daughters died. Chloe was unwise enough to tell some fellow slaves what she had done, thinking they would keep her secret.

But Chloe had not only broken the white man's laws, she also had violated the unwritten laws of slave society as well. In antebellum times, any serious breach of the peace by a slave could bring quick and terrible retribution not only to the violator but also to all the other slaves of the plantation.

Before a white mob could descend to exact its revenge, the slaves resolved to carry out their own form of rough justice—and so preserve their lives.

One dark night they came for Chloe, and seizing her by the arms, they dragged her out onto the grounds and hanged her from an old oak tree near the house. When they were sure she was dead, they cut down her corpse and flung it into the river.

For generations now, successive residents and visitors to the Myrtles have caught sight of an apparition wearing a green turban. The mansion's Green Room seems to be one of Chloe's particularly favorite haunts.

One former owner of the house, Frances Kermeen, was awakened one night to see the turbaned ghost standing over her.

A honeymooning couple staying the night in the 1980s had a similar experience. The bride awoke out of a sound sleep to see Chloe bending over her. She was so terrified by the apparition that she and her husband checked out in the middle of the night.

A baby's cry is often heard when Chloe appears, and by her actions of lifting the veil of mosquito netting around guests' beds to gaze down at them, it is thought that she is still carrying out her duties as a nanny—checking on the judge's children she used to care for.

Chloe's victims are active as well. Two blonde-headed girls with long corkscrew curls, bedecked in antebellum dresses, have been seen peering in through the bedroom windows or standing at the foot of visitors' beds.

Children also have been heard playing in the hallway, and there is an invisible ghost who is fond of jumping up and down on the beds to rumple them. This child ghost is soon followed by another apparition in a black maid's clothing, who dutifully makes the beds after her.

In 1980, soon after a former proprietor of the inn had taken over the historic bed and breakfast, she heard voices calling the name

"Sarah." She was alone in the house at the time, and after checking all the rooms, she could still find no one else there. The voices were low but distinct. It was only later that she learned the tragic fate of Sarah Bradford Woodruff.

The Civil War intruded onto the plantation as well, and there are also reports of ghosts in both blue and gray that appear from time to time.

Reconstruction was a lawless time in the South, and disputes were often resolved at gunpoint. This era, too, left its bloody mark on the Myrtles.

In 1871 the master of the Myrtles was William Winter. A successful lawyer who won many cases, he may also have won some enemies in the courtroom. One night a man on horseback called him out onto the porch, claiming he needed a lawyer. When Winter showed himself, the nightrider shot him, then galloped off into the dark.

Winter staggered back into the house, trying to reach his wife upstairs for help. Climbing the staircase, he made it to the seventeenth step, where he died in his wife's arms.

Every now and then a guest or employee will hear a thumping sound—as of someone staggering across the foyer and climbing seventeen of the twenty steps. The sound always stops on the seventeenth step. On that same step can still be seen a maroon-colored stain—the dried blood of William Winter—and no amount of scrubbing or bleaching has ever been able to remove it.

The Myrtles' bloody history did not end with Winter's mysterious murder. A man was stabbed in the hallway over a gambling debt. The apparition of a slender young man in a fancy vest has been sighted wandering the grounds as well. It is thought that this is the spirit of the young gambler still wandering the grounds.

Then, in 1927, the overseer of the Myrtles was stabbed to death during a robbery attempt. His ghost also is thought to haunt the house. Visitors to this day occasionally report meeting a man in khaki pants who greets them at the front gates and tells them that the inn is not open—that "no one living is here"—and in a sense he is right.

Although unwary guests may occasionally be scared out of their wits by such incidents, aside from the odd candlestick or mantel clock being tossed about, the Myrtles' ghosts are generally a genial lot, despite the house's sad history.

There is, for example, a female apparition dressed in a black skirt who floats a foot off the floor and dances to music no living being can hear.

Another phantom seems to possess the grand piano on the ground floor. Late at night it tries to strike up a tune on the keyboard, playing the same chords over and over again. The music stops when someone enters the room, and it does not resume until they leave.

On occasion, when everyone is in bed for the night, the sounds of laughter, music, and the clinking of glasses can be heard. It's almost as if all the ghosts are holding a cotillion downstairs. Could old General Bradford be acting as host to the ghosts?

Over the years the media has frequently reported on the abundant spectral activities at the Myrtles. The venerable plantation's phantoms have been featured in *Life*, *Southern Living*, and a host of tabloids. Television documentaries have also spotlighted the old house. Its location on the bayou, surrounded by aging oaks dripping with Spanish moss, provides a suitably eerie atmosphere for film and TV productions.

A team of investigative reporters from Mississippi, for example, looked into the Myrtles recently. Their goal was to see for themselves if all the stories about the house and its ghosts were true.

Armed with video cameras and assorted electronic sensing equipment, the crew from WJTV's *Unexplained* succeeded in documenting a number of paranormal phenomena inside the house and on the grounds of the plantation.

Unexplainable drops in temperature, tape recordings of footsteps and whistling in otherwise empty rooms, and photographs of "orbs" and "mists" not visible to the naked eye were only some of the mysteries the prime-time ghostbusters encountered.

One reporter, turning in for the night, watched as the dimmer switch to the room's lights rotated slowly up and down all on its own. No one else was present in the room at the time.

On their first night at Myrtles, two of the crew noticed a gray cat looking at them from the porch. Flashing a light on it, they noticed something peculiar: its eyes did not reflect the light the way those of a normal feline do. When a reporter tried to snap a picture of it with his digital camera, he found the cat had disappeared, seemingly into thin air.

The investigators later found out from the mansion's current owners, John and Teeta Moss, that the cat they had seen was a family pet named Mert. A family cat roaming the property at night might not seem to be a strange event—except for the fact that Mert had died the year before. When the digital photo of Mert was output, all that showed up in the picture were several glowing orbs of light.

The Mosses bought the scenic inn a few years ago, they claimed, without knowing about its supernatural reputation. However, they have adjusted to the notion of playing host not only to real live paying guests but also to a gaggle of ghostly boarders as well. Apparently, all these spirits have found the house too pleasant a place to leave. And should you book a reservation there, you, too, may find it so congenial in spirit that you just might want to stay—forever.

The Myrtles is a historic bed and breakfast open to the public.
For further information on staying there, call or write:

MYRTLES PLANTATION
P.O. Box 1100 • 7747 U.S. Highway 61
Saint Francisville, LA 70775
(800) 809-0565 • (225) 635-6277
fax: (225) 635-5837 • E-mail: myrtles@bsf.net

14

The Witch Queen of New Orleans

Raven hair, ruby lips,
Sparks fly from her fingertips,
Witchy woman, see how high she flies . . .
—The Eagles

MARIE WAS A DUTIFUL DAUGHTER of the Holy Mother Church who attended mass regularly, received the Sacraments, and performed good works. There was another Marie in the Crescent City who wielded nearly limitless power, was said to be in league with the Devil, was feared and obeyed by many, and was accused of the most depraved acts. That these two Maries were one and the same is but one of many enigmas surrounding the occult career of Marie Laveau.

In New Orleans, even more than in the rest of the South, legend and fact merge imperceptibly together—and often the truth turns out to be far more fantastic than the legend. Such is the case with Marie Laveau.

Of Marie's early years, little is known; of her parentage, even less. By one account, Marie was born in 1794 in Sainte Dominguez (Haiti); others assert that Marie was born in *Le Vieux Carre* (the French Quarter) of New Orleans itself. Some say that Marie was born of the union of a wealthy plantation owner and a female slave; others claim Native American ancestry for Marie.

What we know for sure is that she was raised as a strict Roman Catholic, Catholicism being the dominant religion in the Louisiana territory at the time. When first we see Marie mentioned in official records, she is described as a "free woman of color."

Marie began her professional career not as an occultist but as a beautician. Her skill as a beautician won her a following among New Orleans's wealthy elite. Just how her coiffing of hair and dispensing of cosmetic beauty secrets to society *mesdames* and *mademoiselles* led to her later, more famous career as a voodoo queen may not be apparent at first glance. Yet it is true that even today in many parts of Dixie, African-American hairdressers often sell both beauty supplies and voodoo (or hoodoo) charms to their clientele.

It may be that, from listening to her clients' recitals of their marital woes and romantic problems, it was but a short step for Marie not only to give advice to the lovelorn (a favorite pastime of beauticians) but also to dispense love charms and spells to bind a lover or wayward husband closer to his paramour.

Students of Marie Laveau's career have pointed out that in coiffing the hair of the ruling class of New Orleans, Marie was well placed to pick up many close secrets—and even more loose gossip—about the inner workings of the elite of Creole society. Many society women freely told their hairdressers secrets they may have been reluctant to confess to their priest.

In time Marie's uncanny knowledge of nearly everyone's personal affairs would easily convince sophisticated but superstitious Creole matrons that Marie indeed possessed nearly limitless psychic powers—and perhaps she did.

Marie built on this knowledge and recruited others to keep her informed of nearly everything that went on in the area. Throughout New Orleans, Creole ladies often talked freely in front of their house servants, as if they were simply part of the furniture. These servants, either out of fear or gratitude, passed on every little tidbit of gossip to Marie. At the height of her fame, Marie Laveau was often better informed of affairs in Louisiana—personal and political—than even the governor. But Marie was not the first to wield such knowledge and power.

Voodoo (voudoun), originally imported from Haiti, is largely a translation of West African magical and religious practices to the changed circumstances of the New World. Such was its power and influence that in 1782, the Spanish governor of Louisiana, Don Gal-vaez, banned the importation of slaves from Santo Domingo expressly to prevent its spread.

When the United States purchased the Louisiana territory in 1803, many who came to the region were more concerned about lining their pockets with gold than with the state of their souls, and the govern-ment soon lifted the ban. This marked a turning point in the growth of voodoo in the Crescent City. Haitian immigrants, slave and free, started arriving in large numbers. Some came as forced labor, others arrived seeking to avoid the violence of war-torn Haiti. In both cases, the Haitians brought with them their magical beliefs and practices, adding to the psychic gumbo already simmering beneath the surface in New Orleans.

Even before Marie's rise to power, there were already a number of practitioners of the black arts in New Orleans. Foremost of these—and by all accounts Marie's mentor—was an individual known as Doc-tor John.

Jean Montenet, known variously as Doctor John or Bayou John, was the most famous of the conjure doctors and "witch queens" of the early 1800s. If nothing else, he certainly looked the part. Towering above ordinary men, the seven-foot-tall Doctor John had a face heav-ily scarred with tribal markings—red and blue snakes, symbols of the royal clan of Senegal. He dressed entirely in black, except for an immaculately white ruffled shirt, and in later years sported a long, flowing white beard.

By his own account, Doctor John was a prince by birth and had been kidnapped by slavers and sold to a Spanish grandee in Cuba. Even as a young man he had a certain persuasiveness about him; con-vincing his master to grant him freedom, Jean left Cuba, shipping out as a sailor.

Jean returned to Senegal, but finding his father dead and political circumstances unfavorable, he returned to the sea. Eventually Jean came ashore at New Orleans, where he worked loading and unloading cotton bales. The factor for whom Jean worked noticed how other black longshoremen held Jean in awe, and so made him overseer. It was at this time also that Jean became aware of his magical powers.

Jean—now calling himself Doctor John—quickly picked up the tricks of the trade and became the most respected and feared conjure doctor in New Orleans. When and how Marie became his apprentice is not known, but he is credited with teaching her everything he knew about the craft.

Doctor John, by all accounts, was something of an innovator; he was one of the first to mix Roman Catholic ritual with African snake worship, for example. He was also the first to devote most of his powers to healing and reading the future. He was likewise the first voodoo cultist to cultivate a network of spies. All these features Marie eventually incorporated into her own voodoo practice, and it was not long before the student became the master.

In some important respects, however, Marie differed from her mentor. Although a master drummer, Doctor John avoided public displays of his talents for the most part—especially the notorious performances held in Congo Square.

Here, as elsewhere in New Orleans, the curious and the faithful came to watch the sensuous black dancers work themselves into an ecstatic state to the rhythm of African drums. To white sensibilities of the day, such performances were shockingly immoral—and irresistible to watch.

Marie, however, gained particular fame for her dancing at such spectacles. As part of her performance she often employed a large python, whom she called Zombi, as both prop and magical totem—and perhaps as a fertility symbol as well. In African spiritual belief, Damballa was the great snake creator-god; some even believed Marie's snake to be the actual incarnation of that god.

Another area where Marie differed radically from Doctor John lay in the domain of sexual mores. Doctor John was a notorious lecher and maintained a harem of no fewer than fifteen black female slaves as "wives"—as well as a white wife—and was reputed to have sired more than fifty children. His debauchery was part of his legend.

By contrast, Marie remained chaste and pious, at least to all outward appearances. She attended mass daily at the Cathedral of St. Louis, took Holy Communion regularly, and dutifully confessed her sins, receiving absolution from the cathedral's chaplain, Pere Antoine.

Marie is also credited with making the Blessed Virgin a focal point of New Orleans voodoo. Doctor John used icons of the saints and of Mary, but one gets the impression it was more for effect than substance. For Marie, it seems to have been a much deeper, heartfelt, devotion. Anglo-Saxon and Creole society may have regarded Marie's dancing as lewd and lascivious, but in matters of personal morality her behavior seems to have been impeccable.

When Marie was twenty-five, Mademoiselle Laveau married a freeman, Jacques Paris. Pere Antoine officiated over the sacramental marriage, and there is every indication Marie remained faithful to her wedding vows. After Jacques's death, the widow Paris remarried, this time to a man named Christophe Glapion, and this also was reputed to be a happy marriage.

Marie's marital life proved as fruitful as it was successful. Between her two marriages, Madame Marie bore fifteen children, and according to reliable accounts, she was a devoted and loving mother.

It is a basic tenet of Catholicism that to maintain a state of grace and obtain salvation, faith is not sufficient; it must be accompanied by good works. Marie did not neglect this aspect of her faith either. After the Battle of New Orleans, in January of 1815, for example, Marie tended to the Americans wounded in the fighting. In later years she regularly visited convicts in prison, bringing food and comfort to the condemned. During the terrible yellow fever epidemic of the 1850s, Marie was called upon to use her knowledge of herbs and roots to help combat the disease. She rose to the occasion, using all her powers to fight the dreaded plague.

Of course, while Marie was free with her benevolence for the poor, she had no problem charging whatever the traffic would bear for her magical services. Many clients were respectable white Creole matrons who might snub Marie in public at St. Louis Cathedral on Sunday but would come to her in secret the next day to buy *gris-gris* to end their husbands' affairs with their quadroon mistresses.

Marie's greatest case—or at least the one best known publicly—came in 1830. A young Creole gentleman stood accused of murder. Although his wealthy father had retained the best attorneys that money could buy, the case still seemed hopeless. His father sincerely believed his son to be innocent of the crime, but the evidence—and public opinion—was against him.

The father was frantic, his wife was on the verge of hysteria, and both were at their wits' end with concern for their son's fate. In desperation they turned to the only person who could offer any hope: Marie Laveau.

The boy's father was skeptical about employing the notorious sorceress, but what else could they do? The Creole aristocrat came to Marie and recited all the facts of his son's case—no doubt Marie already had learned the particulars of the case from her network of informants—and she listened patiently to the father's petition.

He finished by asking Marie to take his son's case and promised her anything, if she could but rescue the young man from the gallows. The gentleman was prepared to pay a substantial sum to see his son freed, but even he was taken aback by the payment Marie asked as her fee. Marie assured him his son would be acquitted, but in return she wanted title to the father's house on the Rue St. Anne.

Not only was the house one of the finest in that exclusive part of town, her demand openly defied the rigid laws of caste and class that ruled the city. It was simply unheard of for any person of color—regardless of wealth or ability, and much less a woman—to own property in the most exclusive part of *Le Vieux Carre*.

Whatever faults New Orleans's Creole elite of the era possessed (and there were many) they had one solid virtue: to the French-Spanish ruling class, *le famille* was everything. Thus, the father was willing to defy caste and class for the sake of his son and heir, even going so far as to make a pact with *Papa La Bas*—the Devil—if he thought it would do any good. Maybe, just maybe, he already had.

Swallowing hard, the father agreed to Marie's price—if only she could free his son.

The morning of the trial Marie made a pilgrimage to St. Louis Cathedral, where she passed the morning in prayer and deep meditation, all the while holding three Guinea peppers in her mouth. When Marie judged she had gained sufficient spiritual power, she made the short walk across *Le Place d'armes* to the Cabildo, the building which served as the seat of government and the courthouse, and entered unobserved.

Marie persuaded a worker to let her into the empty courtroom. She then proceeded to place the Guinea peppers under the judge's chair, then left.

Later that day the trial took place, and Marie stood just outside the Cabildo in the center of *Le Place d'armes*. After a time, the Creole gentleman emerged, accompanied by his son. The latter had been found not guilty of all charges, by reason of self-defense.

There were those, of course, who tried to rationalize the verdict after the fact. Some claimed Marie had intimidated a witness to change his testimony; others, said the judge was already sympathetic to the young Creole and his family. Whatever amount of truth may lay in these explanations, the fact remains that before the trial everyone regarded the case as unwinnable. Marie's supernatural intervention was universally regarded as decisive.

The Creole father was true to his word and handed over his mansion on the Rue Ste. Anne to Marie. People of all classes and colors united in acclaiming Marie's magic as preeminent, proclaiming her the Queen of Voodoo.

If Marie's new neighbors resented the presence of the voodoo queen next door, they did not show it—nor would they dare to. The Creole elite could at least reconcile themselves to Marie's presence in their midst with the notion that the society matrons would no longer need to travel to the bad part of town to obtain Marie's love potions and charms to keep straying husbands in line.

Marie's Rue Ste. Anne residence, though convenient to her rich clients, was not her only abode. She had a cottage called *Le Maison Blanche* on the shore of Lake Pontchartrain, where she held outdoor ceremonies on occasion and also conducted smaller, private ceremonies in which the actual voodoo work was performed.

Marie's best-known voodoo performances, however, were held at "the Wishing Spot," a place on the banks of the Bayou St. John that was closer to town than the white house by the lake.

Held on June 23—St. John's Eve—these ceremonies were the most important voodoo ritual of the year. Not only did the public attend, but members of the press were also invited by the publicity-minded Queen of Voodoo. Here the faithful and the cynical, black and white, male and female, stood shoulder to shoulder to watch the beautiful Marie and her followers gyrate and contort to the wild rhythms of the African drums. The "secret" ceremonies along Bayou St. John were spectacular performances, equal parts entertainment, magic, and art.

Like other voodoo practitioners in New Orleans, Marie had a keen appreciation for psychological effect in practicing her craft. The black cats, human skulls, and other voodoo paraphernalia that adorned her house—like her large *met tet*, Zombi the snake—were all calculated to instill feelings of awe and fear in her followers.

But it would be a mistake to assume that Marie's magic was all showmanship and no substance. On a number of occasions, for example, Marie was seen in broad daylight in widely separated parts of New Orleans at the same time. Modern biographers have assumed that this was due to the fact that one of her daughters, also called Marie, bore a striking resemblance to her mother. But surely the good citizens of New Orleans could distinguish between so familiar a figure as Marie and a daughter more than twenty years younger.

During the Middle Ages, it was widely believed that two sorts of persons were capable of bilocation (the ability to be in two places at the same time): witches and saints. It remains a matter of dispute which sort Marie was.

That Marie Laveau did many good works is undeniable. That there was also a darker side to the Queen of Voodoo is also true.

During her rise to power in the large occult community of New Orleans, she frequently resorted to intimidation. It is said that she would verbally accost—and sometimes come to blows with—those who would not acknowledge her superiority. Some claimed she also cast spells against her rivals, to weaken their powers and cause them to become ill.

Marie was alleged to be the proprietor of several brothels in New Orleans, houses which were believed to be protected from raids by police because even the local constabulary feared her wrath. If this were true, Marie would be in good company, for many respected citizens of the Crescent City quietly made fortunes from such illicit enterprises. Still, one may question the veracity of such claims, since Marie already enjoyed an ample income from her voodoo practice and was not known to have expensive tastes.

The worst accusations against Marie, however, were made by a leading citizen at the time, one J. B. Langrast. Alarmed at the growing influence of this "free woman of color," he accused Marie and her followers of many crimes, including theft and murder.

It was even alleged that Marie sacrificed abandoned or unwanted children and cooked their flesh. That a woman who gave birth to fifteen children, and was by all accounts a devoted and loving mother, could commit such a heinous crime seems unlikely on the face of it. Moreover, no evidence was ever offered to support this awful accusation—or any others.

At any rate, Marie's followers responded to Langrast's attacks on their queen in typical New Orleans fashion. *Gris-gris* bags began to appear on his doorstep—a sure sign he was being bewitched.

Soon, Langrast's personality began to change; he showed signs of extreme nervousness and paranoia. Finally, whether because of a voodoo curse or simply out of fear of physical injury, Langrast left the city, never to return. Marie Laveau was not a woman one wanted to get on the bad side of.

The turmoil of the Civil War and Reconstruction seems to have fazed the Queen of New Orleans little, if at all. But by 1869 an aging Marie went into retirement. Some claim she was actually deposed as the city's preeminent practitioner of voodoo at a gathering of leading conjure doctors and voodoo queens near *le Maison Blanche*. Supposedly, they voted her out because her powers had waned and she was too old to lead.

Whatever the truth, Marie did cease to actively practice her occult profession and instead focused solely on her Christian faith. She attended mass daily and devoted herself to ministering to those in prison, continuing to do so for as long as she was physically able.

On June 6, 1881, Marie Laveau's physical body ceased to function, and word quickly spread that she was dead. In her obituary, one local reporter summed up the ambivalence many felt toward the passing of one of New Orleans's most famous citizens: "Much evil dies with her, but should we not add, a little poetry as well?"

After her death many tried to lay claim to the power and authority that Marie wielded as voodoo queen, but none was ever quite able to match her. To this day, Marie Laveau is idolized by those who venerate her memory; and her magical powers are still summoned by the faithful.

Marie Laveau's tomb in St. Louis Cemetery No. 1 is festooned with plastic flowers and other small offerings. Triple X's crudely chalked on the sides of her mausoleum serve as mute testimony that some believers still invoke her spirit to obtain favors. In the minds of the faithful, at least, Marie is still very much a living presence. There are those, moreover, who would argue that Marie's spirit is present in more than a mere symbolic sense.

By some accounts, every year on June 23, Saint John's Eve, Marie Laveau rises from her tomb to preside over the great festival on the banks of Bayou St. John. They say she appears on such occasions as she once was, the beautiful young voodoo queen, sensuously writhing and gyrating to the hypnotic beat of African drums, accompanied by her faithful familiar, the python Zombi.

There are also reports of Marie and her daughter ("Marie Deux") floating down the Rue Ste. Anne clad in white gossamer gowns, with Marie wearing her *tignon* (a scarf with seven knots, a trademark of Madame Laveau).

Some denizens of New Orleans assert that the spirits of Marie and her followers still conduct "wild ceremonies" at her house at 1020 Rue Ste. Anne. Residents of a house on Chartres Street—believed to be Marie's first residence—report that her apparition visits their home as well. She is often seen hovering near the fireplace, and the owners of that house are certain it is Madame Laveau because the apparition wears Marie's telltale *tignon*.

In death, as in life, Marie commands respect. For example, when Madame Laveau's apparition appeared in a drug store on Rue Ste. Anne some time ago, a man in the shop failed to acknowledge her presence. She slapped him in the face, then floated up through the ceiling—as the pharmacy owner stood there watching in wide-eyed amazement.

Marie's spirit seems to be most active in St. Louis Cemetery No. 1. Believers and the curious often leave gifts and petitions beside her tomb, and many visitors report that her presence can be felt there—in one form or another.

One man claims he was slapped by an invisible hand while passing her burial vault—seemingly a typical activity of this voodoo queen's spirit. Some in New Orleans insist that Marie often changes into a black dog or black cow, and in this form she has been sighted on numerous occasions wandering the cemetery at night.

Recently, during one of the many ghost tours available in New Orleans, some visitors had an encounter which gives some credence to reports of Marie Laveau's postmortem activities.

In October 1998, just a week before Halloween, a group of tourists was taking the Haunted History Tour—one of many such tours in the city—and had come to the mausoleum containing the mortal remains of the two Maries in Saint Louis No. 1. To heighten the spookiness of the tour, the guide added a theatrical touch by performing a "ritual" he said would "call forth the spirit of Marie."

As the guide was reciting his counterfeit incantation, however, a mist began to rise from the ground around the tomb. One of the visitors was snapping photos of the tomb at the time, and the series of images she captured shows the mist coalescing into the shape of a woman, right before the tomb door. While cynics may try to explain the incident as mere coincidence, it was a most uncanny occurrence—and the photo depicts an uncanny likeness of Marie.

Of course, no matter what evidence is offered, cynics will always scoff at the notion of Marie Laveau rising from her tomb. But in a city where the unusual is usual and the supernatural commonplace, who is to say what can and cannot be? But if anyone could return from the dead, surely Marie Laveau would.

Many of the places associated with Marie are either torn down or not accessible to the public; her final resting place is, however, open to the public and her tomb apparently is still the object of much veneration by practitioners of Voudon:

St. Louis Cemetery No. 1
On Basin St., between Conti and St. Louis Streets

Marie, a devout Catholic as well as Queen of Voodoo, worshipped daily at the city's main cathedral. It too is open to the public, but it is still an active place of worship—and it too is haunted:

St. Louis Cathedral
Jackson Square (Place d'Armes)

15

At the Werewolves Ball

*He who makes a beast of himself
gets rid of the pain of being a man.*
—Samuel Johnson

THE DEVIL AND HIS MINIONS take many forms, and many are well-known below the Mason-Dixon Line. But there are a few of these entities whose dominions do not normally extend to Dixie.

The vampire is a creature believed to be native to the Near East and Eastern Europe. Aside from Anne Rice's fictional characters, the case for vampires in the South is very scanty. While much the same could be said of the werewolf, there is one notable exception.

Although the South is largely free of the bane of the werewolf, that is not entirely so. In the swamps and bayous of Louisiana lurks an ancient evil, the notorious *loup-garou*. It is a transplant perhaps, but nonetheless many claim it is present among us.

For many who live in the Delta, the belief remains strong—and is sometimes backed by facts—that the werewolf, or loup-garou, inhabits much of Louisiana's forgotten domain.

There are legends among numerous Southern Indian tribes about skin-changers or shape-shifters, but the loup-garou seem to have migrated with the French Acadians who fled Canada when the British took their land after the French and Indian War—the people we now call Cajuns. Loup-garou thus arrived in the South by way of Canada from France, where the belief in—and practice of—lycanthropy has long been entrenched.

If one were to believe Hollywood's depictions of this creature, one might assume that jolly Olde England was the main abode of the werewolf and his kin. But while the English werewolf first appears in writing about 1020 A.D., records of werewolves date back as far as pagan Celtic times in France.

By way of illustration, one may look at the evidence of our respective languages. Although English knows but one native word for this fey creature, in France almost every province and department has its own peculiar name for it. In Brittany, it is known as the *bisclavet*; in Alsace, it is the *hogemann* or *masolf*; in the Dordogne, *liberou*; in Normandy, the *garewul*; in Picardi, the *loueroux*. In toto, there are no fewer than sixty-nine different names for the werewolf in France.

When the Cajuns first arrived in Louisiana they were not exactly welcomed with open arms by the French already living there. The French Canadians had intermarried extensively with the Native American tribes, and they were predominantly of working-class origin. The Creole French fancied that they were of purer blood and a more aristocratic lineage than the plebian Cajuns, and so they had little to do with their Gallic brethren.

This did not bother the hardy Cajuns greatly, and they soon spread out into the countryside, settling on lands the Creole planters turned their noses up at: malarial swamps, marshes, and other inhospitable areas of the Delta. But along with these god-fearing Cajuns there undoubtedly came a few of the loup-garou, who also settled in the Louisiana bayous.

Who—or what—exactly is a loup-garou, and how does a person become one? Hollywood would lead us to believe that a loup-garou is a man who is under a curse, for if someone is bitten by a werewolf and survives, that person in turn becomes a werewolf. While this may well be true in a few cases, according to Old World court records and modern Cajun lore, the loup-garou is a more complex creature.

The majority of the loups-garou, say the Cajuns, are people under a self-imposed enchantment. According to one observer in the 1930s, "Loups-garou is them people what wants to do bad work, and changes themselves into wolves." Most such persons, then, are werewolves by choice, not by fate. The Loup-garou is a man-wolf that can walk upright on two legs, has large red eyes and a pointed nose, and appears to be a wolf in every other respect, including having shaggy hair and long, pointed nails.

During the 1930s, WPA workers in Louisiana's bayou country collected a great deal of information about the supernatural from the local Cajuns. Some of the material was pure legend but much was not.

One man, for example, told a gullible government worker that loups-garou used bats as big as airplanes to transport themselves about the bayous at night. When they arrived at a victim's house, they would make the bats drop them down the chimney and then, while the victim slept, the werewolf would bite the person's neck and suck his blood, much as a vampire would do. Once this had been done, the victim would become a loup-garou.

While some victims may have been recruited in this manner, other sources assert that the aspiring loup-garou would transform into a wolf or wolf-man of its own free will.

But whether a person becomes a loup-garou by his own choice or another's, there is one feature common to all Cajun loups-garou that is vastly different from the Hollywood stereotype. In the movies, werewolves are depicted as solitary creatures, loners, outcasts from society. The loups-garou are anything but loners; they are as gregarious as their mortal Cajun counterparts.

When they are not roaming the bayous at night searching for fresh victims or plotting other mischief, loups-garou like to party. "They hold balls on Bayou Goula all the time, men and women both together," claimed one informant years ago. "They dance and carry on just like animals then."

To learn more of the lore surrounding the loup-garou, I consulted an acquaintance who is a certified coon-ass Cajun. Paul is a cab driver in Nashville, and although he has been a resident of Music City for many years, he hails originally from Louisiana. Cajuns are by nature gregarious and loquacious, and Paul is no exception. However, when I started to query him about loup-garou, he gave me a funny look and became uncharacteristically reticent.

The direct approach failing, I decided to take a different tack and invited him to Tebeax's for some food, beverage, and good music—three things dear to the heart of every true Cajun.

In the murky comfort of the tavern off Lower Broadway, I found Paul a little more talkative. While confessing that he had little first-hand experience with the subject, Paul did confirm that tales of such creatures as loups-garou are common in the Delta, although they are most often like stories of the boogey-man. Parents will warn their children to "be good, otherwise loup-garou will get you!"

When asked if he had heard of a *ru-garou*, Paul replied with a grin, "No, but maybe that was what they called them in Australia."

What of loups-garou congregating to dance and frolic? Paul said he had heard something to that effect, but as he understood it, they did so only during a full moon or on one special night of the year—June 23, St. John's Eve—when all the loups-garou from throughout the Delta would gather for a great convocation on Bayou Goula. This convention of werewolves, he said, is somewhat like a Shriner's convention—only a bit wilder.

Did Paul know if the loups-garou did anything besides dance and howl at the moon there on St. John's Eve? He believed so, but he said it was not something I would want to tell my *grand-mere* about.

When I asked if he had ever seen a loup-garou, Paul said he had not, nor did he have any desire to do so. I was about to ask more silly questions, but a Zydeco group replaced the Cajun fiddler onstage and the music began to drown out our conversation.

Bayou Goula is a real place, although why it should be the focal point for the loup-garou social life is a mystery.

Located in Iberville Parish, Bayou Goula lays claim to being the oldest French settlement in Louisiana. Today, it is a virtual "ghost town." Extending along the river road (Route 405), Bayou Goula is now just a marker on the map, part of the township of White Castle. Aside from a stretch of country road, the only notable landmarks are a cemetery, a few old homes, and an ancient chapel on a small bend of the Mississippi.

In sum, Bayou Goula does not seem today a promising place for any sort of convention. But then, if you were a werewolf, perhaps you would not want a lot of eyes prying into your business.

If it is true that most loups-garou become werewolves by choice, the question arises: Why would one wish to become a murderous beast? As one source noted above, one reason that a person might wish to become a wolf would be to commit malicious acts, since such a transformation would allow him or her to do things normally forbidden by the moral standards of our society.

Bloodlust is a primitive drive; and because it is not generally approved of in society, it is suppressed. If one could become a beast, however, then such a primitive urge could be indulged without fear of censure or punishment.

Moreover, the wolf possesses physical strength, agility, guile, and ferocity. By becoming a wolf, a human might also gain access to all these feral powers and more. It is an attractive proposition to some.

In ancient times the wolf—and werewolf—were often accorded a degree of respect, even reverence. Warriors frequently sought to emulate the ferocity of the wolf, and wearing a wolf's head was considered a mark of honor. Warriors known as *berserkers* even wore magic pelts of either bear or wolf skin, which enabled them to transform themselves into man-beasts. These creatures were powerful and ferocious in battle, tearing their enemies limb from limb. Pagan sorcerers freely resorted to this manner of enchantment, and although feared for their powers, they were held in awe because of their abilities.

With the advent of Christianity, the wolf took on a far more sinister cast. Practitioners of the magical art of skin-changing—especially those whose power animal was the wolf—were widely regarded as servants of the Devil. Hounded from the light, the cult of the werewolf went underground.

If not by infectious wolf bite, exactly how does one transform into a loup-garou? One Cajun informant told the WPA in the 1930s that "they rub themselves with some voodoo grease and come out just like wolves is." This also dovetails with what is known of the cult of werewolves in the Old World.

Just as witches were said to use an ointment to enable them to fly, loups-garou too have been known to employ a similar tincture to do their misdeeds. French court records from the mid-eighteenth century relate how one young woman accused of being a loup-garou offered to reveal the secrets of her cult in return for leniency. Skin-changers were regarded as a type of sorcerer and, like witches, were subject to being burned at the stake.

Fetching a pot of the magic salve from her home, the woman applied it to her head, neck, and shoulders, and immediately fell into a death-like coma. When she awoke, she informed her inquisitors that while in the trance she had roamed the countryside as a loup-garou and killed a cow and a sheep. The court sent runners to the places she said she had attacked livestock, and the investigators did indeed find mutilated animal remains.

Some who have studied the subject believe that such sorcerers, through the intercession of the Devil, can transform their physical body directly into that of a beast. Others assert that the loup-garou is capable of bilocation. The loup-garou's human shell stays intact, but the sorcerer projects his or her consciousness into the form of a wolf elsewhere—and it is that astral body that actually commits the offensive acts.

The above methods may be true, but paranormal researchers combing through old accounts have determined that most such creatures employed a magic pelt—a piece of wolf fur that has been enchanted—the mere application of the pelt to bare flesh was sufficient to transform them. The use of the witch's ointment—or "voodoo grease"—was the active ingredient applied to the pelt that completed the task.

Whatever means the loup-garou may use to become a wolf, for folks living on the bayou, a more immediate concern is how best to defend oneself against the loup-garou's onslaught. Ordinary bullets are useless against such a foe, but fortunately the creature is vulnerable to other means of defense.

For one thing, loups-garou are terrified of frogs. Bullets will not ward off an attack, but throwing a bayou bullfrog at a loup-garou is sure to chase him away.

Another remedy—as any Cajun housewife can testify—is plain salt. Salt traditionally has been used as a preservative to ward off corruption. It is said that the Lord of Corruption and his many servants hate it.

Hanging a new flour sifter outside the threshold of a house can also be an effective deterrent. The loup-garou will be compelled to count all the holes in the sifter, and when he does, he can be trapped. Sprinkling salt on the creature as he stands enthralled, counting, will cause his fur to catch fire wherever the salt lands. The loup-garou will step outside his burning skin and then run away.

According to some, loups-garou can also change themselves into other creatures besides a wolf. One man, thought to be a loup-garou, was said to be able transform himself into a mule, so that he could plow his own field!

Needless to say, scientists and others of the same ilk, who firmly deny the existence of anything beyond the limits of the five senses, reject the Cajun belief out of hand. Indeed, on the face of it, the notion that a man or a woman could turn at will into a wolf-like creature may seem absurd, a view that is substantiated by the scarcity of published contemporary firsthand sightings in bayou country.

This scarcity of eyewitness accounts, however, may be due to the traditionally insular nature of Cajun society as well as the continuing taboo against talking too freely about supernatural subjects—especially to outsiders. Ironically, just outside Cajun country there have been several documented contemporary sightings of these creatures.

In 1971 a suburban neighborhood in Mobile, Alabama, was briefly terrorized by nocturnal visits of a creature fitting the description of a loup-garou. Residents in the spring of that year reported seeing a being whose top half was that of a woman, while the bottom half was that of a wolf. All of the sightings occurred at night, and although the police investigated, their findings were inconclusive.

In 1958 a woman living near the town of Greggton, Texas, on the western border of Louisiana, claimed that a "huge, shaggy, wolf-like creature" tried to break into her house through her bedroom window. A flashlight scared it off, and the woman saw the creature flee into a nearby clump of bushes. But what she saw emerge from the bushes a short while later was not some shaggy wolf, but the figure of a tall man, who strode rapidly up the road and was quickly enveloped by the night.

Could these sightings be loups-garou that strayed farther afield? Both states adjoin Louisiana, so it is not out of the question.

Far away to the north, in northern Michigan and Minnesota, there have been scattered accounts of similar encounters with man-wolf creatures. Since these states border Canada and many residents are descended from French Canadians, it is possible that these encounters may also be linked to straying loups-garou.

Another piece of the puzzle that has not been considered before, and which may well point toward this fey creature's existence, involves the many mysterious cases of animal mutilations that have occurred in recent decades. Dogs, cattle, sheep, and other livestock have been found eviscerated, dismembered, or simply drained of blood. Yet in most cases, there are no visible footprints or animal tracks near the carcasses.

Paranormal researcher John Keel has conservatively estimated that in the thirty-five-year period ending in 1994, at least 7,000 cases of animal mutilation were reported. These strange incidents have been blamed variously on UFOs, secret government research, and satanic cults. No single explanation may explain all of these cases, but at least some of the incidents may well be due to the loup-garou and his cousins. Certainly the traditional literature regarding suspected werewolf attacks on livestock has a strong parallel to many of the modern-day mutilation cases.

The swamps and woodlands of Louisiana hold many secrets. If Cajun lore sometimes seems too outlandish to believe, the truth that exists in bayou country is often wilder still. Loup-garou has a long, albeit dishonorable, history among the Cajuns, with roots stretching all the way back to ancient times. In truth, the creature's origins lie deep in the darkness of the human soul.

Unlike the solitary beast of Hollywood fables, however, the Cajun werewolf is a creature as fond of *le bon temps et jolie compagnie* as any mortal.

To those brave souls who would venture into the bayou to find out for themselves if the tales of the loup-garou are true, be advised to bring plenty of salt. And also bear in mind, attendance at *Le Bal Goula* is by invitation only.

If you go ...
More haints and haunts of Dixie to see in Louisiana:

BATON ROUGE
THE SPANISH MOON
1109 Highland Road
Baton Rouge, LA 70802
(225) 383-6066
www.thespanishmoon.com

The Spanish Moon is a rock night club housed in an old firehall that once was a flophouse. The resident ghost is thought to be the shade of a young man who died there when it was still a sleazy hotel. Beer taps turn on by themselves, strange noises and flying glassware have been reported here.

DESTREHAM
DESTREHAN PLANTATION (1787)
13034 River Road • P.O. Box 5
Destrehan, LA 70047
(985) 764-9315 • (877) 453-2095
www.destrehanplantation.org

The ghost of the plantation's former master, Stephen Henderson, roams "the oldest surviving plantation in the Lower Mississippi Valley." Other ghosts have also been reported.

GARYVILLE
SAN FRANCISCO PLANTATION (1856)
2646 Highway44
Garyville, LA 70051
(985) 535-2341 • (888) 509-1756
www.sanfranciscoplantation.org

"Charles" is the resident spirit that haunts this antebellum home.

NEW ORLEANS

It has been said that there are more ghosts in the Vieux Carre (French Quarter) than there are wrought iron balconies; the following are therefore just a small sampling of the many haunted spots in the Crescent City.

THE CABILDO
(AND SPANISH DUNGEON)
701 Chartres Street
New Orleans, LA 70116
(504) 568-6968 • (800) 568-6968
www.ism.crt.state/la.us/cabildo

Located on Jackson Square, this was formerly the city's courthouse and government building, and where Marie Laveau's most famous "case" took place; now a history museum. Various spirits are said to haunt the old public building.

FLANAGAN'S CAFÉ AND PUB
625 St. Philip Street
New Orleans, LA 70110
(504) 522-0300

The resident revenant is "Angela," allegedly the relative of a former owner of the club who committed suicide in the powder room. She has been sighted by guests and staff roaming the grounds of the restaurant.

PIRATE'S ALLEY

Only a block long, running from Chartres Street at Jackson Square (Place d'Armes) to Royal Street, this scenic side street is nonetheless home to a number of ghosts.

CRESCENT CITY BOOKS
204 Chartres Street
New Orleans, LA 70130
(504) 524-4997

A used-book store housed in a nineteenth-century building, the store plays host to educated ghosts. The hauntings here have been investigated by various paranormal research groups.

Louisiana Ghost Tours

NEW ORLEANS

There are nearly as many ghost tours of New Orleans as there are ghosts in the Crescent City. Following is but a sample of some of the more prominent ones.

FRENCH QUARTER PHANTOM GHOST TOUR
Box office in Flanagan's Pub,
625 St. Philip Street
(888) 90Ghost • (504) 666-8300
www.frenchquarterphantoms.com

GHOST AND SPIRIT WALKING TOUR
(Big Easy Tours)
(800) 301-3184
www.BigEasyTours.us

GHOSTS AND SPIRITS TOUR
(Gray Line Tours)
(800) 535-7786 • (504) 569-1401
www.graylineneworleans.com/ghost

HAUNTED HISTORY TOURS
Offers several different ghost tours, including a ghost tour, a voodoo tour, and a vampire tour
97 Fontainebleu Drive
(888) 6GHOSTS • (504) 861-2727
www.hauntedhistorytours.com

NEW ORLEANS SPIRIT TOURS
Daily cemetery and voodoo tours
c/o Royal Blend Coffee House,
621 Royal Street
(866) 369-1224 • (504) 314-0806
www.neworleanstours.net

HAUNTED AMERICA TOURS
Offers ghost tours of New Orleans
www.hauntedamericatours.com

16

The Great International Hoodoo Conspiracy and Other Tales of the Black Art

THE SLEEPY SMALL TOWNS of the Deep South seem an unlikely breeding ground for the occult. Still less does one associate the old stomping grounds of Elvis Presley and William Faulkner with international conspiracies to bewitch, befuddle, and otherwise disrupt the judicial system.

Beyond the pristine picket fences and whitewashed front porches of Dixie exists another realm—every bit as real and a good deal more deadly. For the most part the dark side stays hidden from view. But every once in awhile events cause this sinister undercurrent of daily life to bubble to the surface and be exposed to the light of day.

In the fall of 1988 such an incident happened. It gained local notoriety for a time, briefly illuminating the wormy underside of the rock in Tupelo, Mississippi. In October of 1988 two half-brothers—petty hoodlums by the name of Leroy Ivy and John Henry Adams—became the focus of a case of modern-day hoodoo.

It had started back in July of that year, when twenty-five-year-old John Henry was sentenced to forty years in prison for robbing a gas station. The heist had netted him all of eight hundred dollars. It was seemingly a harsh sentence for such a petty heist, but John Henry had a string of armed-robbery and drug convictions to his credit already, so the good judge had given the unrepentant Adams a suitably long vacation at Parchman Prison Farm, the state penitentiary. Judge Tommy Gardner was not one to suffer fools—or habitual criminals—lightly.

Neither John Henry nor his half-brother Leroy Ivy was terribly happy with Judge Gardner, and the pair resolved to have revenge on the judge in a way that would not implicate them. Not knowing any underworld denizens in Tupelo, and lacking the necessary funds to hire a professional hit-man anyhow, Leroy and John Henry hit on the idea of employing hoodoo—"conjure magic"—to do away with the judge.

Hoodoo is sometimes confused with its close relation, voodoo. While both derive from African magical traditions and share similar practices, voodoo has been more heavily influenced by Latin culture—specifically the rituals and cult practices of the Roman Catholic church. Voodoo employs its own priesthood of sorts and also relies on traditional Catholic iconography to help summon the supernatural powers.

In contrast, while Catholicism had a system of saints and elaborate rituals of a seemingly magical nature, Protestantism had no analogous system to which slaves might adapt their African beliefs. Thus, while voodoo reigned in New Orleans and adjacent areas, hoodoo thrived in those areas outside French and Spanish influence.

Hoodoo—thought to be derived from the African word *juju*—is less formalized and less organized than its Latin cousin. It is also far more widespread, extending throughout most of the South. Hoodoo is not to be confused with the simple reading of signs or omens; rather, hoodoo is the active casting of spells—or the removal of same.

Especially in the antebellum South, hoodoo was a means by which the black slave might obtain some measure of power—or perhaps even control. The awe and mystery of hoodoo was something even bull-whips and chains could not overcome. And when a slave or freeman ran afoul of the white man's law—as they frequently did—hoodoo was often employed as a means of obtaining justice from an unjust system. To this day there are conjurers who specialize in "law" cases.

In 1985, for example, a man standing trial in Winona, Mississippi, on charges of counterfeiting, moonshining, and assorted drug offenses procured the services of a hoodoo conjure doctor to help him. The conjurer poured a line of yellow hoodoo powder at the entrance to the courtroom, and when jurors saw the "goofer dust," several of them refused to cross the line and enter the courtroom.

John Henry Adams and Leroy Ivy, however, were not so much seeking legal assistance as they were revenge. The half-brothers wanted Judge Gardner dead, and through hoodoo they thought they might accomplish this without bringing down punishment on their own heads.

They would first need to obtain certain personal items from the judge that would be needed to create the hex. These objects they would then send to a well-known voodoo priest in New Orleans, who in turn would send them to an even more powerful conjurer in Jamaica. The Jamaican "bush doctor" would actually cast the spell against the judge.

The lengths to which John Henry and Leroy went to secure such a spell were remarkable but hardly unique. However, one may wonder why they hatched such an elaborate scheme instead of hiring a local *cunger* (conjurer) to do the job.

There is a widespread notion among some believers that hoodoo does not work on white people. As Mama Mollie of Jackson once put it, "A Negro cannot conjure a white man." So, perhaps John Henry and Leroy felt they needed the services of a witch doctor outside the United States who possessed sufficient occult powers to cast a death spell on a white judge.

At any rate, in order to cast the spell Leroy Ivy needed to first procure a photograph of the judge and a lock of his hair. Once these were obtained the Jamaican sorcerer could conjure up his malevolent spell. Then, and only then, would the good judge curl up his toes and wither away—or so Leroy and John Henry hoped.

Leroy approached a woman who claimed she had access to the judge's personal effects. Leroy promise her a thousand dollars if she could get him what he needed. One chilly morning in October 1988 he met her outside the local J. C. Penney store.

However, Leroy was only able to scrape up a hundred dollars, far less than the agreed sum. Nevertheless, the woman accepted the money and gave him the photo and an envelope of hair clippings—and within minutes Leroy found himself in handcuffs.

It seems the local constabulary had gotten wind of the half-brothers' international hoodoo plot and set up a sting operation to catch the would-be conspirators. For all their scheming, neither Leroy nor John Henry had taken into account "Jailhouse Jerry."

Informed that there was an elaborate plot to do away with Judge Gardner, Jerry Butler, a.k.a. Jailhouse Jerry of the Mississippi Highway Patrol, assembled a team to investigate the conspiracy.

While Officer Butler may not have put much stock in the hoodoo curse, the law views any threat against a judge as a very serious crime.

Technically, the Highway Patrol could not charge Ivy and Adams with conjuring—it is not illegal in Mississippi. But contriving to kill a state judge is; thus, Leroy and John Henry were indicted on charges of conspiracy "with malice of forethought" to murder Judge Tommy Gardner.

What followed has been described as a media frenzy by some. It had been a long time since anyone was arrested for witchcraft in America, and the circumstances of the case caught the attention of many in the press. Sympathetic lawyers—keeping one eye on the media—called in from all over the country to offer their assistance to the half-brothers' defenders. The small-town crooks were now big-time defendants—all because of hoodoo.

Barry Ford, who was appointed to defend Leroy, stated categorically that "there's no such thing as murder by voodoo." But Michael Throne, John Henry's attorney, had done considerable background research on the case to prepare for the trial and was far less cynical about the black art's efficacy. "Witch doctors actually use some very practical and deadly methods," he told one reporter later.

Even if Ivy and Adams were less than competent conspirators, one should not dismiss the possibility that their hex might have done some real harm. In Haiti and other Caribbean nations where this black art has deep roots, using magic to harm someone is a criminal offense. Hoodoo has been used by generations of Haitians to do away with personal enemies and political rivals. And if the truth be known, malicious conjure magic has been used for countless years in the United States for similar purposes, often with success.

In 1869, for example, the *Nashville Banner* reported a case of "fetish doings" in the Deep South. A black woman by the name of Sarah Robertson, about thirty years of age, had suddenly fallen ill.

When the reporter saw Sarah she was still alive—but failing fast. A hoodoo man from South Carolina had given Sarah some brown sugar, which she believed had been mixed with a secret "fetish" compound.

At first Sarah felt a slight giddiness and a queasiness of the stomach, but that went away. A day or so later, however, the symptoms returned, along with sharp pains in the abdomen and a high fever, followed by vomiting.

Although one might well believe the conjurer who cast the spell on Sarah may have slipped some poison into the sugar, no poison could possibly account for what she began vomiting up: a snake, a quantity of human hair, a large spider, and even several cockroaches.

When last heard from, Sarah Robertson was not expected to survive the conjuring laid against her.

Even in recent times, cases of people being hoodoo'd to death have been documented throughout the South. Unless a conjurer of equal power is brought in to remove the spell, the target of the hex almost always dies.

There was a case in the 1980s, for example, of a man who was admitted to the University of Mississippi's hospital in Oxford, suffering from paralyzing headaches. The man had been hoodoo'd by someone who spread goofer dust inside his hatband. Goofer dust is one of the more important potions used by practitioners of this black art; its active ingredient is dirt obtained from a graveyard.

Doctors and psychiatrists tried to treat the man with modern medical techniques, but nothing worked. Finally the doctors gave up and called in a hoodoo doctor, who counteracted the spell with herbs, chants—and a mojo charm.

Medical doctors often dismiss such cases as "nervous collapse." But the "wise women" and "herb doctors" know better.

In the woods just outside affluent Oxford, Mississippi—hometown of William Faulkner—an aged black woman named Mattie Yarber lives in a run-down shack. Folks thereabouts claim she is a conjurer and has been known to cast a spell or two, even on her own family members—a charge she denies. But Mattie is familiar with the ways of hoodoo nonetheless.

Does hoodoo work? Is it a real force? Opinions differ, and a reporter from up north once posed those questions to her. Even as Mattie huddled over an old woodburning stove to keep warm against the winter chill, she cracked a knowing smile when put to the question.

Can hoodoo kill? Well, as Mattie Yarber put it, "Yes, child, there's things in this world that normal thinking don't quite explain."

17

Curse of the Singing River

THEY CALL IT THE SINGING RIVER, and for as long as anyone can remember, the Pascagoula River has had that epithet. By all accounts, it is a name well earned.

For generations now, fishermen, boaters, and assorted other folk that frequent the banks of the Pascagoula have reported strange sounds coming from the river. Many have heard this weird music, and different stories have been told about its origin, but all agree that in some manner the river is haunted.

Located in the extreme southwestern corner of Mississippi, the Pascagoula starts at the confluence of two smaller streams, the Leaf and the Chickasawhay. From there, near the old logging town of Merrill, the river meanders upwards of fifty miles to the gulf port of Pascagoula.

With its marshes and bayous teeming with fish and wildlife, the river is a hunter's paradise, and so far as we know, it was much the same before the first white men came to the region.

When and how the river first began to make its music is not known for sure, but it is documented that when the French first settled along the coast of the gulf, the Pascagoula River was already singing its siren song.

Etienne de Perier, the French royal governor of Louisiana in the early 1700s, made a tour of newly settled regions in the "Bay of St. Louis," visiting the new French outposts of Biloxi, Pascagoula, and Mobile.

While on his summer inspection tour, he paid a visit to the Pascagoula Indians ("bread eaters") who lived beside the river of the same name. While among the Pascagoula, Governor Perier was invited to go to the mouth of the river to hear the mysterious music for himself.

Midsummer seems the best time to hear the singing of the river, and moonlight nights, when all the country about is quiet, seem particularly conducive to experiencing the wonderment. Governor Perier heard with his own ears the haunting sounds of the river.

Some say the music issues from submerged caverns or grottos in the bed of the river. Those traveling on the river by boat swear the music seems to ooze up through the water from under the vessel's keel and that it sounds like a thousand harps.

To those on shore, especially those standing on the banks near the town of Biloxi, however, it often seemed more like a low humming sound—as of a chorus of hundreds of phantom voices. In any case, the sounds have been clearly heard by hundreds, perhaps thousands of people every year.

What, one may well ask, is the cause of the mysterious music? As with most such wonderments of Dixie, there is a story or two to go along with the mystery. There are different versions of the tale, but the earliest—and as far as we know, the most accurate—dates to the time soon after the white man's arrival on these shores.

About 1539 Hernando Desoto and his troops tramped through this part of the South, leaving the native town of Mauvila (Mobile) in ashes. The Biloxi tribe, which lived on the banks of the Pascagoula River, had managed to avoid the Spaniards' courtesy call. It was not long after this, however, that a white man did appear among the Biloxi.

The man was pale of skin, with a flowing gray beard, and clad in long black robes. The man in the black robes was not like the other whites the Indians had encountered. He came not with sword and armor, or vicious war-dogs, but instead carried with him a wooden cross and a thick black book. These things, he said, would set the Biloxi free and they would live for all eternity.

Because the graybeard came in peace, the Biloxi extended their hospitality to him, although at first they resisted his efforts to convert them to this new religion. The Biloxi, it should be understood, already had a deity to whom they were very much devoted.

It seems that at some time in the distant past, the Biloxi had emerged from the sea, where they said they had originated. They were different from the other tribes, being lighter in complexion and paying homage to a being that ruled beneath the waves.

In the center of their town, the Biloxi raised a large earthen pyramid, surmounted by a temple dedicated to a mermaid goddess. Inside the building was a carving of this creature, to which they gave a tithe of their catch, offering fresh oysters and fish.

Whenever the moon was full, the Biloxi would gather around the graven image inside the temple, and with cunningly wrought instruments of strange shape and voices united, they would make music of great power, chanting the mermaid's praises in unearthly tones the like of which no man has heard before or since. There was powerful magic in that music.

The people of the river were much attached to their mermaid goddess, but the white man in the black robes was persistent. The Biloxi found their gray-bearded visitor to be both kind and sincere, and as he learned to speak their tongue more fluently, the man began to wean these simple fisher-folk from their devotion to the mermaid goddess.

At last, after many months of patient work, the Jesuit's efforts began to bear fruit. A number of the headmen of the tribe consented to be baptized, along with their families, and many more were wavering on the edge—desiring to become Christians yet fearful of the mermaid's wrath should they do so.

Then, at midnight on a summer evening when the moon was full, lighting up the night as though it were day, there arose a great boiling in the middle of the placid Pascagoula.

The water emitted a deep groaning sound and then erupted, as if it had been struck by a whirlwind, sending forth a series of waves outward to both shores in rapid succession.

The water thus disturbed seemed to form itself into a great foaming column. Out of the top of this pillar arose the mermaid. She stood gazing toward the shore with "magnetic" eyes—eyes that had the power to hypnotize and enchant.

Then the mermaid began singing her song, and her dulcet tones proved even more enchanting than her gaze. The siren's song was capable of "fascinating into madness" all who listened to it.

The commotion in the river roused the entire village of the Biloxi from a sound sleep. Rushing to the riverbank, they saw the living embodiment of the being they once had worshipped.

When she saw them, the mermaid refined her tones into a still more bewitching melody, chanting over and over the same chorus:

> *"Come to me, come to me, children of the sea,*
> *Neither bell, book, nor cross shall win ye*
> *from your queen."*

The more the Indians listened to her song, the deeper into a trance they all seemed to fall. At last, as if he were sleepwalking, one of the headmen of the tribe—the first to be baptized—started walking directly into the river, marching straight into the current until his head disappeared beneath the waves.

As the siren's chanting became more intense and bewitching, the whole village fell under her spell. Men, women, and children, one by one, plunged into the river, chanting the mermaid's song, irresistibly drawn into the swirling depths.

When at last the Biloxi had all disappeared beneath the waves, the mermaid cackled a wild laugh of triumph that echoed across the water. Then the river returned to its bed with a roar, and within a few minutes the surface was once again placid, as though nothing had ever happened.

The only surviving witness to the whole affair was the Jesuit priest. Somehow, the man in the black robe had not been affected by the siren's song, or her hypnotic gaze. Perhaps it was the power of the cross he wore, or the sanctity of his holy office—or perhaps the mermaid left the priest behind to spread the tale of what happened.

The priest stood there, stunned, unable at first to comprehend the magnitude of all he had witnessed. Tradition has it that the priest later died of remorse, attributing the victory of the mermaid demon to his own failure—for not having been in a perfect state of grace.

Other versions of the legend of the Singing River hold that the Biloxi's mass suicide was a desperate last resort to avoid enslavement by an enemy tribe. Some even ascribe the tragedy to the ill-starred romance between a Biloxi brave and a maiden betrothed to an enemy chief. In any case, generations of Native Americans in the region who heard the music coming from the river attributed it to the chanting of the lost tribe residing beneath the waters of the Pascagoula, still under a deep enchantment. This tradition in turn was passed on to the whites who later settled in the area.

There is, in fact, some evidence of a mass extinction—if not of the whole Biloxi tribe, at the very least an entire town. Whether this was due to an enemy's wrath, a sudden tidal wave that engulfed the coast, or the mermaid's terrible revenge is impossible to say for certain at this distance in time.

In recent decades the Pascagoula River has been very active with other sorts of paranormal activity as well. In 1973, for example, there was a spate of UFO sightings and close encounters with strange beings, including some sort of underwater entity. Although not directly related to the hauntings of the Singing River, such incidents point to this area being what journalist John Keel has called a "window area"—a zone of intense paranormal activity, where multiple phenomena (hauntings, UFOs, weird beings, etc.) are prone to occur with abnormal frequency.

Along the Mississippi coast there is little doubt that the ghosts of the Biloxi still haunt the wide waters of the Pascagoula. Late on a summer night, when the moon is at its zenith, the chanting wells up from the watery depths. It is then that fishermen along the banks will swear they hear eerie echoes of phantom voices emanating from the river, as loud and as clear as any mortal chorus.

There is a postscript to the story of the Singing River—a part of the story that has yet to be fulfilled.

It is related that on his deathbed, the Jesuit priest declared that there was a way the lost souls of the Biloxi entrapped by the mermaid could be freed from their curse and sent on to heaven.

If, on a Christmas night, at the very stroke of midnight, when the moon is at its fullest, a priest should dare to come to the place where the music is coming forth, then he may free the Biloxi. If he arrives in a boat propelled by himself alone, and drops a crucifix in the water over the chanting, then the souls of the Biloxi will be released from the thrall of the mermaid. However, should the cleric succeed in his quest, then neither priest nor boat will ever be seen again.

To date, no one—believer or skeptic—has been willing to undertake the challenge to see if it proves true. Until then, the ghosts of the Biloxi will continue their chanting.

18

The Devil's Backbone: Ghosts and Haunts of Natchez and the Natchez Trace

LONG BEFORE THE WHITE MAN tread its sinuous paths, the Natchez Trace twined its way across the uplands of Dixie. From the Cumberland Valley to the port of Natchez, by the broad banks of the Mississippi, the Natchez Trace was the main overland route connecting the western settlements of the American frontier to the fleshpots of the Louisiana territories.

As vital as the trace was to the early pioneers, however, it also acquired a sinister reputation, gaining the nickname "the Devil's Backbone." Never was a road's ill fame so justly earned.

Many pioneers returning from Natchez or New Orleans, laden down with Spanish silver and French gold from the sale of their goods, ran afoul of bloodthirsty highwaymen who infested the route. Others never even made it out of the town of Natchez, finding a violent end in one of the taverns, gambling dens, or brothels that dotted the banks of the river like pockmarks.

It was a dangerous time, and Natchez was a dangerous place for the unwary—and the frontier town and the path that led to it left an indelible mark on Dixie's history. Given such a tumultuous past, it is little wonder that the trace has also left an indelible impression on the psychic plane as well. In Natchez and all along the trace, reports of encounters strange or supernatural are commonplace—and often as not are traceable to the violent events of this legendary era.

One of the worst highwaymen to plague the trace was a rogue named John Murrell. Starting young, John quickly graduated from simple theft and pilfering to armed robbery and murder. Near Farmington, Tennessee, along the Natchez Trace, an old house once served as a hideout for Murrell. One of his gang was shot down there in an argument over money, and his blood could not be washed away, no matter what was done. Although the house burned down in 1968, the ghost of the murdered man is still said to be seen haunting the charred ruins.

Farther along the trace, near Tupelo, Mississippi, is a spot called Witches Dance. A long-standing tradition in the area declares that this was a place where witches would gather to perform their infernal rituals. The witches cavorted and danced, and wherever their feet touched the ground, the grass would wither and turn brown, and grow nevermore.

Andrew Jackson—whose interests encompassed both the natural and supernatural—investigated the place and verified that the bald patches did exist. But even Old Hickory could find no rational explanation for them. Indians who traveled the trace shunned Witches Dance, considering it "bad medicine."

A member of this dark sisterhood is reputed to have gotten possession of the skull of one of the infamous Harpe brothers. She ground the skull into powder to use in her potions, for the concentrated evil of Harpe's bones was apparently regarded as a potent ingredient for casting her wicked wiccan spells.

Strange encounters were not uncommon along the twisted byways of the old trace, even by some of its more ferocious denizens. Notorious highwayman Joseph Thompson Hare had supernatural visions along the trace, and he related some of them to his captors. Hare told of seeing a pale-white steed—a ghost horse—which he took to be a divine sign for him to mend his crooked ways. He didn't. Hare was hanged for his crimes in 1818.

As one draws close to the city of Natchez, the frequency of such strange and supernatural phenomena seems to increase.

On the northern outskirts of town, for example, is a place they call the Devil's Punch Bowl. A large circular depression several acres in extent, it was the abode of road agents and river pirates during frontier days.

The wickedness of the place was renowned, and notorious highwaymen such as Murrell used it as a hideout. That it both overlooked the Mississippi and was close to the trace made it doubly useful, for one could plunder passing boats or rob overland wayfarers with equal ease. Its sinister repute was further enhanced by the strange phenomena associated with it.

For instance, compasses on ships passing close to the Devil's Punch Bowl would suddenly go haywire, often spinning round and round in confusion. Some have said the Punch Bowl was formed by the impact of a giant meteorite, and that the iron in that body was what caused the magnetic anomaly. Others claim it was the hoards of pirate treasure buried beneath there that made the compass needles go crazy. Still others flatly assert that it is the Devil himself that causes nature's laws to go so awry.

It is in the town of Natchez itself, however, where one finds the greatest concentration of the supernatural. In many cases, the haints and hauntings there seem to be linked to the frontier era as well.

The greatest concentration of strange phenomena lies in the district called Natchez-Under-the-Hill. Stretching down the steep riverbank and along the shoreline, this area served as the port for the old town. It was here that boatmen, trappers, and merchants rubbed elbows with cutthroats, thieves, and whores in the ramshackle inns and brothels that clustered close to the landing.

In the late 1700s this was Spanish territory, and although it was officially closed to trade for the Yanqui frontiersmen, a bribe to the right official could not only get one a pass to New Orleans but also help in selling one's goods for a nice profit in Natchez.

Whiskey, tobacco, corn, cotton, and lumber were all sold here by the enterprising Americans. As often as not, the money the traders made was soon spent on all manner of vice in that warren of iniquity in Natchez-Under-the-Hill. Many a young pioneer ended up with a knife in his gut or a bullet in his back as payment for all his efforts, and an open ditch or the big river became his final resting place.

Natchez-Under-the-Hill was a favorite haunt of John Murrell in life; in death his ghost is said to still haunt the district. Other spirits jostle with Murrell's shade for attention. For example, phantom Spanish soldiers have been seen on occasion in the alleys and byways off Silver Street, the modern name for what is left of Natchez-Under-the-Hill. Time and the great river have eroded everything else.

Another military apparition sighted Under-the-Hill is thought to be the restless spirit of an American officer. According to local tradition, this anonymous American was a traitor, a man who sold military secrets of the young republic to the Spanish when they ruled Louisiana.

If local lore has forgotten the traitor's name, history has not. In the early 1800s, there was but one American officer known to have had treasonable dealings with the Spanish: Gen. James Wilkinson.

Numerous frontiersmen later brought accusations against this high-placed American commander, the archnemesis of Gen. Andrew Jackson, yet the Jefferson administration repeatedly protected Wilkinson. That he was in the pay of the Spanish from the 1780s onward was common gossip, but no formal charges were ever brought against him.

Although Wilkinson escaped punishment for his treason in life, it may well be that his shade, haunted by guilt, is doomed to abide forever in the city where first he trod the path of treason.

In stark contrast to the lower town, Natchez-On-Top-of-the-Hill stood for all that was lacking in the lower environs. While Under-the-Hill was always "small, straggling, and shabby" (as Mark Twain aptly put it), the upper town was "attractive." Even that sour British snob of the early nineteenth century, Mrs. Trollope, had good things to say about Upper Natchez, describing it as being "like an oasis in the desert." Large stately homes adorn the city atop the bluff, speaking silent volumes of its culture, wealth, and vitality. The two towns have traditionally had little in common, save one thing: both are most thoroughly haunted. For although the residents of the upper city dressed in finery, rode in beautiful carriages, and had all the manners of aristocrats, behind the colonnaded facades lurked violence, betrayal, and pain.

All eras of Natchez's history are represented in this phantom cavalcade. There are antebellum homes such as Dunleith, where the ghost of Miss Percy still wanders disconsolate and heartbroken over her betrayal by a French nobleman. Civil War-era ghosts haunt the unique octagonal house called Nutt's Folly, where the Late Unpleasantness left its spectral mark. A pair of Victorian ghosts haunt Glenburnie and ruined Glenwood, where barefoot Jennie Merrill and the man falsely accused of murdering her still wander the grounds of their respective mansions.

Far and away, however, the most famous—and oldest—of upper Natchez's haunts is King's Tavern. By all accounts, the tavern was there before the city rose on the bluff. The original structure, some say, was actually a blockhouse from the old French fort that had been erected in the wilderness there in the early 1700s.

The region was still Spanish territory when Richard King took a notion to convert the building into a tavern in the 1780s. King took whatever materials were at hand—mainly hewn timbers from the various flatboats and ships that foundered nearby or were sold for scrap—and incorporated them into his enlargement of the original structure.

King did a land-office business in those days, for his tavern was the only place for hundreds of miles around where one could obtain food, lodging, and spirits. As the southern terminus of the famed Natchez Trace, King's Tavern was a convenient place of rest for those starting or ending their travels. For a few, it seems, the tavern also turned out to be their final resting place.

The old building has a checkered past, but today it is close to being what it was originally intended to be—a place to enjoy a hearty meal, good company, and hard spirits. Even one of the old guest rooms has been restored—if you have a mind to stay the night.

Not all the spirits in the modern King's Tavern are eighty proof—at least some are 100 percent supernatural. For some years now, workers at the old inn have had encounters that are hard to classify as anything other than spectral in nature.

Danielle "Danny" Scott, daughter of the proprietor of King's Tavern, often assists her mother in running the venerable establishment. One day Danny was behind the bar tidying up, accompanied by her own young daughter. The little girl, sitting on a barstool facing the bar, asked Danny who the "man in the mirror" was—the one wearing a red hat.

This was a very curious remark, for the bar was not open for business yet and no one else was there. Danny told her daughter so, but the girl insisted that she could see someone in the mirror, adding that the man was "not nice."

The incident was startling but hardly novel. The first time Danny Scott ever visited the tavern, she was sitting in the dining room with her mom, Yvonne, and noticed a beautiful young girl standing by the fireplace. Curious, Danny turned to her mother and asked who the woman was. Looking back, Danny noticed that the girl had disappeared. Mrs. Scott informed her daughter that she had just seen Madeleine, the most famous ghost of the many-spectered inn.

Other workers at the tavern have had their own unusual experiences. A waitress, working in the main dining room, heard a baby's cries coming from the next room. Chastity, the waitress, knew none of the customers that night had a small baby with them; yet the cries from the taproom were quite distinct. Later she learned that another ghost—the "baby ghost"—was believed to haunt the taproom.

During frontier days, the infamous highwayman Big Harpe had grabbed an infant from its mother's arms and smashed its head against the brick wall of the taproom—simply because the infant's wailing irritated him. The resident evil from that vicious act apparently still lingers in that room.

On a number of occasions, news crews have visited the tavern to investigate this and other hauntings. Rarely have they come away disappointed.

Walt Grayson, a television producer based in Mississippi, has investigated a number of haunted sites around the state. By his own admission, Walt's closest encounters with the supernatural were at King's Tavern.

While doing a series of spots in the early 1990s for WLBT-TV in Jackson, Grayson had the occasion to spend some time in the old tavern. At one point he was on the first floor, shooting footage in the main dining room. Although he was alone in the room, he felt secure in the knowledge that an associate was nearby, chatting with one of the waitresses.

For about fifteen minutes Walt shot footage in the room, all the while hearing muffled voices and squeaking of floorboards just above him on the second floor. By chance, he glanced out the window, only to see his friend outside walking with the waitress.

Grayson rushed upstairs to see who had been making the sounds—only to find the place empty. No *living* thing had made those sounds.

More recently, a camera crew from WJTV in Jackson also investigated the tavern, bringing with them Janis Railey, president of the Ghost Preservation League. The CBS affiliate's news crew encountered a number of interesting phenomena.

As they were interviewing Yvonne Scott, the tavern owner, they heard footsteps upstairs. Checking, they too found no one up there.

The news team had brought along some high-tech gear and conducted an electromagnetic survey of the inn. Curiously, areas that initially registered strong levels of magnetic energy later tested abnormally weak. It was almost as if someone—or something—were moving about the house, going from room to room.

At present only one room in the old tavern has been restored as a guest room—the one dubbed "Madeleine's Room." It is believed to be the same room the tavern's young serving wench once occupied.

Madeleine disappeared under mysterious circumstances in the late 1700s. Her ghost is believed to be responsible for many of the strange phenomena in the building.

For example, as the WJTV cameraman was setting up his equipment in Madeleine's Room, he caught sight of a "long flowing shadow" out of the corner of his eye.

Later, this ghost researcher reported a dramatic drop in temperature in the same bedroom. Equipment installed there recorded a temperature drop of twenty degrees within a very short span of time. A microphone set up in Madeleine's Room picked up the sound of a woman's voice when the room was totally unoccupied.

Curiously, a reporter from the *National Enquirer* had had a very similar experience when she visited the same room, only she could see the outline of a young woman with her hands on her hips.

Meanwhile, down at the crew's "command post" on the first floor, just off the dining room, one of the crew was busy setting up recording equipment and other gear. Another man was busy snapping still photographs of the room, and neither noticed anything unusual. Yet, when the still photos were developed, it showed that while the crew was busy with technical details, a stream of glowing orbs was cascading down the nearby stairwell!

Such orbs, invisible to the naked eye, are often closely associated with ghostly phenomena. Many psychic researchers believe these orbs are the actual spirits of those who have passed away. Not only were there orbs in abundance in the dining room, they were also observed out in the garden behind the tavern. One was even captured on film hovering outside Madeleine's third-floor bedroom window. *Something is very active in that tavern.*

Two weeks later—on Halloween—Brenna Willis, another worker at the tavern, was upstairs giving a couple from the Midwest a tour of the tavern. As they were viewing Madeleine's bedroom, a bright light suddenly flashed across the room. The couple thought it was a trick—that the hostess had secretly flipped a light switch. But it was no trick or illusion—just another mysterious occurrence attributed to the ghost of Madeleine.

Unusual things occur with regularity at King's Tavern. Most are more mischievous than malicious, and these are generally attributed to the playful antics of Madeleine. Scalding-hot water is said to cascade suddenly from a faucet not even attached to the water heater. Pools of water suddenly appear on the floor, with no apparent source. Lights are found switched on that the staff had just switched off. Doors swing open on their own, tripping up waiters, and objects are thrown or broken by invisible hands. By now, however, the staff is used to such antics. Whenever such things occur, the workers simply chalk it up to the puckish humor of Madeleine.

While local tradition has long attributed most such hauntings to the ghost of Madeleine, why she haunts in the tavern in death and what actually became of her in life remained two unresolved mysteries until some twenty years ago.

At that time, the tavern's owner was renovating the main dining room. As part of the renovation, workmen had torn up the salon's large brick fireplace. While remodeling a stone wall behind the fireplace, they found a skeleton that obviously had been sealed inside for centuries. The skeleton was that of a young female; a dagger still lodged in her chest told investigators that she had been murdered.

This grisly discovery solved the old mystery. Madeleine, young mistress of Richard King, had disappeared abruptly while King was away on business. The story given out by King's wife when he returned was that the serving girl had up and left one day without so much as a word of explanation. If King had his suspicions, he did not voice them.

The jeweled dagger through Madeleine's heart told the rest of the story, however, for that type of knife was a woman's weapon. While her husband was away on business, Mrs. King, in a jealous rage, had done away with the rival for her husband's affections. Who else but his wife, moreover, would have had access to the dining room long enough to immure Madeleine's corpse behind the wall? Of course, Mrs. King must have had accomplices—men who would do the dirty work of actually burying the girl.

Sightings of a young girl in the dining room near the fireplace and in the old bedroom on the third floor make perfect sense in the light of this discovery. Madeleine's spirit, robbed of full life and a decent burial, has continued to abide by the scene of her murder.

But Madeleine is not the only restless revenant to inhabit King's Tavern. Other murder victims may also be stuck there between two worlds, as evidenced by two male skeletons that were found buried beneath the floor of the building's basement.

What crimes these restless bones betray we cannot know. But many an innkeeper was known to do away with a guest if his purse of silver was large enough. The two bodies also may be linked to Madeleine—perhaps they are the remains of Mrs. King's accomplices, who helped hide the girl's body and were rewarded with death as their payment. After all, life was cheap in frontier Natchez.

What is certain is that more than one male ghost haunts the old tavern, and by all accounts they have a dark aura about them. From the "bad man" in the mirror, to a sinister gent in a black suit and white ruffled shirt who haunts the threshold to the dining room, it can honestly be said that one is never really alone in King's Tavern, the last stop on the Natchez Trace—and the last stop for more than one unwary mortal who has entered its portals.

Under-the-Hill, On-Top-of-the-Hill, and all points in between, Natchez and the trace that bears its name have justly earned their widespread fame. The deeds of men good and evil, great and small, have all left their mark here. The shades of many of those are still anchored to the earthly plane and are still making their mark upon this scenic city that time forgot.

KING'S TAVERN
619 Jefferson Street
Natchez, MS 39120
(601) 446-8845
www.kingstavern.com

NATCHEZ–UNDER–THE–HILL
Silver Street

Time and the river have consumed most of this once infamous district; Silver Street is all that remains. The seedy brothels and shady gambling dens have been replaced by stylish pubs, upscale restaurants and gift shops. The only sternwheelers that dock here now are cruise boats such as the Delta Queen (also haunted). Still, no one has informed the ghosts and it is still worth a look-see.

If you go ...
More haints and haunts of Dixie to see in Mississippi:

MERIDIAN
MERREHOPE
905 M. L. King Jr. Memorial Dr.
Meridian, MS 39301
(601) 483-8439
Open Mon.-Sat., 9 A.M.-4 P.M.

This twenty-room mansion served as headquarters for Confederate Gen. Leonidas Polk, but its resident ghosts are civilians: "Eugenia" haunts the mansion, while a schoolteacher who committed suicide haunts the upstairs.

NATCHEZ
LONGWOOD (1860–61)
130 Lower Woodville Road
Natchez, MS 39120
(601) 442-5193
Open daily

This octagonal Moorish Revival building was labeled "Nutt's Folly" when it was begun, and the outbreak of the Civil War halted its construction. Mr. and Mrs. Nutt's shades both inhabit the house.

MAGNOLIA HALL (1858)
215 South Pearl Street
Natchez, MS 39120
(601) 443-9085
www.natchezgardenclub.com
Open daily

This gracious mansion is haunted by its former master, Thomas Henderson. Guided tours are offered of the first floor; the second floor houses the Natchez Costume Museum and a collection of antique dolls.

OXFORD
ROWAN OAK (1844)
Old Taylor Road
Oxford, MS 38655
(662) 234-3284
www.mcsr.olemiss.edu
Open daily Tue.-Sun.

The home of William Faulkner from 1930 to his death in 1962. Faulkner told a number of stories about the ghosts that haunt his historic home. While those stories are now discounted as fiction, the haunting is real. Phenomena include the sound of ghostly footsteps, a piano that plays on its own, and phantoms in the garden.

Mississippi Ghost Tours

NATCHEZ
NATCHEZ GHOST TOUR, LLC
611 North Union Street
Natchez, MS 39120
(601) 445-4515

NATCHEZ GHOST TOURS
(Moonlight Productions daily driving tour)
(601) 445-8811

VICKSBURG
CEDAR GROVE MANSION INN
Candlelight ghost tours in October
2200 Oak Street
Vicksburg, MS 39180-4008
(601) 661-6100

VICKSBURG HISTORICAL GHOST TOUR
1100 Washington Street
Vicksburg, MS 39183
(601) 636-0611

19

The Devil's Promenade: The Hornet Ghost Light

I N THE EXTREME SOUTHWESTERN CORNER of Missouri, on the border with Oklahoma, exists a mystery that has baffled native Missourians and visitors alike for generations. Local legends abound about it, and numerous scientific—and pseudo-scientific—theories have been proffered to try to explain this disturbing phenomenon. But the Hornet Ghost Light remains a genuine Missouri mystery.

What it is, when it started, and even where to see it are questions that elicit different answers, depending on whom you talk to.

Hornet, Missouri, no longer actually exists as a town—certainly not as a *living* town—its sole claim to fame is the mysterious light that bears its name. Over the years, the spooklight has gone by many different monickers. It also has been known as the Neosho Lights, the Joplin Spooklight, Indian Lights, the Tri-State Light, and the Devil's Promenade.

At present, Neosho, Missouri, is the nearest inhabited town to this strange sight, and it is generally the place to which bewildered ghost-hunters gravitate to obtain directions to see the phenomenon.

Getting to the Hornet Light is not easy, even with directions. It is located about sixteen miles south of Joplin, Missouri, and one must first traverse several remote state and county highways before finally arriving at an unmarked gravel road straddling the Oklahoma border. It is along this isolated stretch of country road that one of the great wonders of Dixie puts on regular performances.

Appearing anytime between sunset and dawn, the light has been known to vary considerably in both size and intensity, and its antics are highly unpredictable.

The Hornet Light often appears to be the size of a baseball. It is commonly reported to zoom down the gravel track "like a tracer round" at an onlooker, only to stop short at the very last second— much to the relief of the spectator. Sometimes it vanishes just before it reaches the viewer only to mischievously reappear a heartbeat later behind the person's shoulder.

At other times the light is seen to bob and weave pendulum-like. It has also been described as being the size of a "basketball or larger." Nor is it solely restricted to the road.

Locals cite numerous anecdotes that lead the serious student of the Hornet Light to conclude that at times it acts with a certain degree of intelligence. It has been seen probing the interiors of cars, as if curious about them. At other times, it acts in a playful manner, as if teasing the onlooker—although some who have been scared out of their wits were less than appreciative of its "humor."

One night, a school bus was returning home to Neosho from a carnival at Quapaw. The driver turned onto Spooklight Road as a shortcut home. Suddenly the light whizzed toward the bus from out of nowhere and perched on the vehicle's rear window, as if it were trying to enter.

Everyone inside the bus immediately became terrified. The driver, blinded by the intensity of the light, was forced to make an emergency stop. The minute the bus screeched to a halt, however, the spooklight tired of the game and wandered off.

Although it has been known to pursue people, the spooklight will suddenly go out if someone tries to approach it, only to pop up again some distance away.

As elusive as the Hornet Light may be, adequate explanations as to its true nature and origin are even harder to pin down.

The local interpretation traditionally has been that it is a manifestation of the spirit (or spirits) of someone who was murdered or died an untimely death. Call it a spooklight, ghost light, or corpse candle, the phenomenon is fundamentally the same as other such haints that are common throughout the South. However, few of these appear quite so regularly or have attained nearly as much fame as the Hornet Light.

Naturally, the professional debunkers have rounded up the usual suspects to explain away the mystery: marsh gas, "foxfire" (bioluminescence), ball lightning, even the after-glow of an alleged mineral deposit. But the favorite explanation of the so-called experts seems to be that the light is simply a reflection of headlights emanating from a major highway nearby.

The "reflected headlight" theory has the virtue of a certain plausibility—until one looks at the facts. Supposedly, the source of the light is vehicles traveling a freeway six miles away, and it is the reflected glow of their headlights that observers see zooming down the gravel road. A number of highly respected scholars have bought into this theory at one time or another.

Originally, the experts said the reflections came from State Route 66, but as that road became less traveled, the experts began to claim the light source was actually Interstate 44. That a high ridge lies between the gravel road and the freeway, effectively blocking any reflection, doesn't seem to have been a consideration when this theory was formulated. The explanation devised to account for this is that certain "freak atmospheric conditions" enable the light to "jump" over the ridgeline and appear on the gravel track.

How these "freak atmospheric conditions" could create the phenomenon first on Highway 66 and then later on Interstate 44, and do so on a quite regular basis, seems to strain both logic and the laws of optics.

The fact that reports of the Hornet Ghost Light were rampant long before either highway was built—and long before automobiles were even invented—would seem to shoot a large hole in the "reflected headlight" theory. The first written record of the Hornet Light dates back to the 1860s, and there are indications that it was active in the area far earlier than that—the first settlers in the region referred to it as the "Indian Lights." In the 1880s the ghost light was so active that it caused the panic-stricken citizens of Hornet to precipitously abandon their town in fear.

While the light's longevity alone would seem to disprove the "reflected headlight" theory, there is also the fact that its location has not remained stationary, even in modern times. Although at present the light is best viewed on an east-west road (E50—now called Spooklight Road), in the 1940s the light was active on a parallel east-west road a mile to the north (E40). Stateline Road, the north-south highway that both of these dirt roads branch off of, is still often referred to as the Devil's Promenade, an indication that the light was active on it at one time as well.

In fact, the Hornet Light has never limited itself to just one stretch of road. Farmers in the area have had personal encounters with it as far back as anyone cares to remember. For example, Chester McMinn of nearby Quapaw, Oklahoma, reported that the light hovered over his field one night—as if to illuminate the area while he did some needed night farming.

In 1979 Sterling Barnett was still a teenager living on his family's farm, just off the Devil's Promenade. One evening he was in the barn doing chores, when a bright light suddenly appeared behind him.

Sterling thought his father had come into the barn with a flashlight to help him see better, but when he turned around to greet his dad, he saw the light hovering by the barn door. Sterling was just fifteen feet from the glowing orb, which was so bright that it lit up the entire interior of the barn. After he watched it for some time in stunned silence, the light disappeared.

Other residents of the area say the spooklight has come right onto their porches. One resident remembers staring out his front window and seeing two big red glowing eyes just a few feet from his house. Others say the light has appeared as a general "big green glow" over the trees in the forest.

Mysterious lights such as the Hornet Ghost Light are known throughout the world. The Hornet Light has become famous because of its regularity. Those who brave the back roads at night to view it rarely come away disappointed.

If scientific explanations of the light have fallen short, there is no shortage of supernatural explanations to fill the bill.

One of the oldest tales of the spooklight tells of a Quapaw brave who fell in love with the daughter of the chief. Because the young warrior lacked a suitable dowry, the chief refused to give his daughter's hand in marriage. In desperation, the lovesick couple eloped and were hotly pursued by the chief's war party. When they were cornered, the couple leaped to their deaths off a bluff into the Spring River.

Ever since, there have been reports of strange lights in the area. These spooklights, according to legend, are the spirits of the star-crossed lovers who are fated to wander the earth together forever.

Another legend holds that an Osage chief was ambushed and killed by a hostile tribe, and that his head was cut off as a trophy and carried away. Ever since, the headless headman's spirit has roamed the scene of his murder, carrying a torch (the spooklight) while searching for his missing head.

Others ascribe the Hornet Light to the ghost of a white miner, who—lantern in hand—is still seeking his children, who were kidnapped by Indians.

It is easy enough to scoff at such native legends and frontier tales. But the fact that a Quapaw ceremonial ground once lay at one end of the Devil's Promenade lends some credence to the Indian connection. It is also why old-timers used to refer to the phenomenon as "Indian Lights."

Then, too, a number of eyewitnesses who have had close encounters with the light have given descriptions of its behavior that indicate an intelligence behind its actions. There are numerous reports that it has investigated cars, become playful with unwary visitors, and the like. All this points to the light being the manifestation of some kind of consciousness, living or dead, and not some natural geological or atmospheric occurrence.

There is also the name Devil's Promenade itself. Apparently an old wooden bridge once connected the back road to the main highway. If local tradition is true, should one slowly walk back and forth across the rickety bridge three times, and then ask the Devil to appear, he would materialize and grant three wishes.

The old bridge is long gone, replaced by a modern concrete structure. But the road's sinister reputation lingers on nonetheless.

Whether it is the result of lost souls, the Devil's playthings, or geophysical anomalies, the Hornet Light seems to defy any easy explanations.

Even those who have earnestly studied the light for years and nurse their own pet theories confess that they don't have all the answers.

And there are some folks in southwestern Missouri who prefer it that way. As one lifelong resident of the area admitted, "I don't really know what it is, and I hope they never find out. It would spoil the mystery."

But there is one thing regarding the phenomenon about which all can agree: The Hornet Ghost Light has been a mystery for countless years—and will remain so for the foreseeable future.

> *The Hornet Ghost Light is most commonly viewed in the area of Stateline Road, south of the I-44 Interstate. As its name implies, the road runs along the Missouri-Oklahoma border. The phenomenon, however, has been known to shift locations to either the east or west of there.*

20

The Lemp Curse:
Lavender Lady, Monkey Boy,
and the Bucolic Brewmeisters

I T IS POPULAR NOSTRUM—spread mainly by the wealthy—that money cannot buy happiness. While there may indeed be some truth to this, most of us probably would hazard that risk to find out for ourselves. Short of that, however, one may look to the sad, sordid story of the Lemps of St. Louis, whose travails and tribulations make the House of Usher seem a clan of Pollyannas by comparison.

In many ways, however, the Lemp saga started as a typical Horatio Alger-style success story. Adam Lemp, the family patriarch, emigrated to America from Germany in 1838. Beginning as a simple grocer in St. Louis, Adam had a dream: to introduce German lager beers to America, where English-style ales were still the norm.

In Germany, brewing was an ancient and honorable art, and the recipe for making good lager was often a closely guarded family secret, handed down from father to son. Adam brought his new brew to St. Louis and felt sure he could find an appreciative—if not thirsty—market for it.

Adam's judgment proved correct, and in time he was able to acquire a grand mansion close to his brewery. It was primarily in this house that the family saga would play itself out.

Underlying St. Louis are extensive catacombs of unknown origin, and Adam Lemp used part of this cavern system to keep his brew cool. He also used the caves to provide an underground passage connecting his house to the nearby brewery.

When Adam Lemp died in 1862, his son, William, became president and brewmeister of Lemp Brewery. Under his leadership, the family business expanded greatly, until the brewery in St. Louis sprawled over nearly eleven city blocks. William also expanded the distribution of the family's beer until it became a nationally recognized brand. Upon his death in 1904, his son William Jr. took over the business.

William Jr. carried on the family tradition, and Lemp Brewery continued to prosper under his direction, especially its premium brand, Falstaff beer. As a result, William enjoyed a lavish lifestyle and Lemp Mansion became more luxurious than ever.

However, Lemp Brewery's heyday came to an abrupt end in 1920, with the advent of Prohibition. Nevertheless, after his brother Will's death in 1922, Charles Lemp continued to reside in Lemp Mansion, albeit in reduced circumstances. Despite this, Charles lived in relative comfort in the house until 1949.

On the surface, then, the Lemps—and Lemp Mansion—enjoyed a relatively long period of prosperity. Yet even at the height of their success, the Lemps were dogged by inner demons. Through it all, Lemp Mansion stood as a silent witness to the unfolding family saga. It was here as well that the darkness that clouded this once fortunate family closed in on them. Some even say it was the house itself that somehow led to their downfall.

The first to fall victim to the Lemp Curse—as it came to be called—was Frederick Lemp, eldest son of William Lemp Sr. Fred was to be William Sr.'s heir and had been groomed since boyhood for the role. Fred worked hard to live up to his father's expectations—perhaps too hard. One day Frederick simply keeled over with a heart attack, brought on by stress and overwork. He was only twenty-eight years old.

William Sr. was badly shaken by the premature death of his favorite son. He had been hard on the boy, trying to prepare him to run the family's burgeoning beer empire. With Frederick's death, however, William Sr.'s self-confidence was shaken to its core, and his carefully constructed personal reality slowly began to unravel.

William Lemp started to withdraw from the world; over time he was seen less and less in public. William would not even walk outside to go to work, preferring instead to use the secret underground passage that led from his house to the brewery. Then, one morning in 1904, William Lemp Sr. was found dead in his bedroom. He had shot both himself and his dog.

Later, in 1920, Elsa Lemp, Frederick's sister, also succumbed to the "savage god" of suicide, ending her life with a handgun in her own home in St. Louis. Her house is also reported to be haunted today.

Although William Lemp Jr. had not been trained to run the family enterprise, his father's suicide and brother's premature death nevertheless left him at the helm of the business. Perhaps in an attempt to overcome the terminal melancholy that seemed to be afflicting other members of his family, Will Jr. started to spend large amounts of money to maintain a very lavish lifestyle.

Will staffed the family mansion with servants, luxuries, and objects d'art, and acquired opulent country estates as well. Much in the manner of European nobility, Will, the beer king, spent freely on fine wines, clothes, and all the other trappings of material wealth. His collection of fine art, for example, was so large that it reportedly overflowed three large storage vaults.

Nor was that all. In the labyrinth of caverns that lay under the house and brewery, Will Jr. constructed a swimming pool, a private theater, and various other amenities for his pleasure.

In 1899 Will Jr. married Lillian Hadlan, the beautiful heiress of a wealthy manufacturing magnate. In Lillian, Will had found a mate with tastes every bit as expensive as his own. She became known publicly as the "Lavender Lady," because of her fondness for wearing clothes of that hue.

But apparently even acquiring a beautiful trophy wife did not satisfy Will Jr. After just a few years of marriage, Will decided to divorce the Lavender Lady. The ensuing divorce trial proved a nasty affair and became the most notorious scandal in St. Louis at the time.

Lillian, who had been outgoing and sociable before her marriage to Will, was broken by the whole affair. She spent the rest of her life in seclusion, far from the public eye. In a sense, she, too, was a victim of the Lemp Curse.

Rumors also circulated at the time that William Jr. had sired an illegitimate child by a maid in his mansion. The boy, it was believed, was born either mentally or physically handicapped in some manner, and to avoid public embarrassment, William kept the youngster hidden from view inside the house, where he was treated more like a caged animal than a son. There is no official record of his sad existence, and he is known today only as "Monkey Boy."

Although William Lemp remarried and continued to surround himself with the trappings of success, material wealth proved more and more hollow to him as time went on. Like his father, Will Jr. became reclusive and started to seek the darkness of the caverns below his house as a refuge from the world above.

The enactment, in January 1920, of the federal Prohibition amendment forbidding the manufacture and sale of alcoholic beverages was the final blow to Will. While other breweries adapted to the times, and made "near beer" or other products, William Lemp Jr. refused to change. On June 28, 1922, the massive brewery complex was sold for only a fraction of its value. Then, one morning soon after the sale of the factory, Will's body was discovered in his office on the first floor of the Lemp Mansion. Following family tradition he had shot himself, in the chest.

Another brother, Charles, inherited the Lemp Mansion,. The family's business was gone now, and with it much of their wealth, but despite this, Charles Lemp clung to the capacious old house. Although it was expensive to maintain, Charles refused to move. In time he, too, became morose and reclusive. He also developed a morbid fear of germs. Finally, in 1949, Charles Lemp followed in the footsteps of his father and sibling, and shot himself to death—choosing the basement as his preferred place of self-destruction.

The last surviving Lemp, Edwin, avoided the family curse and lived to a ripe old age. However, he wisely broke with tradition and, instead of residing in Lemp Mansion, chose to live in one of the family's remaining country estates, Kirkwood. When Edwin passed away at the age of ninety, the Lemp line died out, and the Lemp Curse, too, passed at last into history.

Were the family's misfortunes sheer coincidence? Or were they the result of hereditary mental illness? Or did the family somehow bring down upon themselves a jinx that lasted through two generations, blighting otherwise promising lives?

In St. Louis some have linked the Lemp family's misfortunes to the mansion itself. Some houses have a personality all their own. Just as human personalities are often affected by the trials and tragedies of life, it is thought that a house also may take on an aura based on the emotional traumas that have been experienced within its walls. Such houses retain that aura long after those living there have gone.

According to this theory, the apparitions that haunt many houses are not so much the souls of the dead as they are the preserved memories of past tragic events. Somehow, the house retains the image of those traumatic experiences and replays them over and over again, like some sort of psychic recording.

While this does not begin to explain all supernatural phenomena, by any means, in cases such as the Lemp Mansion, it may provide a clue as to what may be going on within its haunted walls.

The Lemp Mansion passed out of the family after Charles's suicide, and in the ensuing years the elegant house fell on hard times. Its spacious rooms were subdivided, and the dwelling was turned into a boarding house. Inside and out the mansion began to show its age, and the neighborhood around it was no longer quite the socially prominent place it once had been.

At the same time, rumors circulated in the neighborhood that there were other residents within the old Lemp Mansion besides its boarders. Like an aging socialite now fallen on hard times, the old house had begun to get a "peculiar" reputation.

In 1975, however, the grand old lady was rescued from decline by the Pointer family. Richard Pointer bought the house with the idea of restoring it and converting it into a restaurant and inn. Through all the peeling paint and decaying woodwork, he still could see the beauty it once possessed.

But as work began inside, construction workers began to report odd occurrences. Some said they had an overall "creepy" feeling while in the place—as if they were being watched by unseen eyes. Other workers reported tools missing, and still others claimed to hear eerie sounds.

A few workers even reported seeing the apparition of a man in black, dressed in antique formal attire. After several of these eerie experiences, some workers refused to go back inside the mansion.

Mr. Pointer himself had similar experiences. While repainting the opulent master bath, he heard voices and felt someone was watching him.

When the restoration was finally complete, and the new bed and breakfast was open for business, the Pointers and their employees found out for themselves that there was indeed some substance to all the rumors about the mansion being haunted.

In the bar area of the restaurant, for example, bartenders have reported seeing glasses levitate off the counter, as if lifted by some unseen hand. The piano in the lounge has also been known to play all on its own.

One common experience in the Lemp Mansion is hearing the sounds of disembodied voices—as of phantom conversations. The barking of a dog has also been heard, although no canine of any kind resides in the mansion. "Cold spots" are frequently encountered in places throughout the house—a common phenomenon in buildings that are haunted.

A "gentleman in black" is occasionally sighted inside the mansion by visiting guests. The Lavender Lady also makes an appearance from time to time at the inn, her distinctive taste in clothing making her identification as Lillian Hadlan Lemp easy. Lillian's favorite haunts, based on sightings of her, seem to be the third-floor stairwell and the first-floor bathroom of the inn.

Psychics who have toured the house also claim to have made contact with the spirit of Monkey Boy. He does not seem, however, to have manifested himself as a visible ghost.

Nearly everyone who has worked at the Lemp Mansion Restaurant and Inn has had some kind of supernatural encounter, as its present owner, Paul Lemp, will testify. Guests also have their occasional run-ins with the psychic energy that inhabits the house. Some guests even book a room at the inn with that goal in mind.

Given its melancholy history, it is not surprising that the Lemp Mansion is regarded as the most haunted house in St. Louis. The restored dwelling has also been rated as one of the top ten haunted houses in the country—a rare distinction indeed.

Despite its sad, mad history, Lemp Mansion today is a cheery place to dine, and a congenial lodging in which to spend the night. Guests may even reserve the very room in which William Lemp Sr. killed himself.

Should you stay the night at Lemp Mansion, however, there is one thing to bear in mind: No matter which room you stay in, you will probably not spend the night alone.

The Lemp Mansion is located in the heart of scenic St. Louis, a short distance from the Mississippi River. It is open to the public as both restaurant and inn. Tours are available on a reservation basis; the inn also hosts murder-mystery dinner theaters and the occasional Halloween party. For more information, contact:

LEMP MANSION
3322 DeMenil Place
St. Louis, MO 63118
(314) 664-8024
www.lempmansion.com

If you go ...
More haints and haunts of Dixie to see in Missouri:

JEFFERSON CITY
GOVERNOR'S MANSION
100 Madison Street
Jefferson City, MO 65101
(573) 751-7929
www.missourimansion.org
Guided tours available

*The apparition of a little girl has been
sighted in the attic, thought to be
he ghost of the daughter of a
nineteenth century governor.*

NEW MADRID
HUNTER–DAWSON HOUSE (1860)
P.O. Box 308
312 Dawson Road
New Madrid, MO 63869
(573) 748-5340
www.mostateparks.com/hunterdawson
Tours available

*The shades of a former owner roams
the house and has been seen
peering out the window; visitors
often report feeling a "presence"
while touring the house.*

ST. GENEVIEVE
GUIBOURD–VALLE HOUSE (1806)
Fourth and Merchant Street
St. Genevieve, MO 63670
(573) 883-7544
www.stegenevievemissouri.com
/guibourdvallehouse
Open daily April-December

*Three old men dressed in eighteenth-
century costume—thought to be
Spanish officers—have been seen in
and near the house. Their connection
to the old house remains a mystery,
but as St. Genevieve is the oldest
town in Missouri, it does not lack for
reasons for the haunting.*

Missouri Ghost Tours

BRANSON
BRANSON GHOST AND HAUNT TOUR
America by Foot
March-October nightly
(417) 423-7812

ST. CHARLES
ST. CHARLES GHOST TOUR
Nightly year round
P.O. Box 1872
St. Charles, MO 63032
(314) 374-6102
www.ghostsinmissouri.veryweird.com

ST. LOUIS
ST. LOUIS GHOST TOUR
Ghost Ride Tours
(618) 451-2381
(314) 849-3211

ST. LOUIS SPIRIT SEARCH
(314) 776-4667

21

The White Doe:
The Mystery of Virginia Dare

ONE OF THE EARLIEST and most haunting mysteries of America surrounds the first English settlement in the New World—the "Lost" Colony of Roanoke—and the first white child born in America: Virginia Dare. The many unanswered questions concerning the fate of the Lost Colony's inhabitants—and in particular that of Virginia Dare—have made for an enduring enigma that continues to fascinate and engage our interest.

Every schoolchild is (or ought to be) familiar with Sir Walter Raleigh's ill-fated attempt to establish an English colony in the New World in the 1580s. The colony was to be called Virginia, in honor of Queen Elizabeth, "the Virgin Queen," although the initial landing and settlement, Fort Raleigh (Raleigh Cittie) was built on an island off the coast of modern North Carolina.

On an exploratory cruise in 1585, the English made the acquaintance of two Indians from the area, Manteo and Wanchese, whom they took back to England with them. The two Native Americans were quite a novelty in London, where they were treated as celebrities, met the queen, and were feted by the upper class. Raleigh even authorized that Manteo be given the title of "Lord"—the only Indian ever to be granted that accolade by the English.

In 1787 Raleigh dispatched a shipload of settlers aboard the *Lion* to the new land to establish the colony. John White was in charge of the expedition and was to be governor of the new settlement. With him were some 115 colonists, including his daughter Elanor and her husband, Ananias Dare. Also accompanying the settlers were the two friendly Indians, Wanchese and Lord Manteo.

From the previous voyages, it had been determined that the Chesapeake Bay region would be the best site for the settlement. The Portuguese captain of the ship, however, was eager to raid Spanish shipping, so he instead landed the settlers far to the south of their destination, on Roanoke Island, where the colonists knew a previous expedition had built a small stockade fort.

Soon after the group was established at Raleigh Cittie, Governor White's daughter gave birth to a beautiful baby girl. Like her mother, the baby was born with golden hair, and her parents named her Virginia, in honor of both the queen and the new colony.

The first explorers had given glowing reports of the Roanoke area and its inhabitants; so when the Portuguese mercenary put them ashore at the wrong place, Governor White was not unduly concerned.

What Raleigh's previous expeditions had neglected to mention, however, was that Fort Raleigh had been built close to a malarial swamp. Moreover, the previous ships' crews that Raleigh had hired to explore the coast of the New World had a secondary profession: piracy. These part-time pirates had letters of marques from good Queen Bess to legitimize their acts, but given their background, their methods of conflict resolution with the natives left something to be desired.

The Native Americans had very different notions than the English regarding private property and real estate. So when a local chief from the mainland near Roanoke took a liking to a silver cup belonging to the ship's captain, the captain interpreted that as theft. In response, he ordered the village pillaged, burning down houses and crops and putting to the sword any native that was caught, regardless of age.

So, when White's party of hapless settlers landed two years later, the local natives were not exactly waiting to welcome them with open arms. John White had no inkling of the hornet's nest that awaited his charges there. However, he did realize that to survive, the colony would need further succor and aid. Though he was reluctant to leave his daughter and granddaughter, While felt compelled to return to England immediately to secure more manpower and supplies. He would be back in a few months at most, he thought.

But when Governor White reached England in October 1787 the nation was bracing for invasion. The Spanish Armada was bearing down on the island, and every man and ship was needed for war. Therefore, instead of three months, it would be nearly three years before White could mount a relief expedition.

When White's party finally arrived at Roanoke, they found the fort deserted and no sign of anyone, living or dead. The only hint as to the fate of the Lost Colony lay in a cryptic carving on a nearby tree: *Croatoan* was all it said.

The fate of the Lost Colony of Roanoke is one of history's great mysteries. An even greater mystery, however, is why, when John White found the deserted settlement, he made no effort to find the settlers, even though his own family was among the missing.

Before he returned to England, White had arranged for the settlers to leave a sign if they were in peril or had to abandon the settlement. They were to carve the name of their destination on a tree—if they left voluntarily, it would be the name alone; if they left by force or under duress, they would carve a cross above the name.

White found no cross atop the inscription, and that should have given him hope that his family and the other colonists had been safe when they left Roanoke island. Moreover, the governor knew the Croatan Indians, who lived not far from the island, were a friendly tribe.

Despite this, after staying but a few days White sailed for other parts.

With White's departure, history drew a veil across the scene, leaving generations to ponder the fate of the Lost Colony and little fair-haired Virginia Dare.

But if the white man's history is mute, the Native American's legends are not. According to tribal accounts, the settlers at Fort Raleigh learned of their peril not long after the *Lion* disappeared over the horizon.

Manteo, learning of an imminent raid on the tiny settlement by a hostile tribe, resolved to warn his white friends and bring them to safety.

Using a hidden tunnel, Manteo led the settlers away from the imperiled fort to waiting canoes. By rowing through the night, the colonists evaded the hostiles and passed safely into the territory of the Croatans, Manteo's folk, whose lands stretched along the Carolina coast from Hatteras to Beaufort.

The Roanoke settlers were adopted by Manteo's tribe and so survived by the grace of the native leader's benevolence. That, at least, is the legend.

There are, in fact, some tantalizing hints in the early records of the Jamestown colony that support this lore. In 1608 the Jamestown colonists received word that in at least two Indian villages there were "seven of the English alive . . . who escaped the slaughter at Roanoke." These included "fower men, two boys, and one young mayde, who escaped the massacre, and fled up the river Chanoke."

Was this "young mayde" actually Virginia Dare? Virginia would have been twenty one at the time, and the description seems to fit her. But what actually became of Virginia Dare?

Here again, native tradition speaks to us where the English records fall silent. And a haunting tale it is they tell.

When Eleanor and her daughter were taken in by the Croatans, they were afforded special treatment. Eleanor, whose pale complexion and flaxen hair were a novelty to the Indians, was called "the White Doe," and little Virginia, the first white infant seen by the natives, was given the name "Little Fawn."

Virginia was a golden child in more ways than one, for her blond tresses were far more than a curiosity to the Indians. They believed that any pale-hued creature was touched by the Great Spirit, and thus was holy, a source of great power.

As Virginia Dare grew to womanhood, she developed both grace and beauty. She was held in high esteem by everyone in the tribe and, in the manner of the Croatans, was given the rank of Beloved Woman, or prophet. In time she also inherited her mother's Indian name, White Doe, as well.

To Native Americans, spirit power is not some mere intellectual abstraction; it is a very real force that courses through all living things and all of nature itself. To harness this force was to obtain great magical ability and personal power—which could be used for either good or evil.

There was a medicine man of the tribe who wished to marry White Doe—not out of any affection for her but because he wanted to obtain the power the Great Spirit had imbued her with, in order to enhance his own magical abilities.

The medicine man, Chico, asked for Virginia's hand in marriage. Virginia, though disposed to be friendly toward the shaman, didn't want to be his wife and rejected the offer. Chico grew wrathful at her rebuff and vowed that if he could not have her as his wife, no man would.

Luring Virginia back to the place of her birth, the medicine man laid an enchantment upon her. Stepping ashore onto Roanoke Island, Virginia Dare was immediately transformed into a snow-white deer.

Soon, word spread among all the tribes of the coast of the white deer of Roanoke Island. She was a magic deer, it was said, for although several great hunters had shot their arrows directly at her, she seemed immune to harm. The deer was often seen, it was said, at the ruins of old Fort Raleigh, facing eastward, as if staring across the great sea to the land of the White Queen.

No one could catch the swift white doe—nor did they know whether she was an omen of good or evil for the Indians. One young brave, however, suspected the truth. Wanchese, son of old Chief Wanchese, had a suspicion that the magic deer was none other than Virginia Dare, placed under an enchantment. The two had grown up together, and although he had long loved the golden-haired maiden, he never declared his feelings for her. Then, one day Virginia disappeared. The medicine man Chico was suspected of some sort of bedevilment, but nothing could be proved against him.

Wanchese had inherited a silver-tipped arrow from his father. Chief Wanchese had been given the arrow by the White Queen, when he had visited her lodge across the great eastern sea, and it was believed that it could break even the strongest of enchantments. With it Wanchese hoped to dissolve the spell set upon Virginia and so restore her to human form.

It was in November 1615 when Wanchese set foot on the island to hunt the White Doe. Through marsh, across sand hills, and into the woods he pursued the fleet-footed, milk-white deer until at last he caught up with her at Kill Devil Hills. Taking careful aim, Wanchese loosed the silver arrow.

The shaft found its mark, and the snow-hued doe collapsed on a nearby sandhill. As Wanchese had been led to believe, the silver arrow did indeed break the spell. There, before his eyes, the doe was transformed back into the form of a fair-skinned young woman, clad in a white buckskin dress.

But Wanchese's aim proved too true. The arrow, instead of finding a fleshy part, had pierced her heart, and now Wanchese watched in dismay as Virginia looked up at him with large fawn-like eyes, sighed, and then breathed her last.

At that very instant, Wanchese looked up to see another white doe before him, bounding away into the forest. It was the departed soul of Virginia Dare, which had taken on the form of the white doe for all eternity.

The legend is, as one historian describes it, a "pretty tradition," and one is free to accept or reject it as such. But it is a legend handed down, in one form or another, from the white man's earliest days in North Carolina and on that account should not be summarily rejected.

From time to time ever since those early days, hunters on Roanoke Island have occasionally caught a glimpse—albeit a fleeting one—of a pure-white doe.

That these rare sightings might actually be an albino deer is not out of the realm of possibility. However, its close association with Roanoke Island and the fact that the white doe is sighted only at night, when spirits roam the earth, may suggest other answers.

The mystery of the Lost Colony and Virginia Dare is a powerful tale that still resonates among the inhabitants of the North Carolina coast.

A play that has been presented each summer since the 1930s in Manteo, North Carolina, dramatizes the events surrounding the founding and disappearance of the Roanoke Colony. Actors in period costumes re-enact the dramatic events of the 1580s. In recent years, however, several actors have reported seeing individuals dressed like themselves but who are definitely not part of the cast. A few actors even claim to have seen Virginia Dare herself.

It is likely, therefore, that whatever fate befell the inhabitants of the Lost Colony in life, their spirits, like that of Virginia Dare, continue to linger along the sandy shores of Roanoke island.

22

Belinda and the Brown Mountain Lights

THEY ARE A MYSTERY AS OLD AS THE MOUNTAINS themselves. The Indians told tales of them; the first white men over the mountains encountered them; engineers and scientists have studied them. Yet all who have experienced the Brown Mountain Lights have come away baffled.

Even today travelers on the scenic Blue Ridge Parkway will occasionally sight the fey array of lights dancing before the slopes of Brown Mountain. Near mile marker 310 on the parkway is an overlook called Lost Cove Cliffs. At a height of 3,800 feet, it affords one a panoramic view of the North Carolina countryside.

At night from this vantage one may gain an easy glimpse of the uncanny display of lights in the distance. Like flaming balls shooting from a Roman candle, these multi-colored orbs of light appear to rise higher and higher in the air, sometimes darting about, sometimes zooming straight up the slopes.

Area residents agree, however, that the best place to view the lights is a spot called Wiseman's View. Located atop Linville Mountain, it is difficult to get to, accessible only by means of an unpaved U.S. Forest Service road. But the view is well worth the effort.

Surrounded by wild gorges and soaring mountaintops, Wiseman's View by day is a naturalist's delight. Pitch-black at night, this vantage point affords a breathtaking front-row seat to view the light show that Brown Mountain offers.

Seen from Wiseman's, when the lights first rise over the mountain, they appear to be about twice the size of a star, and the orbs often have a sapphire-blue or ruby-red hue to them. Eyewitnesses often report that when the lights appear, they sometimes are moving so fast and in such numbers that it is impossible to count them all. Some lights fade away as they rise; others, however, expand as they ascend and then burst in mid-air like silent fireworks.

No one questions that the Brown Mountain Lights exist, but what they really are—natural occurrence or supernatural phenomena—has been a matter of much dispute over the years. Certainly, of all the spooklights in the South, Brown Mountain's are by far the most famous and best studied.

But the lights are by no means just a recent phenomenon. Accounts of them have been handed down by the Cherokee for generations. They claim that centuries ago a great battle was fought on the mountain's slopes by the Catawba and Cherokee tribes. So fierce was the battle and so terrible the slaughter that the dead lay in heaps on the mountainside.

As night descended on the battlefield, the Indian women ascended the mountain, torches in hand, to search for their husbands and fathers among the fallen. The lights we see today, according to native tradition, are really the ghostly remnants of those ancient torch-lights as the phantoms of the Indian women still search the slopes for their lost loved ones.

In 1771 the first white man to view the lights had a more prosaic explanation. Gerard Willum de Brahm, a military engineer, believed that "the mountains emit nitrous vapors, which are born by the wind and when laden winds meet each other the niter inflames, caliphates and deteriorates."

De Brahm was working for the colonial British government and had designed Fort Loudoun in Cherokee country, among other tasks. De Brahm would not be the last government official to try to explain away the lights, and his theory, like those that followed later, proved false.

There were eyewitness reports of the Brown Mountain Lights

throughout the nineteenth century, and numerous stories arose to explain the phenomenon, but no serious scientific attempts to solve the mystery were made until the early years of the twentieth century.

The lights must have been particularly active in the spring of 1908, for in June of that year an "expedition" was dispatched from the nearby town of Morganton to discover their cause. The sortie by the local gentry proved a failure.

However, in 1913 the U.S. Geological Survey studied Brown Mountain and its lights. Government scientists confirmed that the lights did exist, but they airily dismissed them as simply the reflection of train headlights from the valley below. Railroad tracks did indeed wind around the base of Brown Mountain as they passed through the Catawba Valley. The government explanation seemed reasonable at the time.

But in 1916 a big flood hit the Catawba Valley, washing out tracks and trestles and downing all power lines in the area. Despite the fact that no trains ran for weeks—and that there was not any electricity in the valley—the lights continued to appear undiminished.

Undeterred, federal authorities investigated the lights again. This time investigators determined that the lights were caused by the spontaneous combustion of "marsh gas," and any other light seen was simply a reflection of brush fires on the ground.

Well, that mule didn't plow with the residents around Brown Mountain either, any more than the previous government report had. For one thing, there are no marshes anywhere near Brown Mountain, so there were no places where marsh gas could arise. For another thing, the people who lived near the mountain were quite able to tell the difference between the glow of a wildfire at ground level and the erratic airborne orbs that appeared over Brown Mountain.

Other scientists also questioned the marsh-gas theory. They pointed out that such phosphoric combustion was unlikely to be seen at any distance—unlike the Brown Mountain Lights—and that such lights would appear brighter, not dimmer, as one approached them. The notion that the lights were actually the fires of illegal stills was also rejected.

Some have theorized that the lights are really a form of Saint Elmo's fire—a kind of electrical discharge known to occur around ships and planes. But here again, the facts don't fit: Saint Elmo's fire occurs only on the edges of (usually moving) objects, never in mid-air as these lights do.

In recent years scientists have tried to revive the optical-effect theory. In 1977, for example, the Enigma Project decided to investigate the lights in association with ORION, the Oak Ridge Isochronous Observation Network. This project bounced a giant arc light off Brown Mountain from Lenoir City, some twenty-two miles away, and succeeded in creating stationary colored illuminations similar to the lights. ORION therefore concluded that the lights were merely a reflection, or a mirage.

Like the older train-headlight theory of the early 1900s, this attempt to explain away the lights fails to account for the fact that the lights preceded modern electric lighting and automobiles by decades, perhaps centuries. Then, too, local residents have reported a second series of lights—rarer and less well known—at the base of the mountain. This second series of lights flits about just above the tops of the trees. It is impossible for this second layer of lights to be a long-distance reflection.

If all of these scientific explanations have fallen short of solving the mystery of Brown Mountain, local lore has no problem explaining them.

About 1850 a young girl named Belinda lived with her parents in the hills near Brown Mountain. In those days, mountain girls married young—so young, in fact, that a girl would scarcely finish playing with dolls before she was raising a real baby of her own.

Belinda was young and sweet, and it was not long before men were paying court to the beautiful girl. One man in particular caught Belinda's eye.

His name was Jim. He was a big brute of a man, older than Belinda by far, but he was fair of speech and face and easily turned the young girl's head with romancing. Had she heeded the advice of those relations who knew him, she would have known he had a mean streak a mile wide and deeper than a blue hole.

Belinda's parents had a bad feeling about Jim as well, and they did their best to dissuade their naïve young daughter from marrying him. But Belinda had fallen head over heels for Jim, and her heart overruled all advice.

For a while, Belinda and big Jim lived near her family; but soon Jim wanted to move up the road a piece. Against her parents' wishes, the

couple moved out of the hollow to the more remote slopes of Brown Mountain.

As Belinda had been warned, once they were away from her parents' watchful eyes, Jim started to change. His mean streak came out more and more, and with each new day he became more sullen and hostile. He began to drink heavily and often beat the young girl at the least provocation.

Things got worse when Belinda found that she was pregnant. Far from being filled with joy at the prospect of fatherhood, Jim grew resentful—and more violent.

Worse than Jim's cruelty was his neglect. He began to disappear for days at a time, with scarcely a word of explanation or apology. When Belinda could extract a civil word out of Jim, he would mumble that he simply had been out hunting.

But local gossip had another tale to tell. It was rumored that Jim had tired of his young bride, now that she was with child, and was stepping out with another woman.

Indeed, Jim was seeing a woman named Susie. He was crazy about her, romancing her with sweet words and fine gifts—and Susie didn't much mind that Jim was already married. But the nicer he was to Susie, the meaner he became to Belinda.

Things came to a head when the baby was born. Maybe Jim half hoped his wife would miscarry and die of natural causes, neglected as she was, giving birth all on her own without a midwife or anyone else to help her. But the will to live is strong, and a mother's love for her child stronger still, and the two survived the ordeal.

Saddled now with a family he no longer wanted, Jim's cruelty waxed fiercer still. Exactly what happened next is unclear, since only Jim and Belinda knew for sure.

Some say that Belinda, learning of her husband's infidelity, finally worked up the courage to leave him. She was packing her belongings while he was out "hunting," but he discovered what she was up to Others say that Jim, in a drunken rage, declared he'd had enough and decided to finish what neglect had failed to do. Whatever the motivation might have been, Jim grabbed an axe and started swinging, chopping off Belinda's beautiful head. Then, for good measure, he killed the infant and hid both the bodies.

Telling everyone that his wife and child had disappeared without

trace, Jim feigned great concern and even enlisted his neighbors to help search for the missing pair. The small, tight-knit community turned out to a man to look for Belinda and her babe, and the search continued day and night, when scores of torches could be seen dotting the slopes of Brown Mountain as the mountain folk hunted in vain for the missing mother and child.

Some say the lights we see today are the phantom images of those restless revenants still searching for sweet Belinda.

But those who knew Jim and Belinda began to have suspicions that the young mother had met with foul play—and Jim was their prime suspect. When Susie moved in with the "grieving" husband so soon after his wife's disappearance, tongues began to wag.

Belinda's bonnet was found in the woods, caked with dried blood. Relations of the missing girl confronted Jim, but the mountaineer claimed ignorance regarding her whereabouts. The local constabulary refused to intervene, claiming there was not enough evidence to make an arrest.

It was about this time, old-timers say, that the lights began to appear on the mountain. Soon after, big Jim disappeared—lit out for other parts, it was said, to avoid further questioning about his wife's disappearance. That, at least, is what the local inhabitants told the county sheriff when he came to inquire about Jim's sudden disappearance.

Now, it's no secret that in Appalachia mountain folk had their own way of dealing with situations—especially before the Civil War. The real story of what became of Jim was never fully revealed publicly, and even today many who know the truth are reluctant to discuss it.

When the lights began appearing on the mountain, it was taken as a sign that some evil had indeed befallen Belinda. According to mountain lore, such ghost lights are always a manifestation of those who have died a violent death.

Two mountain women felt sure the ghost lights were trying to say something. So one night, when the light appeared, they followed it across the craggy slopes of Brown Mountain, whale-oil lamps in hand.

Finally, the two women arrived at a spot over which two balls of light seemed hover. On the ground beneath lay a heap of rocks that appeared to have been freshly stacked. Returning in the daylight, the women dug into the stones, finding beneath them the skulls of an adult and a newborn.

As every child in the mountains knows (or leastways *used to* know), the skulls of murder victims don't rot or decay, and when the victim's skull is held over the head of his murderer, the accused is incapable of lying about his crime.

Straightaway, a party of "Regulators" was organized and paid a late night visit to the cabin of the "bereaved" widower Jim. As one man held the skulls over Jim's head, one of the two wise women put the question to him.

Knowing he could not lie his way out of the situation, big Jim chose to say nothing at all. The silence was deafening.

Mountain justice can be swift and sure, and what the sheriff was unwilling to do, the folks who dwelt near Brown Mountain took care of in their own quiet way. Jim had been judged by his peers and found wanting, and from the verdict of Judge Lynch there was no appeal.

Although the skulls of Belinda and her baby were recovered, the rest of their bodies were not. It is said that the lights will continue to bob and sway at night as they seek to point the way to the place where the bodies were hidden, until the day that some kind soul finds them and gives them a Christian burial, finally putting their souls to rest.

According to a few who claim to know, a third unmarked grave lies somewhere on the slopes of Brown Mountain, and a light marks the way to this one, too. It is a fiery red light, they say—as red as the flames of hell—but for this restless spirit there will never be any peace, for there is no rest for the damned.

Mile Marker 310 on the Blue Ridge Parkway has a scenic overlook which provides a good panoramic view of Brown Mountain.

Wiseman's View, near Linville Falls is also a favorite viewing place, although less accessible for those not familiar with the area. It is located on Highway 105, outside of Morganton.

23

A Night on
Bald Roan Mountain

ORTH CAROLINA'S MOUNTAINS HAVE LONG held many mysteries. Ghost lights, haints, and similar wonderments attract the curious, the serious seekers, and the outright bewildered in growing numbers every year. Beyond the many strange occurrences, though, are a few which can be heard but not seen. Such is the case with the mysterious music of Bald Roan Mountain.

The "balds" of North Carolina are a curious phenomena to start with. A bald is a spot on a mountain that for whatever reason has been stripped of trees and other heavy cover. How they came to be is something naturalists cannot agree upon.

Some say that when woolly Mammoths roamed the land, they grazed the mountain tops bare, and the mountains simply stayed that way. Others assert that these summits attract lightning from the heavens, which in turn sets off fires that prevent trees and shrubs from growing there.

But in the highlands of North Carolina, tradition often strikes closer to the mark than scholarly theories. The early settlers used to say that the Devil himself once walked these hills, and that wherever

Old Scratch put his foot down, the ground around would wither for-ever—so creating the balds.

Before the white man came to the region, the Catawba Indians lived in the shadow of the Roan mountain range. According to oral tradition, a series of battles took place there between the Catawba and their rivals. The warring tribes chose the summit of Roan Mountain and its sister peaks as their battlefield, so they could be closer to the Great Spirit when they fell in combat.

It is said that the slaughter on the mountain's slopes was so terrible that blood dyed the flowers crimson. The Catawba claim the spirits of the slain still reside there, and because of this, only grass and the red-stained flowers will grow on the spot. As proof, they say, you can still hear the ghosts of the slain warriors chanting prayers to the Great Spirit.

An Indian myth of even greater age relates that a monstrous bird once took to roosting on the summit of Roan. It would swoop down to devour helpless children at will, until the tribe resolved to scale the heights and destroy the creature. But when the warriors reached the top of the ridge, they found a whole family of such monsters, in numbers beyond counting. Seeing that they would be helpless before an onslaught of such terrifying creatures, the natives threw down their weapons in fear and began beseeching the Great Spirit for mercy.

No sooner had their chanting risen up to the heavens than silent lightning began to flash down from every quarter of the cloudless sky to pound the mountaintop where the horrible beasts stood. When the divine fire was at last spent, everything on the mountaintop was burned beyond recognition—but the creatures were gone. The Indians raised their voices again, this time chanting their praises to the Great Spirit. Many believe their ghosts continue to chant an aboriginal *te deum* to this day.

While giant, prehistoric-looking flying creatures such as the myth describes have been sighted in modern times in the South and Midwest (some eyewitnesses have described them as being as big as a B-52 bomber), anthropologists generally have interpreted such stories as a symbolic memory of an ancient catastrophe. The Thunder-bird, these scientists say, was symbolic of some great natural disaster—probably an earthquake or a volcanic eruption—which had the bald range as its epicenter. Still, this scientific interpretation does not begin to explain the unearthly singing and chanting that wafts down from the mountain's heights from time to time.

There is little doubt that something uncanny manifests itself atop Bald Roan Mountain. In the more than two hundred years since the white man began to inhabit this region, many people have reported hearing the ghostly choir chanting from the mountaintop. Some have even dared to spend the night there.

In 1799 a member of a surveying party running the state boundary between Tennessee and North Carolina reported a most unusual wind atop Bald Roan. It was so strong, he said, it could blow holes in solid rock. Farmers in the area said the wind was "circular"—that the clouds whirled around the mountain in a complete circle—and that, they claimed, had something to do with the phantom chorus.

Cattle herders in the valley below have long sworn they hear an angelic choir when the wind blows down the mountain. The music, it is said, is clearest just after a thunderstorm. Starting low and rising gradually in volume, it grows wilder and faster as it reaches its peak.

For many, the phantom choir of Bald Roan Mountain was thought to be just a legend until after the Civil War. Then, in 1885, Gen. John T. Wilder opened the Cloudland Hotel atop Bald Roan. Wilder had been the Yankee commander of Wilder's Brigade during the war, and after ravaging a good part of Dixie, he later took a mind to settle there.

In addition to the spectacular view from the top of Roan—one can see all the other bald peaks strung out in a row, like stepping stones—the mountain, Wilder thought, would also be a prime location for a health resort, an ideal spot for those suffering from hay fever or lung ailments.

General Wilder didn't quite get the public response he expected to the opening of the Cloudland. Guests who stayed there complained about the "demon wind," saying that, besides the unearthly music, the wind made them feel like prisoners in a ship's hold. The hotel's stone structure tended to sway back and forth when the wind was high. However, Wilder did attract some curiosity seekers—people who sought to unravel the mystery of the mountains.

One such person was a gentleman named Henry Colton. Colton wrote extensively about the Southern landscape, and the mystery of the Roan chorus was one phenomenon that he couldn't resist investigating for himself. He checked into the hotel determined to find the cause of the strange sounds on the mountain.

One evening, when the ghostly choir was particularly active, Colton ascended the peak of Bald Roan, along with General Wilder and a few other adventurers. Standing there, high above the world, Colton listened intently, trying to analyze the sound.

Some had tried to explain the music as simply the collective humming of a large swarm of bees. But Colton concluded that could not possibly be. The music was more like the sound of glass jars snapping together he said, than that of insects. Moreover, the uncanny sound was often heard at times of the year when insects were dormant.

Henry Colton verified the reality of the phantom choir, analyzing it as best as he could. But in the end, he, too, was unable to solve the mystery.

Then one summer day, a brash young stranger checked into the Cloudland. His name was Libourel, and he also had heard about the phantom choir. He was confident he could find its source where others had failed.

Fog hung heavy on the mountainside the morning Libourel set forth on his quest. General Wilder knew the moods of the mountain well, and by all appearance this was not a good day to challenge Bald Roan.

Wilder tried to dissuade the young man from venturing out. It was not advisable to go climbing alone under any circumstances, he warned, and it was all too easy to get lost in the thick fog—or worse still, to fall off a cliff. Moreover, Wilder said, it would likely rain in the afternoon—as it generally does in the summer there.

But the young adventurer could not be talked out of his quest—and he left the Cloudland without even taking food or water with him. When he left he was dressed in a checked shirt and navy blue pants, and his only protection was a stout walking stick.

Libourel ascended the slopes, trying to track the source of the demon wind. As the day progressed, the weather turned wicked, as the general had warned. As the wind grew stronger, Libourel felt sure he was approaching its source. Then he heard it.

Amid the roar of the wind, but distinct from it, came an unearthly humming. It seemed almost like the sound of a thousand lost souls, chanting together. The thunder began rolling violently, almost bowling him over with its force, and lightning started flashing all about, streaking down onto the treeless slopes.

Between the force of the driving rain and the danger of electrocution, Libourel was forced to seek shelter. He found it underneath an outcropping of rock, where he huddled for dear life, waiting for the tempest to end.

At the Cloudland Hotel, John Wilder was becoming concerned over his guest. As he had warned, the weather had turned foul late in the day, trapping the brash young visitor on the upper slopes.

It was impossible to mount a rescue party while the storm raged, and it was equally foolhardy to try to search for him after dark. If young Libourel did not make it back before nightfall, the general would try to organize a search party in the morning.

Libourel finally did make it down from the treacherous crags of the south face of the mountain. Wilder and the others were relieved to see him back safely, but they were shocked at his appearance.

The well-dressed young man they had seen leave that morning was gone, and in his place was a gaunt figure with haggard eyes. His blue pants and red-checked shirt were now snowy white, and the bark on his walking stick had been stripped down, exposing bare wood.

Without saying a word, Libourel went straight to his room, packed his bags, paid his bill, and left. General Wilder never did find out what had spooked the young man so.

It was many years before Libourel would be willing to talk about his experience on Bald Roan. When he was finally able to discuss it, he claimed that he had indeed found the source of the wind—and the phantom choir as well. He wished he hadn't.

As he clung to life in the small rock shelter that evening, a cave suddenly opened up behind him. Perhaps it had been there all along and he hadn't noticed it; but somehow it seemed grow wider. Stranger still, Libourel felt himself being sucked into it.

Whether he fell or was drawn into the cavern he could not tell for certain, but once inside he encountered firsthand the phantom voices.

The singers, he later insisted, were neither angels nor dead warriors, as some had thought. Rather, he claimed, they were the spirits of the damned. Some wore leather shoes, not Indian moccasins; others were covered in the tattered remnants of European-style clothing. But aside from that, there was little human left to them.

All of the spirits seemed to have died violent deaths—some had deep gashes about their heads and faces; others were missing limbs; still others had rotting flesh falling off in large shreds from their bodies. These were the lost souls of hell, he realized; the voices of Bald Roan Mountain were a chorus of the damned.

Somehow the young man managed to claw his way out of the cave, and after a long while made it back down the mountain slope to the hotel. He had found what he was looking for—and got far more in the bargain than he intended. To his dying day, Libourel swore he had been caught in the middle of a monumental struggle between the forces of heaven and the winds of hell.

Today, a line of stones marks the place where the Cloudland Hotel once stood. But Bald Roan Mountain remains as majestic as it has always been. And, as has been the case for centuries, its craggy slopes echo with the eerie music of a chanting chorus.

Whether it is, as the young man claimed, a chorus of demons, or a choir of angels, or something else entirely, no one can say for sure. But until the day that someone unlocks the secret of this uncanny phenomenon—or some brave soul rediscovers the doorway to hell—the music of Bald Roan Mountain will remain a mystery.

If you go ...
More haints and haunts of Dixie to see in North Carolina:

ASHEVILLE
THE BILTMORE ESTATES
1 Approach Road
Asheville, NC 28803
(800) 411-3812 • (828) 225-1333
www.Biltmore.com

This luxurious tourist venue is haunted by a "Lady in Black" who occasionally is spotted throughout the mansion.

FOUR OAKS
THE HARPER HOUSE
Bentonville Battlefield
5466 Harper House Road
Four Oaks, NC 27524
(910) 594-0789
www.ah.dcr.stat.nc.us

The house was commandeered for use as field hospital during the bloody Civil War battle that raged all around it. Civil War ghosts and been reported in and around the grounds of the old house, now part of the battlefield park.

WILMINGTON
THE PRICE-GAUSE HOUSE (1843)
(Wilmington Visitors Center)
314 Market Street
Wilmington, NC 28401
(919) 762-2611

Phantom footsteps have been heard on the steps, and a strange tapping coming from the walls have been reported by visitors. A ghost was photographed on the stairs in 1967.

WINSTON-SALEM
THE SINGLE BROTHERS HOUSE
Old Salem
600 South Main
Winston-Salem, NC 27101
www.oldsalem.org

Located in a Williamsburg-like recreation of the city's original settlement, a "Little Red Man" occasionally appears near the Brothers house—the shade of a man tragically killed while excavating a basement in colonial days.

North Carolina Ghost Tours

ASHEVILLE
ASHEVILLE GHOST WALK

(America by Foot)
(828) 355-5855
www.hauntedghosttours.com

BEAUFORT
BEAUFORT GHOST WALK
(252) 342-0715
www.tourbeaufort.com

OCRACOKE ISLAND
GHOST WALK OF OCRACOKE

Seasonal by the "Village Craftsmen"
170 Howard Street
P.O. Box 248
Ocracoke Island, NC
(252) 928-6300
www.villagecraftsmen.com

WILMINGTON
GHOST WALK OF OLD WILMINGTON

Also offered is a Haunted Pub Crawl (adults only)
(910) 794-1866
www.hauntedwilmington.com

24

An Affair of Honor

Yet this inconstancy is such
As you too shall adore;
I could not love thee, Dear, so much,
Loved I not Honour more.
— Richard Lovelace, *To Lucasta, on Going to the Wars*

HISTORY AND HAUNTINGS HANG EQUALLY HEAVY in the atmosphere of Charleston, South Carolina. Enter any home in the old part of town and one may easily agree with Margaret Rhett Martin's dictum that "every Old Charleston house has its ghostly visitor." Even a short sojourn there reveals to the visitor that Charleston has ghosts in abundance.

From its beginning, Charleston has been a bastion of the values of the Old South. Foremost among these, for good or ill, was the Southern Code of Honor. No tale of old Charleston better illustrates this fact than the events surrounding the death and afterlife of Dr. Joseph Brown Ladd.

Joseph Ladd was born in the Rhode Island colony in 1764, the son of an honest farmer of modest means. As a boy Joseph was an avid reader, and he developed a flair for poetry as he grew older. In time, he earned a degree in medicine and set out to establish his reputation as a physician.

Joseph no doubt would have lived a long and happy life in New England had it not been for Amanda. The two met, it is said, in a library. The handsome, bookish young doctor immediately became smitten with the beautiful young heiress and began wooing her with poetry of his own devising. She, in turn, soon declared her love for Joseph.

But Amanda was an orphan—a rather wealthy orphan—and her guardian did not want to lose the income he realized from managing her estate. When Joseph proposed marriage, the guardian opposed it vigorously and began to spread terrible rumors, slandering the young doctor in hopes of blackening his reputation and thereby breaking up the romance. His underhanded tactics worked.

Bewildered and humiliated by this turn of events, Ladd left Rhode Island and the love of his life, traveling south to rebuild his reputation and seek his fortune, so that he might again be deemed worthy to ask for Amanda's hand. And so it came to pass that fate led Ladd to the bustling port of Charleston.

No sooner had his buckle shoes touched the cobblestones of Charleston's streets than Ladd made the acquaintance of one Ralph Isaacs, a gentleman of the city. Isaacs took the young doctor under his tutelage, helping him steer clear of some of the more unsavory local characters and introducing Ladd to Charleston society. The two soon became good friends.

Joseph secured lodging in the home of two respectable spinsters, Fannie and Dellie Rose, who lived in a spacious house at 59 Church Street that was built in 1735 by their now-deceased father, Thomas Rose. It was from here that Doctor Ladd began to reestablish his medical practice and—of equal importance—cultivate a favorable reputation among Charleston's elite.

Joseph corresponded faithfully with Amanda, often writing passionate love poetry dedicated to her. When not busy with his patients or writing, Ladd frequently attended society functions. With his good looks, charm, and cultured intelligence, the young doctor soon was in great demand on Charleston's bustling social scene.

All seemed to be going well for the good doctor. With his reputation restored and his fortune assured, it appeared that Ladd would soon be able to regain his heart's desire.

But Joseph's success also proved to be his undoing. Isaacs, who had befriended the young doctor upon his arrival from Rhode Island, began to resent how others now monopolized Ladd's time. Isaacs fancied that the physician was ignoring him, now that he had become the toast of the town, and he began to nurse a secret grudge against his old friend.

Things came to a head when the two attended the theater one evening. An argument arose over the quality of the performance of an actress on stage. It was a seemingly trivial matter—local accounts don't even agree on the performer's name—but somehow the disagreement mushroomed out of all proportion. Soon, the two men even began to trade insults openly in the *Charleston Gazette*, Isaacs going so far as to label the doctor a "scoundrel" and a "disgrace" to humanity.

It had been public slurs on his reputation that had caused Joseph to move to Charleston in the first place. Now a friend was seeking to slander him publicly in the city where he had rebuilt his life. To let these insults pass unchallenged would undo all that he had achieved. Moreover, his new circle of friends advised Joseph that the Code of Honor left him with no other choice if he wanted to preserve his good name: he must challenge Isaacs to a duel.

On a chill November day in 1786 the two men met, their seconds attending with dueling pistols primed and loaded. Ladd had not sought this confrontation, but now he was convinced it was necessary to see it through to preserve his honor.

But when they took aim at each other, Dr. Ladd refused to fire on his old friend, instead shooting his pistol into the air. Ralph Isaacs, however, was not so honorable. He fired directly at Ladd, hitting him in the legs and maiming them.

Ladd's seconds carried him back to his Church Street lodgings, where the Rose sisters attended to his wounds. Although the injuries were not initially life-threatening, infection set in, and Joseph Brown Ladd's health began to fail.

The Rose sisters wrote to Amanda and tried to let her know about Joseph's condition. Amanda yearned to be by Joseph's side, but her cold-hearted guardian got wind of her plans and had her watched closely by day and locked her in her room at night. Joseph died with Amanda's name on his lips. He was buried in Charleston.

Doctor Ladd's love for Amanda and his tragic death at such a young age stands as a haunting tale of love undone by the Southern Code of Honor. It is a story that has been told and retold in Charleston for generations. But Dr. Ladd's death was not the end of the tale, by any means.

Since Dr. Ladd's death at 59 Church Street in 1786, successive residents of that house have often experienced inexplicable sounds and various other odd occurrences.

The most commonly encountered phenomenon in the Thomas Rose House is the sound of phantom footsteps.

Andrew Frost, now in his eighties, has worked in the Church Street house for a score or more years. Although he has never seen a ghost there, Frost said he has often heard the sounds of someone walking around and slamming doors on the second and third floors—usually on cloudy days.

The first time Frost heard the ghostly sounds, he called the cook to see if she was making the noise. He was surprised to find the cook had been downstairs at the time.

Andrew has not heard the ghost recently, however. One day a few years ago Frost became fed up with all the clattering throughout the house and yelled out, "Damn you, dead! Leave me alone!" Since then, the ghost—a gentleman even in death—has complied with Frost's wishes.

Others, however, continue to encounter Doctor Ladd. Workmen called in to do renovations and repairs to the old house in recent years have reported seeing a man walk by when no one else was in the house. An exterminator was so badly frightened by the apparition that he refused to come back ever again.

The house has been in the present owners' family since 1941; Cathy Forrester and her husband are the third generation of her family to reside there. While Mrs. Forrester protests that she doesn't believe in ghosts, she nevertheless admits to having had at least one spectral encounter shortly after moving into the house.

It seems that one night, as she was trying to settle her children in their respective bedrooms on the third floor, both youngsters became restless for no apparent reason. While going from one bedroom to the other, Mrs. Forrester caught a glimpse out of the corner of her eye of a figure standing on the landing. It was "of a man *not* dressed in contemporary clothes," she recalled.

The apparition lasted but a moment; and when she brought her full concentration to bear on it and looked squarely at it, the figure disappeared.

Visitors staying in the guest bedroom on the second floor—where it is believed Doctor Ladd died—will occasionally hear the sound of someone walking up and down the stairs in the middle of the night. A quick search of the staircase, however, reveals no one there.

Juliette Staats—Cathy Forrester's grandmother—occupied the same second-floor bedroom for several years. She, too, heard the sounds of someone walking about outside her room.

Previous residents in the house have also testified to hearing the sound of soft whistling from time to time. Doctor Ladd evidently was not only fond of poetry, he loved music as well.

Joseph Ladd was neither the first nor the last to seek his fortune in a distant place in hopes of winning his heart's desire. But the story of his tragic life and death, of love's labor lost, has left its imprint on his adopted city—much as his spirit has left its mark on the elegant dwelling he once called home, the golden-hued house at 59 Church Street.

25

The Gray Man

A YOUNG WOMAN WALKS ALONG the sandy shore, barefoot, the surf lapping gently onto the beach occasionally engulfing her feet to the ankles. It is a warm, sunny day, and she is enjoying her stay on one of the many islands that grace the Carolina coast like jewels on a necklace.

Suddenly, out of nowhere, a man approaches her. He is dressed strangely, in a gray cap and gray work clothes, and his pallid complexion strikes an odd note on this sun-filled island. He tells the young woman to flee the island immediately, for her life is at hazard if she stays.

Whether it is his odd demeanor or strange attire, something about the ashen-faced stranger causes her to heed his warning. Without exactly knowing why, she cuts her vacation short and heads back to the mainland.

A short time later, a hurricane slams into the Carolina coast, causing extensive damage and loss of life. The woman is one more person who owes her safety to an encounter with "the Gray Man."

For more than a half-century this same scenario has played itself out on the sands of Pawley's Island, South Carolina. It seems the idyllic retreat possesses a far more accurate forecaster of dangerous weather than the National Weather Service.

According to local lore, the Gray Man has appeared to residents of the small island resort on a regular basis for well over a hundred years, giving timely warnings of major storms.

The Gray Man is a unique specter in the annals of the supernatural. Not only does this phantom regularly haunt the scenic beaches of Pawley's Island, but he also seems to possess both prophetic and protective powers.

Those who heed the Gray Man's warnings to depart the island say he seems to preserve more than their lives. For when the predicted storm has passed, those to whom he has appeared invariably find that their homes have not been touched by the Atlantic's fury. Other dwellings may be ravaged by wind and surf, but those who have seen this guardian spirit are convinced that they, as well as their real estate, are under a special benediction.

But who is the Gray Man? And why has he made protecting the inhabitants of Pawley's Island his special mission?

As is the case with many ghosts, the origins of the Gray Man are somewhat hazy. One account holds that the ghost is that of a nineteen-year-old man who was betrothed to a girl whose parents lived on the island.

In the early 1800s, after a long absence, the man returned to Pawley's Island and, hurrying to be with his beloved, took a shortcut across an inhospitable marsh.

Riding a bit ahead of his manservant, the young gentleman's horse suddenly jerked to a halt. In his haste, the man had unwittingly ridden into a patch of quicksand, and he and his horse were mired and sinking fast. Unable to help, the manservant looked on in horror as his master rapidly sank out of sight.

When his fiancée heard the news of his demise, she was devastated. It all seemed like a bad dream: his unexpected death, the funeral—everything happened so suddenly.

To clear her mind, and as a way to deal with her pain, she did what she always did when confused or distraught; she took a walk alone along the beach.

The young woman strolled along the same beach where she and her beau had walked many times before, talking about their plans for the future. The wind was up, and the surf seemed a little wilder than normal, but she paid little heed, for she was lost in a deep reverie.

Suddenly, her meditations were interrupted by the sight of a man approaching. He seemed somehow familiar, although she could not at first place him. As he drew nearer, she recognized him—it was her dead fiancé.

For a moment she seemed to have awoken from a dream—all the bad news had been just a nightmare. But then she realized that his death was all too real, and the figure approaching her was a wraith, not a human.

Yet such was her affection for her lost love that she felt no fear, and strode forward to meet him. When she came close, he spoke to her:

"You must flee the island immediately," he told her. "Your life is in danger. Flee!" And with that, he disappeared.

The girl rushed home to her parents and related her encounter on the beach. She was a good daughter and level-headed, so her parents had no reason to doubt her truthfulness. Her sincerity in relating her encounter with her dead fiancé and her urgent pleas to leave the island convinced them to heed her warnings.

By dawn the next day the family had left Pawley's Island and traveled some distance inland. That night a ferocious hurricane hit the coast, devastating the island. When the family was able to return to inspect the damage, they discovered that their home had been spared the wrath of the howling winds. Since then, it is said, the woman's dead fiancé has returned to warn others of impending danger.

Some who are steeped in the lore of the Carolinas reject this traditional account of the Gray Man's origins. They assert that the Gray Man is really the ghost of Plowden Weston, who built what is now the Pelican Inn as his summer home in the 1840s.

The Westons were fabulously wealthy and owned expansive mainland plantations, most of which were dedicated to the cultivation of rice. But Plowden was most fond of his summer home and the isle on which it lay.

Although he was personally opposed to secession, when the Civil War began, Weston joined the Confederate army as a captain of local volunteers. However, while away on military duty, Weston developed consumption—tuberculosis, also known as "the Gray Plague"—and died of the wasting disease before the war's conclusion.

It is thought by some that Plowden's fondness for Pawley's Island in life caused him to return there in death, to look after the island and warn its inhabitants in time of danger.

The founder of the island community, Percival Pawley, has also been suggested as a candidate for the Gray Man, and for similar reasons.

In recent decades, however, a local historian, Julian S. Bolick, has done a great deal of detective work, unearthing evidence that points to yet another possibility as the ghostly guardian of Pawley's Island.

It has been known for some time that the Pelican Inn is also haunted. On a number of occasions, a stern-looking woman has been seen in different parts of the hostelry, as if overseeing the employees to make sure their work is done properly.

A previous owner of the inn, Eileen Weaver, has sighted this ghost many times. The female phantom, dressed in gingham, appears to be so real that one often does not realize at first that she is a ghost. Mrs. Weaver thought the specter's features made her appear to be French.

One spring, for example, Mrs. Weaver's daughter-in-law Gayle was assisting the family with spring cleaning. She was hard at work upstairs, cleaning the hallway and guest rooms. Taking a break, she sat leafing through an old journal when she felt a tug on her arm.

Gayle at first ignored the tugging, thinking perhaps that it was one of her in-laws teasing her. But when she felt the insistent pull once again, she looked around—and found that no one was there; nor was there any way someone could have approached her without making a noise on the creaky wooden floor. Gayle was convinced that she had had an encounter with the family's guardian female ghost, irritated at her for taking a break from her cleaning chores.

Although not so frequently seen as this female apparition, a male presence has also been detected around the Pelican Inn on several occasions. It, too, seems to be a protective spirit.

A few years back, Julian Bolick of nearby Georgetown showed Mrs. Weaver a lineup of old photos, including one of Plowden Weston and his wife, Emily. But when Eileen looked at the pictures, she identified Mr. and Mrs. Mazyck—relatives of the Westons—as the ghosts she had seen.

Emily Weston, widowed prematurely, died childless. When she passed, the Mazycks inherited the Westons' summer home and converted it into the Pelican Inn, an upscale summer resort. Mrs. Mazyck evidently ran a tight ship, keeping a weather eye on all aspects of the operation; Mr. Mazyck apparently was equally protective of the island as a whole. Circumstantial evidence would seem to indicate that Mrs. Mazyck is still looking after the inn from the other side of the grave.

The Gray Man is somewhat harder to pinpoint, since his features often appear less distinct than those of the house ghost. But Mrs. Weaver has seen the Gray Man as well, and given the protective nature of this duo of ghosts, the identification of Mr. Mazyck as the Gray Man seems quite likely.

The last known documented sighting of the Gray Man was in 1989. That year, a couple walking along the beach at Pawley's Island encountered a thin man wearing a gray fishing cap and drab workman's clothes. As the phantom had done with many previous visitors, he warned the couple to leave the island at once.

Having heard tales of the Gray Man, they were inclined to take the stranger's warning seriously and made haste to escape to the mainland. They drove inland all night, finally reaching Kentucky. Two days later, Hurricane Hugo struck South Carolina.

Over the years the Gray Man has saved perhaps thousands of lives. Needless to say, this specter is held in high regard by the local populace. In fact, almost everyone on Pawley's Island has a tale or two to tell about the Gray Man—all of them good.

The Pelican Inn remains a haven from the workaday world, welcoming visitors from all around the country who come to enjoy its good food and scenic views. But be forewarned: if you should encounter that spectral gent during your stay, by all means heed what he has to say. And if you are at all wise, before the next sun rises, you will be far, far away.

THE PELICAN INN
506 Myrtle Avenue
Pawley's Island, SC 29585
(843) 237-2298
www.evanspelicaninn.com

26

South Battery Hauntings:
The Battery Carriage House Inn

STROLLING ALONG CHARLESTON'S SOUTH BATTERY, immersed in the present, images of the past still flood the senses. Throughout the district rise rows of stately town homes, each a monument to the city's heritage. Behind each graceful façade·is an unwritten novel—of lives lived, storms survived, sieges endured, loves won and lost—and the spirits, past and present, who watch over it all.

DeBose Hayward, author of *Porgy and Bess* and an unreconstructed Charlestonian, once observed that "an old city without legends is like a cow without a cud." Certainly, an old city such as Charleston has no shortage of legends—or ghosts.

Three buildings down from the DeBose Hayward House on the South Battery stands an edifice which serves to confirm his dictum.

The Stevens-Lathers Mansion, at 20 South Battery, is one of those grand homes that seem particularly steeped in legend and lore. Since its construction in 1843, its owners have included wealthy cotton merchants, anti-secessionist entrepreneurs, and financiers; visitors have included soldiers, socialites, shady ladies, and even the famous politician and orator William Cullen Bryant.

During the nineteenth century, the South Battery was the favored neighborhood of South Carolina's elite, and the Stevens-Lathers House was its crown jewel. Built for cotton factor Samuel N. Stevens, the house was originally done in the Greek Revival style. During the 1870s its third owner, Colonel Lathers, extensively renovated the house to give it the "Second Empire" look it has now. A native Carolinian who had taken a Unionist stance during the Civil War, Lathers also added the house's distinctive "fish scale" mansard roof.

After the war the colonel had hoped to reconcile North and South by attracting Northern capital to help rebuild Charleston and the Carolinas. But his loyalty to the Union doomed his efforts, in part because bitterness from the war was still too fresh in the minds of Charlestonians to allow them to have anything to do with Yankees. In the end, Lather sold the house and moved north.

Andrew Simonds bought the mansion from Lathers in 1874. Simonds, who had been a staunch supporter of the Confederacy, had managed to preserve much of his fortune after the war. Charleston society found him far more congenial to its sensibilities than the home's previous resident had been, and soon the mansion became a meeting place for the city's elite as well as distinguished visitors from near and far.

The current owner of the house, Drayton Hastie, is the great-great-grandson of Andrew Simonds. Thus Hastie's efforts to restore the home and its outbuildings have been something of a mission of filial devotion.

Hastie's grandmother, Sara Calhoun Simonds, for example, spent her summers here as a young girl—but she almost didn't survive her childhood. One summer, while playing in the area above the grand ballroom's skylight, she slipped and fell through the glass portal.

Sara surely would have been killed by the fall had not she grabbed hold of the crystal chandelier as she plunged through the skylight. Dangling in mid-air, high above the ballroom floor, she managed to cling to the fixture's fragile framework until the family's servants were able to climb up and rescue her.

Squire Hastie is the guardian of many such bits of family lore and history as well as an earnest collector of material related to the ghosts of his ancestral home. Between his grandmother's era and the time he and his wife purchased the home, however, the house had a somewhat checkered reputation. During the 1920s and early thirties, it seems 20 South Battery was not a home—although it definitely was a *house*.

During that period many of Charleston's elite frequented the mansion—but they made sure not to bring their wives. By all accounts, strip-teasers performed in the carriage house at the rear of the mansion, while the richly appointed bedrooms of the main building may have been reserved for more discreet entertainment.

Although succeeding decades saw the mansion enjoy a somewhat less scarlet career, time took its toll on the structure, and by the latter decades of the twentieth century, the Stevens-Lathers mansion was sorely in need of major repairs. In 1989 Hurricane Hugo did extensive damage to the house, further adding to its problems.

Grand mansions such as the Stevens-Lathers House had gradually fallen out of favor with many of the affluent. They were immensely expensive to maintain, and the fast pace of modern life meant that such an abundance of living space was no longer needed. So the old mansion lay vacant for several years until Drayton and Catherine Hastie rescued it.

Today, the upper stories of the house comprise the private residence of the Hasties, who converted the garden level and the carriage house into a cozy but elegant bed and breakfast—the Battery Carriage House Inn. And given its long and colorful history, it's not surprising that the inn is also the abode of more than one spectral guest.

The best-known phantom inhabiting the inn is the specter known only as "the Gentleman Ghost," whose favorite haunt seems to be Room 10. He is a most amiable spirit and is particularly fond of female visitors—especially young women.

Described as short and balding (and given the carriage house's somewhat lurid history, one would not be surprised to find his name was "John"), the Gentleman Ghost has been known to climb into bed with female guests in the middle of the night.

Of a considerably less congenial disposition is the apparition that haunts Room Number 8. This ghost seems to date to the Civil War era, when the city was under blockade by the Union fleet and, toward the end of the conflict, subjected to almost daily bombardment—a random shelling of residential areas designed to terrorize the inhabitants. Many innocent civilians—men, women, and children alike—were killed.

The ghost in Room 8 is known as "the Headless Torso," so called because of his penchant for appearing to guests without his head. It is thought the apparition is that of a Confederate soldier who was killed during the siege of Charleston, although this is not certain. The phantom might just as easily be a civilian victim of the shelling by Yankee gunboats, which would account for his aggressive attitude.

The Headless Torso would not win awards for congeniality, for, according to various accounts, he is not overly fond of visitors. Although he has never been known to harm anyone, the sudden appearance of his headless body at one's bedside in the middle of the night can be a terrifying experience.

In 1992, for example, a man who was staying in Room 8 had a close encounter with the specter. An engineer by trade and a practical sort of person by nature, the man was not prone to flights of fancy. That evening, however, he awoke from a sound sleep and was overcome by a strange feeling—as if he was being watched—although he knew that was impossible, since he had securely locked the door to the room.

But when he opened his eyes, however, the visitor saw the torso of a man floating in the area between his bed and the wall. The apparition, broad-shouldered and with a large chest, was just inches away from him and seemed to make a deep gasping sound—as if he were having difficulty breathing. The man later said the ghost was so close that he could make out details of his long overcoat.

On an impulse, the engineer reached out his hand, half expecting the apparition to disappear into thin air. But as soon as he made contact with the specter, it began to emit a low-pitched, loud, unearthly sound, something like a cross between a growl and a howl. Needless to say, the engineer quickly terminated his stay at the inn.

While some visitors are nonplussed by their encounters with these spectral entities, other guests actively seek out such confrontations.

One young lady, when asked by her mother what she wanted as a birthday present, replied, "To see a ghost!" With this in mind, the mother made a reservation at the Battery Carriage House Inn, booking Room 9, as her daughter had requested.

The daughter had heard that the spirit that haunts Room 9 is one of a guest who had stayed at the inn before the Civil War, and that he had jumped to his death from the window of this particular room. Local lore has it that the man had an adopted slave boy who stayed with him.

Guests staying in Room 9 say they have heard the sounds of children's laughter—even though no one under twelve is allowed to stay at the inn overnight.

The birthday girl and a friend roomed together in Room 9 one night in December (Halloween having been all booked up), but whatever spirit resided in the room did not make an appearance that evening—or so she thought. When the girl processed the film she had taken during her overnight adventure, all the photographs of the room were strangely distorted. Further, one shot she knew she had taken never showed up on the negatives. Her girlfriend's camera completely malfunctioned when she tried to photograph the room, yet it worked normally when away from the inn.

Although their spectral encounter was not so dramatic as some at the inn, the teenage visitors nevertheless were convinced that *something* was in Room 9, even if it did not wish to reveal itself.

More recently, a woman returned to the Battery Carriage House Inn after a long hiatus. The lady was a psychiatrist and paid a courtesy call to Catherine Hastie to show her a photo she had taken at the inn many years before, during a previous stay there.

The woman and her husband were vacationing at the inn during that visit. Wanting to get a picture of the antiques in her room, she took a photo of Room 9's layout.

But when her photos were developed, she was surprised to find not a shot of the furniture but the image of a woman in the foreground— a woman with long, dark flowing hair. The image was slightly blurred, but it was nonetheless distinguishable as a person.

The psychiatrist was quite sure her roll of film had been a fresh one, and she was equally certain that no one had been in the frame when she snapped the picture.

Could this "unexpected development," this unknown female in the photo, be the apparition of one of the several shady ladies who worked there in the 1920s?

For now, at least, the ghost in the photo remains yet one more mystery to ponder, and one more ghost story to discover involving the elegant inn at 20 South Battery.

THE BATTERY CARRIAGE HOUSE INN (1843)
20 South Battery
Charleston, SC 29401
(843) 727-3100 • (800) 775-5575
www.batterycarriagehouse.com

If you go ...
More haints and haunts of Dixie to see in South Carolina:

BEECH ISLAND
REDCLIFFE PLANTATION (1859)
181 Redcliffe Road
Beech Island, SC 29842
(803) 827-1473
Open Thurs.-Mon.

Home to a former governor, Redcliffe is now a state historic site. James Hammond is believed to be the principal ghost here, and his apparition follows certain visitors; other shadowy figures have also been reported.

CHARLESTON
THE OLD EXCHANGE AND PROVOST DUNGEON
122 East Bay Street
Charleston, SC 29401
(843) 727-2165 • (888) 763-0448
www.oldexchange.com

Pirates and other enemies of the state would have been thrown in the dungeons beneath the old government building to await execution—or simply to rot away—in colonial days. The ghosts of the innocent and the guilty dwell thickly in this old building converted to a history museum.

POOGAN'S PORCH RESTAURANT
72 Queen Street
Charleston, SC 29401
(843) 577-2337
www.poogansporch.com

Like many buildings in Charleston, this venerable home has been rededicated to serve the needs of a bistro hungry public—only no one notified its previous resident, Zoe St. Amand. The woman frequently seen staring out the unoccupied second-floor window is believed to be her apparition.

McCLELLANVILLE
HAMPTON PLANTATION
1950 Rutledge Road
McClellanville, SC 29458
(803) 546-9361

Strange sounds emanate from the upstairs bedroom of the Rutledge family ancestral mansion.

South Carolina Ghost Tours

BEAUFORT
GHOSTS OF THE SOUTH
Candlelight walking tour
(843) 575-4917

CHARLESTON
BULLDOG TOURS
Offers four different ghost tours of the city: Ghosts and Dungeons Walking Tour, The Dark Side of Charleston (Rated "R"), Ghosts and Graveyards, and Haunted Jail
(843) 822-TOUR
www.bulldogtours.com

GHOSTS OF CHARLESTON

(Walking tours by Tour Charleston, LLC)
(843) 723-1670 • (800) 854-1670
www.tourcharleston.com

GHOST WALK

*Tour led by a twelfth-generation
Charleston socialite with a deep
knowledge of the city's history,
heritage, and hauntings.*
(843) 720-TOUR
www.ghostwalk.net

HAUNTED HARBOR TOURS

*The only nautical ghost tour of
Charleston Harbor.
(Sandlapper Tours)*
Charleston Maritime Center
P.O. Box 21540
Charleston, SC 29413
(843) 849-8687
www.sandlappertours.com

THE GHOSTS AND LEGENDS WALK

*Nightly tours by
The Original Charleston Walks*
(843) 577-3800
(800) 729-3420
www.americabyfoot.com

COLUMBIA
GHOST OF CAROLINA

Walking tour of Columbia
(888) 328-1272
www.columbtours.com

GEORGETOWN
HISTORY AND HAUNTED TROLLEY TOUR

Bus tour
(843) 833-2939

WALKING SHADOWS GHOST TOUR

Walking tour
(843) 543-5321

MYRTLE BEACH
MYRTLE BEACH GHOST WALK

Ghosts and Legends Theatre
Barefoot Landing
4818 Highway 175
North Myrtle Beach, SC 29512
(843) 361-3700
www.ghostshows.com/ghostwalk

27

The Haunting of Reelfoot Lake

I N THE NORTHWEST CORNER OF Tennessee stands a large shallow lake. Where fish now reside and ducks abide, fields of corn once grew, a placid stream once flowed, and a bustling little Indian town called Reelfoot once lay. How that sunlit land became a mist-shrouded swamp, and what befell the people who dwelled there, remains a matter of considerable discussion.

If you listen to the folks in the white lab coats, they will tell you all about plate tectonics, fault lines, and such. But the people around Reelfoot Lake have a different tale to tell, one handed down from the Chickasaw, of a great earthquake, and a lake, and a love that dared defy the very heavens.

It all began in 1811. From the beginning of the year there were signs to warn the wary that something was amiss. For one thing, a great comet appeared in the sky—one with a forked tail, at that—and any fool knew that a comet was always a presentiment of some great impending disaster.

Then hunters in the woodlands west of the mountains began to notice that something was up. Squirrels by the tens of thousands were seen heading southward, fleeing some nameless terror. Moreover, all the great rivers of the West—the Mississippi, the Ohio, and the Missouri—

flooded badly that spring, and no sooner had the floodwaters receded than a "bilious fever" struck many who lived along their banks. It was a puzzlement that the white man was at a loss to explain.

The red man, however, had no doubt what was behind the strange occurrences. The Great Spirit was angry, they told one another, and he was about to lay a severe chastisement upon his people.

The great Shawnee chief Tecumseh thought he knew why the Great Spirit was angry. He journeyed south that fall to warn the tribes there that selling off of their sacred lands to the whites had incurred divine wrath. Their punishment, Tecumseh declared, would not be long in coming if they did not repent their ways and join the Shawnee in a great alliance against the pale-skinned intruders.

All the southern tribes welcomed Tecumseh and his brother, and heeded their words—all, that is, except the Chickasaw, for the Chickasaw had been at peace with the Americans the longest and had cultivated the deepest friendship with them. The Chickasaw rejected Tecumseh and his brother as false prophets.

The Great Spirit finally did castigate the tribes that year, but when he did, there were those among the Chickasaw who thought they knew the *true* cause of his wrath.

In those days the land beyond the great bluffs that overlook the Mississippi close to the Kentucky border rolled away to a quiet side river, by whose banks was a small Indian town. The chief, or "mingo," there was called Kalopin. His name, it was said, translated into "Reelfoot" in English, and both the village and the adjacent stream were named that in his honor. It was said that Kalopin was called Reelfoot because he had been born with a clubfoot, which caused him to reel from side to side when he walked.

Despite this infirmity, Kalopin had become chief, for his mother's lineage was noble and he also outshone all the other young men of the village in manly pursuits. Swifter than a jackrabbit, more keen-eyed than an eagle, braver than the bear, Kalopin always came back with game after a hunt. Even in the village ball play, Kalopin always emerged as the champion.

The young braves of the town looked to Kalopin as a leader, despite his clubfoot. But with the maidens of the village it was otherwise. None of the young women of Reelfoot looked upon Kalopin with loving eyes, and although Kalopin, as chief, was respected by many, his lodge remained empty. The Southern tribes used different colors to describe emotions, and many said of Kalopin's sadness, "His face was blue."

To fill the emptiness in his heart and the vacant spot beside his hearth, Kalopin resolved to embark on a quest to find a wife. Somewhere south, he thought, he would find a woman who could see beyond his infirmity and into his heart.

So, provisions and handsome bridal gifts were obtained, and three of his most loyal braves volunteered to accompany Kalopin on his journey. There was Osceola, which means "Singing Eagle"; Nashoba, or "Wolf"; and Biwier, "Living White Oak." With three such mighty warriors by his side, a chief had little to fear from either man or beast.

After the Green Corn Festival all was at last in readiness, and Kalopin and his party set out on their quest.

For many days the group traveled along the great river the Choctaw called Mishasi-pokni Huch-cha, "He Whose Age is Beyond Counting"—and the whites called Mississippi. The days passed swiftly, for the journey was pleasant and the companions were enjoyable.

At last the shores of the Choctaw Nation came into view. The Choctaw were a large tribe and less warlike than their neighbors. The stillness of the woodland creatures told Kalopin and his comrades that they were fast approaching a large and important Choctaw town.

Kalopin and his companions pulled their canoes onto the riverbank. Kalopin then sent a herald to inform the chief of the town of his arrival, and to reassure the mingo of his peaceful intentions.

The mingo of this town was named Copiah. He was a mighty chief, a man of many winters and many followers; a leader not so wise, perhaps, but wily in his own way. Informed of Kalopin's arrival, Copiah made ready to greet the Chickasaw chief with suitable hospitality.

A young maiden of royal blood was sent to the landing to escort the Kalopin and his braves to the royal lodge. Her name was Laughing Eyes, and she was aptly named. She stood out from the other village maidens at once: raven-haired and fair of face, she walked with an air of nobility and grace, and her eyes were a startling hazel color which seemed to flash whenever she talked.

Kalopin had but to gaze into her cheery, animated eyes and listen to the sweet sound of her voice to know that his quest had not been in vain.

Kalopin and his companions were ushered into the presence of Copiah Mingo and the village elders, and the usual pleasantries were exchanged.

With great eloquence and much excess wind, Chief Copiah welcomed his noble guests from the north and offered them the freedom of the town. Kalopin replied in kind, praising the Choctaws and their chief and thanking them for their hospitality.

After a hearty feast, the pipe of peace was passed around, and in the roundabout way of the Indian, Copiah at last inquired about the reason for Kalopin's visit. As Copiah Mingo puffed away on the ceremonial clay pipe, Kalopin replied.

He explained his quest to find a suitable bride among the Choctaw women, who were renowned for their great beauty and domestic skills. Copiah nodded contentedly in agreement to all this, but when Kalopin began to relate how one maiden in particular had caught his eye and won his heart, and described her in detail, the old chief's countenance suddenly changed.

If Kalopin did not know the bright-eyed maid's name, Copiah most certainly did, for Laughing Eyes was his very own sister's child, whom he loved as dearly as a daughter. She was doubly cherished, for she was of royal lineage, and among the Choctaws descent was traced through the female line. It was from Laughing Eyes' loins, therefore, that the tribe's next chief would come, when she entered the fullness of womanhood and took a husband. She would also inherit the rank of "Beloved Woman," or priestess, as her mother had been before her. Laughing Eyes' destiny and the tribe's future were as one.

Before Kalopin had finished talking, Copiah burst out in a fit of anger, denouncing his guest in no uncertain terms. He told Kalopin that it was forbidden for Laughing Eyes to marry outside her tribe. Moreover, Copiah said bluntly, he did not want his closest blood-relative and heir to marry a cripple—much less an upstart Chickasaw.

Despite the barrage of insults, Kalopin still sought to press his courtship, at which point the village medicine man intervened.

The Great Spirit had spoken to him on this matter, the shaman told the assembly, and had declared that such a union was forbidden. If Kalopin should disregard the warning and marry the princess, the Great Spirit himself would come down and "stamp his foot"—Kalopin and his entire tribe would suffer a terrible fate.

Even after the Medicine Man had spoken, Kalopin still wished to claim the hand of the royal maiden, even though everyone else seemed set against it. Copiah, "red" with anger, seized the peace pipe, hurled it to the ground, and then stamped on it, smashing the pipe to pieces.

The Choctaw laws of hospitality forbade doing injury to guests, yet such was the wrath of Copiah that the Chickasaw made haste to return to their canoes, lest they share the same fate of the fire-roasted venison they had just consumed. Even so, it was only with great difficulty that his companions persuaded Kalopin to leave, so love-struck was their chief.

Osceola, Nashoba, and Biwier paddled hard to put as much distance between themselves and the Choctaw village as possible before dark. Kalopin was little help, for both his head and his heart were elsewhere. As the miles slipped by, Kalopin began to come to his senses, after a fashion.

Throughout that summer Kalopin's friends tried to keep him busy, engaged in hunting and fishing and all the things that formerly had made him happy. But Kalopin's thoughts remained in the south, dwelling in the land of the Choctaw.

When the maize had been gathered for the year, and shadows grew long upon the land, Kalopin resolved to take by stealth what had been denied him openly.

On a dark night after the harvest moon, Kalopin and three warriors crept through the shadows into the heart of Copiah Mingo's town. Entering the lodge next to the king's, they emerged a few moments later, with Kalopin carrying a large object slung across his broad shoulders. So quiet were the four raiders as they left the village that not even a dog's barking protest marked their departure.

Laughing Eyes at first was terrified. True, she had been strangely attracted to the Chickasaw chief when first they met, and his eloquence and passion in describing her beauty and pleading for her hand had moved her heart. It was also true that when Kalopin looked at her, she had returned his gaze—and for any other Choctaw maiden, that would have been sufficient to win her hand.

She had thought that Copiah Mingo's fiery anger and the medicine man's dire warning doomed any hope she might have of her seeing the passionate Chickasaw chief again. But now her slumber had been abruptly broken by the four intruders, and feelings of fear, confusion, and helplessness all flashed through her mind. Even when they reached the canoes and she recognized Kalopin, she remained terrified—both for herself and for him.

However, Kalopin's soothing words and his sincerity soon put Laughing Eyes at ease. And as the days passed on their journey north, the flame that burned bright in Kalopin's heart finally ignited passion in her heart as well. By the time they reached the Chickasaw Bluffs and were drawing close to Reelfoot's village, Laughing Eyes had consented to be his bride.

On the day of their marriage, the people of Reelfoot gathered atop an ancient mound in the heart of the village to celebrate the marriage of their chief to the Choctaw princess. Kalopin was dressed in his finest clothes and his face was daubed with white paint—a symbol of the joy in his heart. Laughing Eyes wore the finest white buckskin dress, adorned with bright beadwork. Bride and groom both were festooned with eagle feathers.

The tom-toms drummed a heart-beat rhythm as the Reelfoot women danced around the couple, chanting a bridal song and stamping their feet in cadence with the drums. And as their feet struck the ground, it shook, and the dancers shook their rattle-gourds in answer.

Even as the medicine man bedecked in a wolf's-head said words of benediction over the couple, the shaking of the ground seemed to grow in intensity with the dancing. The low rumbling of the drumming also seemed as if it were waxing louder and louder by the second as the ceremony progressed.

Then, as Kalopin and Laughing Eyes said the words that would bind them as one, the shaking of the earthen mound became noticeably stronger. It suddenly dawned on the villagers that the low rumbling was not coming from the drums but from within the belly of the earth itself.

In an instant, joy and celebration were replaced by bewilderment and fear. Terror ensued, as Reelfoot's hide-covered lodges and hewn log cabins began to sway and shake, and then tumble to the ground.

The Great Spirit had been as good as his word, and no sooner had Kalopin made Laughing Eyes his bride than the shaman's prophecy was fulfilled.

The Great Spirit stamped his foot, and Reelfoot's town and the surrounding land slowly began to sink—as if from the downward pressure of a giant invisible foot. Those who tried to run for their lives did not get far, for the shaking of the sinking earth made them reel from side to side and then fall, just as the whole village of Reelfoot was doing.

Then the Great Spirit summoned Mishasi-pokni Huch-cha and told the river to flow backward and flood the land of Reelfoot. And so the waters of the great river gathered up into a huge wave that overspilled its broad banks and roared over the quaking land. It is said by those few who survived that the last they saw of their doomed leader, Kalopin, he was still standing beside his bride upon the mound where they had wed. He made no attempt to escape his fate; he and his Choctaw princess stood gazing intently into each other's eyes, holding each other tightly.

The cries and shouting of the villagers were soon drowned out by the roaring sound of the waters of the great river. Then all was silent.

The Chickasaw have a saying, *Neetak intahah*, which means "the days allowed him were finished." And so it was with Kalopin and his people. They vanished as if they had never existed, and all that was left was a lake, a legend, and a haunting legacy.

A curse lay heavy on the land of Reelfoot after the great earthquake of 1811, and though fish and foul and all manner of wildlife were abundant, Indian hunting parties shunned the place. So, when a few years later the Long Knives came with their chain and pole and "land-stealer" (surveyor's compass), the Chickasaw did not resist the white men's pressure to sell off the land.

While today some may question the story of Kalopin and Laughing Eyes, there is no denying that many Native Americans died in the quakes of 1811-1812. That so many died such violent and premature deaths is itself sufficient cause for the spirits of the dead to continue abiding there.

Ironically, what to the Indians had become a cursed land seemed a sportsman's paradise to the whites. But if Reelfoot Lake's natural abundance has been a boon to generations of hunters and fishermen, reminders of the great tragedy that occurred there still haunt lake and land.

When all is still, and a mist hangs heavy about the lake, fishermen swear they can hear the faint sound of tom-toms beating out a heart-beat rhythm. Sometimes the drums are accompanied by the faint but audible sounds of chanting. Both sounds emanate eerily from beneath the still waters.

At other times, duck hunters waiting patiently behind blinds on shore have seen an Indian canoe gliding silently across the surface of the lake. The canoe bears an Indian brave and his Indian maiden, all decked out in bright beads and feathers.

There are also those who even aver that the sun glinting on the surface of Reelfoot Lake is but a reflection of Laughing Eyes' brightly colored bead necklace.

Then too, there is the curious fact that a band of eagles appears over the lake each year on the anniversary of the great quake, stays several months until the time of the year that the last tremors shook the region, and then disappears as mysteriously as it arrived. It may be just a coincidence—but it also may well be that the Great Spirit's enchantment of Kalopin's band of befeathered braves continues to this very day.

In the hustle and busy of the city, it is easy enough to scoff at the tale of a man who defied heaven and earth for love—just as it is easy to doubt other uncanny encounters that have occurred in the wilderness. But around a lonely campfire by the lake on a chill autumn night, such stories become harder to dismiss.

So, should you go to Reelfoot Lake on a frosty December morn, in the blue-gray twilight before dawn, as an eagle soars overhead, just try telling yourself that the strange sounds coming from the lake are not the mournful chanting of the restless dead.

Reelfoot Lake is a popular destination for tourists, nature lovers, hunters, and fishermen. In addition to the many private resorts in the area, there is also a state park, which includes a museum featuring the history and lore of the region. For information, contact:

REELFOOT LAKE STATE PARK
Route 1, Box 2345
Tipton, TN 38079-9799
(731) 253-7756 • Museum: (731) 253-9653

28

Clara and Lizzie:
A Memphis Mystery

F AR AND AWAY THE GREATEST mystery Memphis has ever seen—one which still enthralls and baffles residents to this day—was the chance encounter in 1871 between two girls at the Brinkley Female College. The meeting might not have aroused such keen interest had not one of the girls been dead at the time.

Brinkley Female College stood, in all its antebellum glory, near the corner of Georgia Avenue and DeSoto Street in Memphis—at what today is 683 South Fifth Street downtown. In those days, the school building—a white-washed frame house that somehow seemed larger than its two stories would allow—stood in a grove of shady trees, its classical lines graced by ornate fluted Ionic columns soaring the full height of the structure. Inside, fourteen-foot ceilings and finely crafted woodwork created a feeling of awe and grandeur.

Dr. J. D. Meredith was president of the institution, which was highly regarded among Memphis's social elite.

Among the school's fifty-odd students was a thirteen-year-old named Clara Robertson, whose father was a respected attorney in town. The Robertsons lived at 261 DeSoto, just a few blocks from the school—within easy walking distance for young Clara.

By all accounts Miss Clara was big for her age, but she had lustrous blue eyes and thick blonde hair that hung loosely over her shoulders. Her face was expressive, reflecting a high degree of intelligence. She was considered very advanced for her age.

One afternoon late in February 1871 Miss Clara was upstairs at the college, practicing études on the piano. The notes echoed off the high ceiling and walls, hanging in mid-air before gradually fading away as new chords replaced them in the ether.

It was a gray, somber winter's day, and Clara was all alone in the music room, intent on her practice, when the room suddenly became totally still, much like the feeling one gets just before a storm. Clara sensed somehow that there was another presence in the room, although she could see nothing untoward.

Turning about, she beheld a young girl standing there in a pink dress. The girl looked to be about eight years old, but she was quite obviously not one of the students.

Focusing more closely on the girl, Clara perceived her sunken, lusterless eyes, her emaciated figure, and pale skin that was almost transparent—like parchment. The girl's pink dress, once pretty, was now dingy, tattered, faded, and covered with a greenish, slimy mold. A sad expression was apparent on her face. As she concentrated on the figure before her, Clara discovered she was standing face to face with a ghost.

The grim visage filled Clara with terror as the realization sank in, the fear redoubling as the apparition started to move toward her. Clara fled the music room in panic.

Running into an adjacent room, Clara collided with the bed of a schoolmate, who was lying there sick with a fever. Clara leaped into the bed next to the girl, hoping the apparition in the next room would disappear.

The phantom in pink followed her, however, its emaciated arms outstretched. The phantom slowly and noiselessly advanced to where Clara lay cowering. The phantom placed a bony finger on the pillow next to Clara and seemed to be trying to say something.

Scared out of her wits and too terrified to scream, Clara tried to motion the apparition away. Finally the girl in pink disappeared through a side door, exiting as noiselessly as she came.

With the apparition gone, Miss Clara ran downstairs to tell some-one—anyone—about what had happened.

Some of the girls believed Clara's tale, others doubted it, and still others ridiculed her story outright, which brought Clara to tears. The teachers did not believe her either, nor did her parents, who scolded her for making up such foolishness. When she expressed her fears about returning to school the next day, they ordered her to go back.

Reluctantly, Clara obeyed her parents' command and returned to Brinkley College the next morning. Nothing out of the ordinary hap-pened that Wednesday at school, and Miss Clara began to calm down after her traumatic experience of the previous day. In fact, she was ready to chalk up the incident as simply a malicious prank played on her by another student.

On Thursday Clara went back to the music room to practice her piano lessons, taking two of her female friends with her. Clara's nerves were still on edge as she began to play her études.

Just then, Clara was startled by an odd noise, which her friends thought sounded as though someone had dashed water onto the floor. They all turned in the direction of the strange sound when they saw it—the emaciated phantom all dressed in pink and covered with mildew and mold that reeked of the dampness of the grave. The three schoolgirls scrambled for the door and fled the room in terror.

With witnesses to corroborate Clara's story, her classmates no longer scoffed at her tale of seeing a ghost, but the adults still would not take her seriously.

The following Tuesday, a week after the first encounter, the phantom in pink materialized in the upstairs room again. Miss Clara fled the room again, running downstairs where, trembling like a leaf, she told one of her teachers, Miss Jackie Boone, the phantom had returned.

Thinking to put an end to this foolishness once and for all, Miss Boone insisted that Clara return with her to the music room at once.

Climbing the steep staircase to the music room, Miss Clara opened the door slowly and the two peered inside. Clara could still see the bony apparition in the pink dress, but Miss Boone did not. However, the instructor did see something—a vague shadow hovering in the middle of the room near the piano. Another of Clara's classmates, who had followed them up the stairs, also looked into the room and she, too, saw the phantom in pink, just as Clara did.

Urged on by her teacher, Clara approached the specter and asked why she had come to the room and what it was that she wanted. The girl in pink pointed her bony finger in a southerly direction and told Clara that under a stump, some fifty yards away from the house, were hidden some things of value.

"I want you to take them and use them to your advantage," the apparition told her.

Miss Boone could hear a rumbling noise in reply to Clara's query but could make no sense of the sound. The other schoolgirl, however, was able to hear the ghost reply almost as clearly as Clara did.

Once the girl in pink had spoken to Clara, the phantom vanished.

This latest encounter had the whole school in an uproar, and it was at this point that the Reverend Doctor Meredith intervened. Although he accepted the trio's sincerity, the schoolmaster was skeptical of the whole affair. He was convinced that the two girls and the teacher were all victims of some elaborate hoax or practical joke. Dr. Meredith told Clara to go into the yard while he questioned the other witnesses separately.

Clara walked quietly around the school grounds, sharpening a pencil as she went. When she was about fifty yards from the house, the specter materialized once again, this time no more than six feet away from her.

Clara tried to scream, but the ghost spoke to her in a mild, soothing tone of voice:

"Don't be alarmed, Clara," she said, "My name is Lizzie. I will not harm you."

Still filled with fear, Clara stood motionless as Lizzie told her again of the buried treasure. The specter explained that all of her kin were dead and no one else was left to claim it—Lizzie had been the last of her family to die.

Even before this latest encounter, word had gone out through Clara's classmates to their families and friends of her weird encounters with a ghost at school. As the haunting continued and became even more bizarre, rumors spread beyond the college community to the city at large.

It was not long before the newspapers got wind of the strange happenings at Brinkley Female College, and their pages soon were filled with the latest twists and turns of the uncanny incidents.

The years after the Civil War had been traumatic for the city of Memphis. It had survived Union occupation intact, but newly freed slaves had swarmed into the city after the conflict ended—more than the city's resources could handle. Law and order had almost broken down, with roving gangs of white hoodlums—called "mackerels"—assaulting merchants at will. Added to this were sporadic outbreaks of cholera and yellow fever. All these disasters and plagues had set the residents' nerves on edge, and folks in Memphis were only too willing to seek answers to their woes on the spiritual plane.

News of the ghostly visitation at Brinkley College pushed nervous Memphians over the edge; the whole city was agog with a mixture of excitement, wonder, and fear. Children cried if left alone; women left their lamps lit at night to chase away the dark, and consumed heftier doses of their favorite patent medicines. Even the bravest men gave dim doorways and dark alleys a wide berth at night. Not to be out-done, the city's bartenders concocted something called a "ghost cock-tail," on the theory that the best way to ward against wayward spirits was to fortify oneself with other spirits—of the liquid kind!

By now Clara's father was convinced of the reality of his daughter's spectral encounters. In an effort to solve the mystery, he called in a noted psychic—Mrs. Nourse—from St. Louis to help solve the mystery.

Mrs. Nourse was versed in the latest techniques of Professor Mesmer, and putting Clara into a deep trance, she handed her a pen and paper, hoping to elicit answers from the spirit through "automatic writing."

Glassy-eyed, Clara took the pen in her fingers, and it began to move—seemingly without any conscious action on her part. At first, the characters she wrote were "strange, indistinct, and unreadable." Bit by bit, however, her scribbling began to become legible.

Those present at the séance asked questions of Clara while she was in the trance state, and Clara, still apparently unconscious, answered in writing.

During the séance the ghost was quizzed about the buried treasure. As before, Lizzie replied that it was buried under a stump in the garden, but this time she added that the cache was sealed in a large glass jar.

The ghost writer also elaborated on her identity. She said she had been called Lizzie Davidson when she lived on earth. This piece of information proved significant.

Upon investigation, it was discovered that a Colonel Davidson had been the original owner of the building that now housed the Brinkley Female College. His daughter Lizzie had indeed died there in 1861, at the age of eight.

As news of the ghost's identity became public knowledge, citizens came forward who recalled details relating to young Lizzie's burial. It was an almost inviolate custom in those days that little girls be buried in white—symbolic of innocence and purity. Instead, her father had had her buried in her favorite dress—a pink party dress.

With his daughter's testimony now corroborated by others, Mr. Robertson resolved to carry out the specter's request. He hoped that by doing so he would be able to solve the mystery haunting his family and lay Lizzie's restless shade to rest.

That Sunday night, beneath the light of a cold and ghostly moon, J. R. Robertson and some Negro laborers began to dig in search of Lizzie Davidson's buried glass jar. Working through the night, the excavators' only reward was old bits of brick and masonry. It seemed to some that they had been duped by the specter.

Early the next morning Miss Clara was playing in her backyard of her DeSoto Street home, when Lizzie suddenly appeared. By now Clara was no longer afraid of the apparition and stood there and listened as the ghost spoke to her.

Lizzie scolded her mortal friend, telling Clara that her father's workmen would never find the treasure on their own—Clara must seek it herself. Clara ran inside and told her family of Lizzie's latest visit. Then, with a neighbor, she hurried over to the school, where the laborers were just about ready to give up their search.

Acting as if she were possessed, Miss Clara got down on her knees and began clearing away the dirt, digging in the exact spot where Lizzie instructed her to dig. With all the excitement and exertion, Clara fainted, but her father took up the pick and shovel himself and soon broke through a brick structure, revealing a glass jar. Lizzie had told true after all.

It was a large jar—the five-gallon kind used by apothecaries—and showed every sign of having been underground for a long time. It was encrusted with rust, mold, and dirt. Through the dirty and dingy glass sides one could make out several bags and packages, along with what appeared to be a yellow envelope.

Supposedly, a disembodied voice had warned the searchers not to open the jar for sixty days, so Mr. Robertson whisked the treasure off to his house for safekeeping.

With the discovery of the mysterious jar, excitement and interest in the city rose to a fever pitch. People were clamoring to be present when the jar was opened, but neither the Robertsons' home nor the college could begin to accommodate them all.

The enterprising attorney announced that the jar would be opened on the stage of the Greenlaw Opera House on Second Street when the sixty days were up. Moreover, an admission fee was to be charged. Half the fee was to go to Clara, as compensation for her ordeal, and the remainder was to be donated to a church or local orphanage.

Throughout the next sixty days, a number of séances were held, during which Lizzie communicated with Clara on a regular basis. Psychics, spiritualists, and assorted fortune tellers flocked to Memphis, and there was an almost infectious fascination with the supernatural in the city. Pink ghosts began to be spotted in outlying towns as well.

At old Cochran Hall on North Main Street in Memphis, in particular, nightly séances were held, all of them well-attended. A flock of "spirit guides" went through the whole repertoire of table tapping, bell ringing, and slate writing.

By now Miss Clara had become accustomed to the ghostly visage of Lizzie. They had even become good friends, after a fashion. Mainly communing with Lizzie by means of séances now, Clara would get up on stage, accompanied by professional spiritualists. Then, pencil in hand, Clara would go into a trance and, glassy-eyed, would write the latest message from Lizzie.

As the end of the sixty-day waiting period neared, everyone in the city grew anxious to learn the contents of the jar. But just a few days before the opening, a most unusual event took place.

Mr. Robertson was entertaining some friends in the parlor of his DeSoto Street home when he heard a strange noise coming from the backyard. Getting up to investigate, he excused himself, assuring his friends he would only be a moment.

The minutes dragged by but Mr. Robertson did not return. At last Joe, Robertson's black house servant, ran in, shouting that Mr. Robertson was dead.

Robertson's friends, accompanied by Joe, ran into the backyard, where they found the attorney lying in a pool of blood, near a small stable. They carried his limp body back into the house.

Perceiving that there was still life left in him, his friends sent for a nearby physician, Dr. H. J. Shaw, and then summoned the police.

Fortunately, Dr. Shaw was able to revive the attorney, who then related what had befallen him.

Robertson said he had gone out back to investigate the noise. As he stepped into the privy, he noticed some men nearby in the dark. The villains rushed up and seized the lawyer by the throat, shoved a pistol in his face, and threatened to kill him if he did not reveal the where-abouts of the glass jar.

Fearing for his life, Robertson revealed the mystery jar's location— it was tied to a rope in the privy hole. Once the thieves took what they had come for, they proceeded to choke the attorney. Robertson's pleas for his life were cut short by a heavy blow to the head.

The mysterious jar had vanished, and with it the solution to the mystery that had beset the Robertson family. What did the jar contain? Who were the men behind its theft? Was the ghostly visitation real, or was the whole affair simply a hoax? These and other questions were on everyone's mind that spring of 1871.

One positive result of the haunting incident was that Clara Robert-son ultimately became quite a medium in her own right. Although Lizzie never materialized again, Clara was able to go into trances at will and ostensibly communicate with her. Following the assault on her father, Miss Clara—now Miss Clairvoyance—was able to clearly distinguish the faces of her father's four assailants and was even able to put a name to one of them. The police, however, either were unable to use the information or were unwilling to take it seriously.

During another séance, Lizzie supposedly revealed the contents of the stolen jar—two thousand dollars in gold, gold jewelry, a diamond necklace, and certain important papers. The papers, she said, included deeds which she claimed would prove the rightful ownership of cer-tain valuable property belonging to Lizzie's kith and kin.

The whole incident had been a wonderment, that is certain. But there was a vocal segment of the city's inhabitants who were less than impressed—in fact, were highly skeptical of the whole affair. They felt it was either an outright hoax or the ravings of a mentally ill girl. Some accused Clara of hiding the jar under her hoop skirt, then dropping the vessel into the hole dug by her father's laborers. Others, claiming inside knowledge, accused Mrs. Nourse, the "meejium" from St. Louis, of masterminding the whole thing to drum up business for her public séances during the sixty-day waiting period.

Certainly there are some things about Clara's psychic adventures that seem suspect—the theatrical nature of the séances, for example. Also, Clara's description of Lizzie seems closer to a gothic romance novel's notion of what a ghost should be than to any description gleaned from a modern encounter. Then too, the convenient disappearance of the jar just prior to its scheduled opening raised more than a few eyebrows in Memphis and went a long way toward discrediting both Clara and her father.

Granting all these difficulties with Clara's story, there is still much about her uncanny experience that rings true. For one thing, Clara Robertson was not the only person to see the ghost; her teacher and several other students witnessed the apparition as well. None had quite the clarity of vision that Clara had experienced, but they did encounter something supernatural on the second floor of the Brinkley Female College.

As for Clara's father, there is no reason to doubt his basic veracity. He was a successful lawyer, with little to gain from the affair, and there is little doubt that his involvement in his daughter's spectral affairs seriously damaged his reputation and professional standing. To defend his name, Robertson later published affidavits by respected citizens who were eyewitnesses to the unearthing of the jar and testified to its authenticity. Then, too, the nearly fatal assault on the attorney was certainly no hoax either.

Some critics, while not doubting Clara's honesty, ascribed the events to "nervous derangement," which led Clara to experience hallucinations. They cited the fact that some months before, Clara had attended a revival meeting at the Greenlaw, and had been greatly affected by it. But another interpretation is possible.

It may well be that the ecstatic religious state Clara experienced during Dr. Earle's revival meetings at the Greenlaw somehow awakened in Clara dormant powers of a psychic nature. The revival may have made her more receptive to things of the spirit, more sensitive to the supernatural. While her teacher just saw a hazy gray apparition and heard nothing but a low, rumbling sound, Clara, who was perhaps more attuned to psychic vibrations, was able to focus far more clearly on the entity.

For most Memphians, however, the theft of the glass jar marked the end of nearly three months of almost continuous excitement. Things returned to normal—or as close to normal as they can be in a bustling river port.

For a time Dr. Meredith's academy in the old Davidson mansion returned to normal as well. But the Brinkley Female College began a gradual decline—perhaps brought on by the "pink ghost" furor—and eventually closed it doors.

By the beginning of the twentieth century, the once proud mansion had been split up into a number of cold-water flats, for use first as a boarding house for railroad workers and then later as a "Negro tenement." The neighborhood, once suburban and affluent, had become just another run-down inner-city district. In 1972 the graying and decaying Davidson mansion was finally torn down to make way for a business.

The Wurzburg Paper Company built a warehouse and offices on the exact spot where Clara once played and Lizzie haunted. With the razing of the school building, the last vestige of the famed haunting was gone—sort of.

It seems that since construction was completed on the Wurzburg warehouse between Fourth and Fifth Streets in downtown Memphis, several strange incidents have occurred inside the building. Many who have worked there believe the structure is haunted.

In 1985, for example, telephone company workers were inside the building late one night making repairs to the phone system. Unable to locate the main power switch in the dark, one of the workers used his cigarette lighter to see by.

Suddenly, the phone worker heard an odd rustling sound coming from behind him. Turning, he saw papers flying off the shelves. No draft or breeze could be felt, yet stacks of papers acted as if an unseen hand were flinging them about violently.

Cold spots have also been reported in the warehouse, and again there is no evidence that such phenomena were caused by a draft or an open window. Workers claim they have felt a deathly chill come over them, and those who have experienced the sensation say it as unlike any natural cold they have ever encountered.

Warehouse management, of course, denies any supernatural doings and simply attribute the mysterious disturbances to underground creeks that run beneath the building, or passing freight trains. Others, however, remain unconvinced by such rationalizations.

In the annals of parapsychology it is not unusual to read of incidents where a ghost associated with a particular structure or place will also haunt succeeding buildings that occupy the same location.

Could it be that Lizzie—and perhaps Clara—still dwell within the bounds of the old college property? Like the mystery that spawned the legend of the two girls, it all depends on whom you wish to believe. Although the Davidson mansion is long gone, the Memphis mystery it spawned remains.

29

The Oak and the Hackberry

FOR SEASONS UNCOUNTED, THE TWO trees grew side by side. One, a royal oak, was tall, erect and strong. The other, a hackberry, was graceful and lithe, its curving limbs intertwining with the thick limbs of the mighty oak.

The two trees had stood together for as long as anyone could remember in the small community of Athens, Tennessee. The arboreal pair were unusual in several respects. For one thing, these two species of trees were not known to associate with one another in nature, their roots normally being hostile to each other. For another, according to local lore, the trees were haunted—possessed by the spirits of two lovers.

How these haunted trees came to be is an old tale handed down in Athens from the Cherokee Indians. Although accounts differ in their details, there is no reason to doubt the tradition's basic veracity.

Long before the coming of the white man, this region was the domain of the Overhill Cherokee. A proud and warlike race, they feared no one. Yet, for their own benefit, the Overhill Cherokee eventually sought trade and amity with the English, whose colonies still lay east of the mist-shrouded mountains.

So it was that the Overhill towns began to tolerate the presence of a few English traders and packmen, who brought with them iron tools, buckram cloth, and vermilion paint—all greatly desired by inhabitants of the Overhill towns. In return, the traders and packmen came away with fine deer skins and buffalo hides, and such other items as the virgin forest gave its native children.

After a time the English offered to protect the Overhill Cherokee from the "bad white men"—the French—whom the English said meant to do them harm. A fort would be built deep in the Cherokee homeland for their protection—and as a symbol of English power. The site chosen for this fort, Fort Loudoun, would be close to Chota, the "Beloved Town," capitol of the Cherokee nation.

Where before there were but few whites in their midst, now there were many score, as soldiers of the English king marched into Overhill country to begin building their mighty fortress along the banks of the Little Tanasi River.

At first all was well between the Overhills and the English. The king's soldiers, tall, pale and muscular, were well-behaved and treated the natives with respect. In fact, many of the maidens of the tribe soon came to the English camp, ostensibly to sell ripe fruit and fresh vegetables, but in truth they were curious about the newcomers and eager to get a closer look.

The main architect of this alliance between the Overhill tribes and the English was a great leader named Attakullakulla, or "Little Carpenter." Though diminutive in height, he was great in stature, respected by the Indians and whites alike. His piercing glance, it was said, could reach deep inside a man's soul and divine its contents instantly. Little escaped his attention—even if he did not always give any outward sign of noticing.

As a skillful carpenter will dovetail the ends of logs from different trees to make them fit more snugly together when constructing a sturdy cabin, so too did Attakullakulla seek to draw the two races closely together in friendship. So, when many of the maidens looked at the young Englishmen and they looked back, Little Carpenter thought it was a good thing for the friendship he was trying to cultivate between the two peoples.

One of those maidens who looked with affection on a soldier of the king was none other than Attakullakulla's daughter. Her name was

Nocatula Coweenah, which means "Sun Shining on Dew Drops." Fair of face and noble of bearing, she was lithe and graceful as a doe running in the dappled forest. Her long, silky black hair and large chestnut eyes further accented the beauty of her face and form. Many brave warriors throughout the Overhill country sought her hand in marriage.

Colonah, "the Raven," was one of those warriors who tried to win Nocatula for his wife. Although Raven was brave in war and respected around the council fires, his gaze made Nocatula shudder, as if the north wind were blowing through her soul.

Colonah lived in a town near the Hiwassee River, but such was the renown of Attakullakulla's daughter that he was drawn to Chota to seek her hand. When Nocatula Coweena shunned the offer of marriage from this fearsome warrior, the jealous Raven vowed that if he could not have Nocatula as his wife, no other man would either.

The beautiful maiden, however, looked with wide eyes at one of the English soldiers, and when she did, a great hatred arose in Raven's heart for the man—and for all whites. He resolved to have his revenge, even if it should take many, many moons.

As the fort neared completion, other voices arose around the Overhill council fires, questioning the alliance between their nation and the English. In particular, Ostenaco, Attakullakulla's chief rival, spoke in favor of the French.

Were not the French gorgets and silver medallions as bright and shiny as those of the English? Were not their blankets as warm, their vermilion as red? Did not the French Charlesville muskets belch forth fire and smoke like the Brown Bess guns of the English? These and other things Ostenaco and his followers said around the great council fire of Chota, until at last many of the Overhill began to turn a deaf ear to the words of Attakullakulla.

Although amity still reigned between the garrison at Fort Loudoun and their native neighbors, elsewhere relations between the two races became less cordial—and more bloody. To the east lay Fort Prince George, in South Carolina, whose commandant suspected the Cherokee of treating with the French. Fearing their deceit, he exceeded them in treachery. When a party of friendly chiefs from the Lower Towns of the Cherokee came in peace to parley, he seized them as hostages. When the surrounding natives became hostile as a result, the English officer murdered his hostages in cold blood.

The entire Cherokee nation was outraged, the Lower Towns and Overhill alike equally inflamed, and Little Carpenter was driven from the council fire at Chota with threats of death. The English garrison at Fort Loudoun, though innocent of wrongdoing, was closest to the Beloved Town, and the first to feel the Cherokee's wrath.

Soldiers and packmen who strayed outside the fort were slain and scalped. Oconostota, "the Great Warrior," paramount chief of the Cherokee, began a siege of Fort Loudoun in March 1760, for its walls were too thick and too tall to storm. Oconostota forbade anyone of the nation to supply the garrison with food.

But Nocatula and the other Cherokee women at first scoffed at the threats of the Great Warrior and continued to supply the men in the fort with food. Secure behind the walls of their fortress, the king's men of Fort Loudoun had every hope of holding out until a relief column could arrive from over the mountains to rescue them.

But as spring turned into summer, Oconostota tightened the siege. Those Indians sympathetic to the whites were restrained by force from coming close to the fort's walls. As the siege dragged on, stocks of food ran low inside the walls.

By the end of July 1760 all hope of relief had fled from those at Fort Loudoun. Reluctantly, on August 7 Capt. Paul Demere, the British commandant, sent emissaries to Oconostota asking for terms. From the Great Warrior, his lieutenants brought back word that the English should take their men and guns, their banners and drums, and leave the land of the Cherokee. Depart in peace, they were told, but leave the fort, its cannon, equipment, powder, and shot intact.

The English soldiers could keep their muskets and a few rounds each of shot with which to hunt game, and they were free to return over the mountains—but they must never return. Oconostota promised as well to escort the soldiers to guarantee their safety.

So, on August 9, 1760, the Union Jack was hauled down and the garrison formed up and marched out of the fort, the men in the scarlet jackets taking leave of the land of the Cherokee. No sooner were the gates opened than the Indians rushed in to loot the fort—the headmen making sure, however, to secure the stores of gunpowder and shot.

The English marched but ten miles toward home that day before making camp beside the waters of Ball-Play Creek. Oconostota began to accompany the crimson-coated column, but claiming he had forgotten his match coat, he turned back for Chota. Later, Ostenaco visited the camp briefly, but he also disappeared.

Some say the Cherokee warriors were dissatisfied with the small amount of booty they found inside Fort Loudoun. Others claim that Captain Demere, by ordering his men to fill their powder horns, had broken his promise to leave the stores of gunpowder intact. Still others aver that the offense to Cherokee honor by the massacre of their chiefs at Fort Prince George could only be erased with blood. There was one warrior, at least, who had his own personal motives for revenge against the English.

On August 10 the English arose to the sound of the drummer beating reveille. In short order the soldiers were dressed and ready to resume the march.

Suddenly, two shots rang out from the woods, and Captain Demere slumped to the ground, wounded. A war whoop went up, followed by a volley of musket fire and showers of arrows from the forest. Seven hundred warriors, their faces painted red and black, charged out of the surrounding woods before anyone in the column had time to think.

Attakullakulla had known what was about to happen but was powerless to prevent it. Nocatula, unaware of the ambush, was downcast when she learned that the English had been ordered to leave and never return. Her sadness quickly turned to fear, however, when she heard the musket fire in the distance and realized what was happening.

Racing to the scene of battle, she was horrified by what she saw. Bodies and parts of bodies lay strewn about the area, and many of the English had been stripped naked and scalped. Captain Demere, badly wounded and scalped but still alive, had been forced to get up and dance until he bled to death. Others had been taken alive, to be used as slaves or saved for slow torture.

Nocatula looked for her Englishman among the captives, but he was not there. Looking among the fallen, she found him, grievously wounded but still alive. To save him from the scalping knife, Nocatula claimed him as her own lawful prize of war. With her father's help, she carried him safely back to her lodge, where she could tend his wounds.

Although his injuries were serious, the soldier could have had no better physician to nurse him back to health. Like many women of the

Cherokee, Nocatula had learned from her mother about the various healing roots and herbs the forest held, and she used her knowledge to cure her beloved captive.

In the eyes of the Cherokee, the young soldier was Nocatula's slave, a prize of war. As a prisoner of war, it was a soldier's duty to try to escape; yet the Englishman felt no desire to flee from his captivity. As the days passed and his health returned, the devotion between the soldier and Nocatula grew, until, far from seeking his freedom, the man desired to make his bondage permanent.

When spring came again, the two were wed at the Green Corn Festival, and the British soldier was adopted into the tribe. He was given the name Connestoga, which means "Oak," for he was tall and firm of limb like an oak. Although her full name was Nocatula Coweena, Connestoga called her simply "Weena."

For a time the two lovers were as happy as any two people could be. At any given time, they could be seen together in a warm embrace, their limbs intertwined, his tall body towering over her petite frame.

Connestoga was a skilled marksman, and his hunting abilities drew the admiration of the other Cherokee villagers. So, when autumn came once again to the forest, he was invited to participate in the fall hunt. Not wishing to be separated from her beloved, Weena insisted on coming as well.

In search of meat and hides, the hunting party wandered far from their native town. As was the custom, the men split up to increase their chances of finding game.

Intent on stalking a deer, Connestoga did not hear a rustling in the bushes behind him. Suddenly, someone sprang upon him, wielding a knife. It was Raven, with hatred in his heart and murder in his eyes— he had waited a long time to catch Connestoga alone and unprepared. Without a moment's hesitation Raven plunged the knife into Connestoga's back, and the hunter slumped to the ground with a groan.

Not stopping to take his rival's scalp, lest his treachery be discovered, Raven started to flee the scene. Still conscious, Connestoga was able to make out the figure of his assassin leaving the clearing. With his last bit of strength, Connestoga raised his musket and fired. Raven fell to the ground, a bullet through his heart.

The other members of the hunting party found Connestoga, alive but mortally wounded, and sent for Weena, who was still in camp nearby.

No medicine could cure Connestoga this time. Nocatula knelt beside him as he breathed his last, tears streaming down her face and mingling with his blood. Overwhelmed with grief, Weena drew out the fatal dagger from her lover's back and, before anyone could stop her, plunged it deep into her own breast. She fell across her husband's chest in a final embrace.

When Attakullakulla was summoned to the scene of the tragedy, he ordered the two lovers buried where they lay. In the palm of Connestoga's right hand he placed an acorn; in his daughter's he put the seed of the Hackberry tree; and an earthen mound was raised above the two.

When the next spring came, two shoots were seen sprouting from the mound. This was interpreted by Attakullakulla and his people as a sign of divine approval.

The two trees flourished, and as they grew their limbs wound around each another, like two lovers embracing. Even after the land was settled by whites and the forests were cleared, somehow these two trees escaped the woodsman's axe. In time the city of Athens, Tennessee, sprouted there, and a small college grew up around the trees.

The two trees on the campus of Tennessee Wesleyan College whispered and sighed, they say, especially in the spring, at the full of the moon. For generations, the story of the hackberry and the oak was handed down on campus and in town, and the trees' intertwined limbs indeed looked very much like two lovers embracing. Countless students who passed by the pair of trees that stood near Ritter Hall would swear they often heard the sound of two voices talking in tender tones. Even members of the faculty gave credence to the tale, for forestry experts they consulted informed them that hackberry and oak trees do not naturally grow next to each other.

The area beneath the two trees became a favorite trysting place for young couples in love, and while some ascribed this solely to the power of the legend, many who stood beneath the twin boughs claimed that there was an undeniable aura connected to the place, an ambience imbued with the spirit of love.

For nearly two centuries the pair thrived on the campus of Tennessee Wesleyan. In 1945, however, a new campus administration, claiming the hackberry was diseased, had the tree cut down. Strangely, soon after that the oak, which had been strong and healthy, also became sickly and began to wither. By 1950 it, too, was gone.

But if the trees have gone, the spirits of the two lovers may yet reside there. In the years since, students have often reported seeing phantom figures standing near the spot where the trees grew, while others claim to have heard voices still holding quiet conversations in the dark, whispering "I love you" beneath the sighing boughs of the trees that remain.

There will always be those who scoff at such things as mere superstition. But the fact that two inimical breeds of trees could live side by side in peace indicates—at least to some—that, like the Indian maiden and her English lover, even in the darkness of hatred and war the bright flame of love can serve as a beacon, enduring beyond the bounds of death and folly.

TENNESSEE WESLEYAN COLLEGE
204 East College Street • P.O. Box 40
Athens, TN 37371
(423) 745-7504 • (800) 745-7504
www.twc.net

The site of the two lovers' graves on campus is marked. In recent years, the school administration has come to appreciate the legendary lovers' presence a great deal more than before. The fact that so many alumni first fell in love with their future wives at that spot may have had something to do with the change of heart. In any case, some alumni are currently sponsoring the creation of Nocatula Garden, to create a beautiful setting for the lover's final abode. No doubt donations to the project by visitors would not be refused.

If you go ...
More haints and haunts of Dixie to see in Tennessee:

KNOXVILLE
BIJOU THEATER (1817)
803 S. Gay Street
Knoxville, TN 37902
www.knoxbijou.com

Originally a hotel, in 1909 the front part of the building was converted into a theater. The venerable theater remains an entertainment venue to this day, and some loyal patrons refuse to leave—even after death. The ladies room on the second floor is haunted by a mischievous spirit, while ghostly voices have been recorded throughout the theater.

MEMPHIS
GRACELAND MANSION
2491 Winchester Road
Memphis, TN 38116
(901) 332-3322
www.elvis.com/graceland

Former home of The King, the numerous post-mortem sightings of Elvis in and around his mansion lead one to conclude that he has not left the building.

QUETZAL INTERNET CAFÉ
668 Union Avenue
Memphis, TN 38103
(901) 521-8388 • (888) 673-4181
www.coffeeandcocoa.com

The upstairs has been identified as the source of much spectral activity. A local paranormal research group has even put a web cam on the second floor to catch a glimpse of any random phantom.

NASHVILLE
BELMONT MANSION
1900 Belmont Blvd.
Nashville, TN 37212
(615) 469-5459
www.belmontmansion.com

Once the home of fabulously wealthy Adelicia Acklen and later a young ladies' finishing school, the mansion is now part of a modern university campus. Over the years, students have had spectral encounters with what is believed to be the spirit of the willful Adelicia.

RYMAN AUDITORIUM
116 Fifth Avenue North
Nashville, TN 37219
(615) 889-3060
www.ryman.com

Originally a religious revival hall but better known as the home of the Grand Ole Opry for many years, the grand old hall has acquired a number of ghosts in its long history, as has the nearby Tootsie's Orchid Lounge across the back ally from the theater's old stage door.

Tennessee Ghost Tours

APPALACHIA/EAST TENNESSEE
APPALACHIAN GHOST WALKS

*Offers year-round tours of more than
nine cities in East Tennessee*
P.O. Box 153
Unicoi, TN 37692
(423) 743-9255
www.AppalachianGhostWalks.com

CHATTANOOGA GHOST TOURS
(423) 821-7125
www.chattanoogaghosttours.com

GHOSTS AND GHOULS
WALKING TOUR

*Nightly downtown candlelight tours
offered in October*
Blount Mansion
Knoxville, TN

GATLINBURG GHOST AND HAUNT
TOUR

(America by Foot)
www.ghostandhaunt.com

GATLINBURG HAUNTED GHOST TOUR
(888) 651-1107
www.pigeonforgetours.net

FRANKLIN
GHOSTS AND GORE TOUR

(Franklin on Foot)
Saturdays (weather permitting)
(615) 400-3808
www.Franklinonfoot.com

MEMPHIS
HAUNTED MEMPHIS

Walking tour
(800) 979-3370
www.backbeattours.com

MEMPHIS GHOST TOURS

Walking tour
(888) 478-1476
www.memphistours.us

NASHVILLE
NASHVILLE GHOST TOURS

Walking tour
(888) 844-3999
(615) 884-3999
www.nashvilleghosttours.com

NASHVILLE HAUNTED GHOST TOUR

Walking tour
(888) 881-3279
www.nashvillesightseeing.com

30

The Devil's Dominion

It has also been made to doubt by some whether there are any such things as Witches . . . but no . . . Age passes without some apparent demonstration of it.
— Cotton Mather, 1689

COLONIAL MASSACHUSETTS TRADITIONALLY has been accorded the dubious honor of being the most witch-infested region of early America. In truth, however, its sister commonwealth, Virginia, was every bit as beset by practitioners of the dark arts as was Puritan New England.

In 1613, for example, before the Massachusetts Bay Colony even existed, the Old Dominion had already gained a sinister reputation in some quarters. One observer complained that the Virginia plantation had been made to "resolve" the works of the Devil, that in Virginia, "Satan visibly and palpably raignes . . . more than any other known place in the world."

The first recorded case of witchcraft in Virginia was in 1622, when charges were brought in Jamestown against one Goodwife Wright. "Goody" Wright was accused of "spelling" a young couple and their baby. It seems the couple had dismissed Goody as their midwife prior to the birth of their child on the grounds that she was left-handed—a sinister omen in folk belief, to be sure. Soon after the infant was born, the family fell on hard times, and they laid the blame on Goody Wright.

In testimony during her trial, witnesses cited examples where she had accurately foretold the death of several members of the community. That much of the accusation seems to be true. But Goody's uttering of prophetic statements that later came true was not in itself proof that she actually cast malicious spells—it may be that she had psychic abilities. In any case, there is no record of Goodwife Wright's conviction or punishment.

In contrast with the Puritans of New England, the magistrates of colonial Virginia were cavalier, not only in their political orientation but also in their attitude toward witchcraft. In general, the gentry of the Old Dominion didn't seem to have harbored the same sort of fear of Satan that filled the Yankee justices in the Northeast. By and large the Virginia courts more often acted as a restraining influence on popular fears of witchcraft rather than further inflaming public opinion.

Between 1622 and 1702 at least nineteen cases dealing with witchcraft were tried in Virginia. There were no executions; in fact, many of the cases involved the person accused of witchcraft suing his or her accusers for slander.

However, of all Virginia's witches, real or alleged, far and away the most famous case of witchcraft ever in the commonwealth was that of Grace Sherwood.

The daughter of John and Susan White, Grace was born about 1660 in Princess Anne County, along the coast of Virginia near what is today Virginia Beach. Sometime around 1680 she married James Sherwood, at which time her father deeded James fifty acres of land in the township of Pongo as a dowry. To the best of anyone's knowledge, the marriage was a happy one, with Grace bearing three sons by James.

What first set off neighbors' suspicions about Grace is unclear, but it is known that she was unconventional in a number of respects.

Grace Sherwood liked to go about dressed in men's clothing, sporting a pair of breeches, a ruffled linen shirt, and a set of riding boots. Such attire no doubt was more practical for doing farm work than the multiple layers of long petticoats typical of women's clothing of the period. While this would scarcely raise an eyebrow today, it was virtually unheard of for a woman to do so then. The male clothing, although scandalous, would have shown off Grace's figure to greater

The Sherwoods also sued Anthony and Elizabeth Barnes for slander. It seems that Mrs. Barnes had had a nightmare—or rather, she had *become* a nightmare.

Elizabeth claimed that Grace had come into her room and transformed her into a horse, and then had ridden her throughout the night. When Grace had finished, Elizabeth said, the witch changed into a black cat and left through a keyhole in the door.

If Elizabeth Barnes's testimony sounds absurd to modern ears, it should be remembered that it was commonly accepted at the time that witches could transform a sleeping mortal into a horse—literally a *night-mare*—and ride him or her at will through the countryside. The witch would return the victim to the bedroom before dawn and change the person back into human form.

Generally, a person who had been abused in this manner would have no memory of the event per se. The only "evidence" would be that the victim would feel a heaviness in the chest at night and awaken the next morning feeling winded and more tired than when he went to sleep. What is different about Elizabeth Barnes's case is that she had full memory of the bewitchment.

By this time suspicions about Grace in the little town of Pongo seemed to have hardened into a certainty, for in both of the cases filed by the Sherwoods, the court found for the defense. Apparently even the magistrates in Princess Anne County had come to believe that Grace was a practicing witch—and if that were true, then no slander or defamation could be proved against those who called her one.

Still, no actual indictment for witchcraft had yet been handed down. In Virginia at that time, malicious witchcraft was a capital offense, following the rule of the Old Testament as stated in Exodus: "Thou shalt not suffer a witch to live." Local laws added that the witch should be executed "without benefit of clergy."

So far, allegations against Grace were mostly washday gossip, and no one was yet willing to file formal charges against her.

In 1701, however, James Sherwood died, leaving Grace a widow with three young sons to raise and a farm to tend all alone. But if she thought her loss would soften the hearts of the women of Pongo, she was mistaken.

Now that Grace had no husband to defend her honor and good

advantage than the voluminous women's dresses, and men ogl
attractive Mrs. Sherwood would have been guaranteed to arou
jealousy of other women in the community.

Local tradition also holds that Grace had a mischievous strea
was fond of hiding things from friends and neighbors as a pra
joke. This easily could have been misinterpreted, and some may
believed that she had bewitched the object in question to make it
appear.

In addition, Grace was knowledgeable about herbs and their m
icinal uses. Such knowledge was not uncommon, but as was the c
with women skilled in midwifery, possessing it could open one up
accusations of witchcraft. This was not an unreasonable assumptio
since knowledge of herbs and the making of potions was part and pa
cel of the practice of witchcraft.

There is a local tradition that credits Grace with introducing the
herb rosemary to America. Needing rosemary to sweeten her lard, it is
said, Grace sailed to England and back all in one day—in an eggshell!
Rosemary had never been known to grow in America before the time
of Grace's alleged magical trip, but afterward it grew without any cultivation in many parts of the New World. In any case, the tongues of
Pongo's residents must have been wagging about Grace long before
1697. On March 3 of that year James Sherwood brought suit in county
court against Richard Capps for defaming his wife, Grace.

It seems that Capps had openly accused Grace of casting a spell
that caused his prize bull to shrivel up and die. Several years before,
the Princess Anne County Court had decreed that anyone who slan-
dered a woman by falsely accusing her as a witch would be liable to
pay a stiff fine—one thousand pounds Sterling (payable in tobacco)
and also face the possibility of "further censure." No verdict was ren-
dered, for Richard decided to settle out of court with the Sherwoods,
no doubt worried that the court might rule against him.

James and Grace emerged victorious, but settling the lawsuit was
not enough to stop the gossip. The next year, the couple filed two separate lawsuits—both on the same day.

On September 10, 1698, James and Grace Sherwood sued John and
Jane Gisbourne for defamation of character. Apparently the Gisbournes
blamed Grace for bewitching their cotton crop—alleging that she had
somehow nipped all of the cotton buds and so caused a bad crop.

name, the women of Pongo started acting more boldly toward, almost like a pack of ravening hounds chasing a fox.

In December 1705 Grace was back in court, this time suing "Luke Hill and Uxor" for "trespass of assault and battery." The *uxor* (a Latin legal term for wife) in question was Elizabeth Hill.

Mrs. Hill had come to believe that Grace had "spelt" her. She evidently was so convinced of this that she took matters into her own hands. Not willing to stand by passively while the witch down the road hexed her, Elizabeth stormed over to Grace's farm, barged into her home, and "assaulted, bruised, maimed, and barbarously beat" the Widow Sherwood.

Grace filed suit, asking for fifty pounds Sterling in damages plus court costs. The jury did indeed find for Mrs. Sherwood, and she was awarded court costs. But the amount the court awarded in damages gives an idea where its sympathies lay: Grace received a paltry twenty shillings.

Even though the monetary award was a mere token, Beth Hill was not about to let the Widow Sherwood's court victory go unchallenged. Less than a month later, Mrs. Hill, with her husband in tow, filed formal charges of witchcraft against Grace Sherwood.

A jury was summoned—this time composed of twelve women—to "make due inquiry and inspection" of Grace and determine if there was evidence that she was a witch. The forewoman of the jury was none other than Elizabeth Barnes!

One reason for empanelling an all-woman jury was so that Grace Sherwood's body could be closely searched for signs that she was communing with the Devil. The "witch's teat" was the most commonly accepted sign of complicity with the forces of darkness. This could be almost any piece of flesh that was hard to the touch or had a bluish tinge to it.

Given the fact that Elizabeth Hill had beaten Grace black and blue, it was probably not too difficult for the twelve female jurors to find a blue "mark." The women also found two black spots (moles?) on Grace's "private parts," which they also interpreted as being witch's teats.

At this point, the Princess Anne County court had reached the limit of its authority. It had found evidence that Grace Sherwood was a witch, and it now referred the case to the colony's general court (the governor and his council) as a capital case.

But the colony's attorney general was less than impressed with the evidence against Grace, and he referred the case back to the county court, saying that the charges were "too general" and that no specific crime had been alleged.

The Princess Anne County court again summoned twelve women, but this time the ladies refused to show up—probably fearing that Grace would bewitch them.

It was only by threatening the women with jail for contempt of court that the authorities were able to assemble another jury. The women heard further testimony and found the same "marks" as before.

But the matter continued to drag on for several months. Finally, to resolve the matter, Grace agreed to submit to "trial by ducking." She would be bound, thumbs to toes, and then submerged in water. If she sank, she was innocent, but if the water rejected Grace and she floated, it was sure proof she was a witch.

July 10, 1706, was the day set for the trial by water. Some of the older women of the village first searched Grace's person for any herbs, amulets, or other magical devices that might skew the results of the test.

Then, around 10 A.M., Grace was loaded onto a wagon and taken down the dirt track to the Lynn Haven River. Ever since then, the road has been known in Virginia Beach as Witch Duck Road.

It was a sunny summer day, and given the notoriety surrounding the trial, a large crowd gathered at a point on Harper's Plantation where the river flowed to watch Grace's test.

"You hypocrites!" she is reported to have told the gathering. "You have come hither to see me ducked, but before you reach your home tonight, it is you who will get the ducking of your lives!"

The authorities then bound the Widow Sherwood, rowed out to a deep part of the channel, tied a rope around her to prevent her from drowning, and then threw Grace into the river.

To the surprise of some—but to the confirmation of the majority—Grace did not sink. Rather, she bobbed to the surface, even though she was still awkwardly bound hand and foot.

After the dunking, the sapphire-blue sky began to cloud over, turning first gray and then black. Then low, rumbling thunder began rolling rapidly toward the assembled multitude.

As they carted Grace back to jail, the heavens unleashed a down-pour the likes of which folks in Pongo had never seen. Torrents of rain pummeled the townfolk as they walked along the road, and they began slipping and tripping in the mud. The wind, howling like an angry demon, toppled many people and blew them into ditches. Some among them even fancied that they could hear in the angry wind howling shrieks of laughter—the mocking laughter of Grace Sherwood.

Having been proved a witch—at least to the satisfaction of the good people of Pongo—Grace's case was again remanded to the general court in Williamsburg. Much of what transpired there is lost to history, for most of the general court's records from the period were burned by Union troops when they captured Richmond in 1865 during the Civil War.

But based on what is known, one may surmise that the gentry at the provincial capital were still not impressed with the evidence against her. Grace faced an all-male tribunal in Williamsburg—and as any trial lawyer will attest, it is extremely difficult to gain a conviction against a woman on a capital charge when the woman is beautiful and the jury is male.

Such appears to have been the case here, for had the general court found Grace guilty, it would have been obliged to execute her. Yet Grace Sherwood is mentioned in local court records in a case involving tobacco in 1708, and she is reported to have lived to a ripe old age, dying in 1740.

It is related that when Grace was buried, it rained for seven days and seven nights. On the eighth day, her coffin floated out of the grave. Her three sons drained the grave and re-interred their mother, but again it rained and again her casket floated out of the grave. It was said by many in Pongo that the water rejected her because she was a witch—just as it had during her trial by water.

The next day, a passer-by spotted a black cat sitting atop her coffin. The traveler spread the word that Grace had come back as a cat, setting off a near panic—some residents abandoned their home and moved away; others went out and shot every cat they could find.

To this day, it is said that when the moon is full, all the cats in the community come out and sit next to Grace Sherwood's grave and howl. In response, her spirit rises and takes the form of a black cat and joins in with the chorus of felines.

Anecdotes and traditions aside, the question remains: was Grace Sherwood a practicing witch, or was she the innocent victim of persecution?

Certainly, many in the community of Pongo were sure of her guilt. Elizabeth Hill was so convinced that Grace had put a spell on her that she physically assaulted the woman in her own home. That goes beyond mere jealousy and gossip.

That there were those during the colonial era who practiced the black arts is not to be doubted. Practitioners continued to conduct their rites in secret throughout the nineteenth century, and if the informants who talked to the WPA researchers in the 1930s spoke truly, some were still actively practicing the craft in Virginia in the early part of the twentieth century.

The trial of Grace Sherwood was by far the most famous case in colonial Virginia—perhaps in all of Dixie. Many, many tales were told of her occult powers, and while some sound fanciful, they can't all have been spun out of thin air.

Yet Grace Sherwood remains an attractive and sympathetic personality, even at three centuries' distance. Much mystery surrounds her life and times. Bewitching beauty and a wicked sense of humor were a dangerous combination, and given all of the accusations of occult powers that flew about her, one can't help feeling that with all that smoke, there must be some fire—hellfire.

31

The Haunted Homes of Robert E. Lee

O F ALL THE FIRST FAMILIES of antebellum Virginia, surely none was more distinguished and honored than the Lees of Virginia. Related by marriage to George Washington, and including in their ranks the famed Revolutionary War hero "Light Horse Harry" Lee, the Lees of Virginia were blessed with great wealth as well as fame. Their most illustrious scion, Robert E. Lee, remains one of the most venerated figures in American history.

But behind the honors, the glory, and the opulence, the Lees har bored a secret shame that haunted the family and the homes in which they lived.

Arlington is best known today as the site of a National Cemetery, where America's honored dead are laid to rest. Tourists come from all over to pay homage to our nation's heroes, past and present. Originally, however, Arlington Plantation was the family estate of Robert E. Lee.

A tour of the Lee home at Arlington is often something of an afterthought for many of the visitors to cemetery. Nevertheless, a visit to Arlington mansion is well worth the effort, for the experience of wandering its halls extends far beyond viewing the beautiful architecture and priceless antiques. Here one can get a real sense of the life and times of the man who, despite his decision to side with the Confederacy, is still widely regarded as a great American hero.

There is a deep spiritual presence about Arlington and its grounds that many who have visited there can confirm. Some, however, claim that presence may also include the restless spirits of the Lees.

Overlooking the Potomac River, the soaring columns of Arlington mansion rise majestically on a Virginia hillside offering a panoramic view of Washington, D.C. Originally built in 1802 by George Washington's adopted grandson, George Washington Parke Custis, Arlington was intended in part as a memorial to the nation's first president and was built near the site of his birthplace.

Custis's only child, Mary, married young Robert E. Lee, son of Revolutionary War hero "Light Horse Harry Lee," in 1831, and the newlyweds took up residence on the estate. Their domestic tranquility at Arlington, however, was fated to be repeatedly disturbed.

In 1846 Lee was called away to serve in the Mexican War, and in 1852 Robert left to become superintendent of West Point. Lee had been home but a few years when the secession crisis came to a head and he was forced to chose between his allegiance to the Union and his devotion to his native soil.

With Robert away at the war, it was not long before Federal troops moved to occupy the estate and seize the house, which was confiscated in part to punish the Rebel general and his family. Federal authorities started burying Union battle-dead on the estate—temporarily at first, but later the site was designated as a permanent burial ground.

Rumors have circulated for years that the area about the cemetery is haunted. Recently, a driver chauffeuring a Marine chaplain to Arlington for a funeral started visibly shaking, sensing that spirits of the dead were all about him. At first the chaplain laughed at the driver's reaction, but on reflection he had to concede that the cemetery at times gave him goose-bumps as well. From tales of Native Americans swimming the nearby Potomac to reports of Civil War soldiers heard marching down an old military road on the grounds, the cemetery resounds with the aura of ages past.

But it is in Arlington mansion itself where encounters with the spirits of the past have been best documented.

It was a dreary Veterans Day afternoon in 1980 when three sisters paid a visit to Arlington house. Two of the them, Katy and Maryanne, were in town to visit their married older sister, Joan. The three decided to see the sights in town while together. It was chilly and wet by the time they reached Arlington, so they opted to tour the house instead of walking around the cemetery.

Although it was a national holiday, overcast skies and intermittent rain had apparently discouraged many visitors from coming out. The house was open, though no guides were there to greet them at the front door. Nor were there other visitors anywhere in sight.

The women called out into the cavernous hallway to see if it was all right to enter, but no answer came from within. With some hesitation, the three stepped into the dim hall and slowly walked past rooms roped off to prevent entry by visitors. They were still unsure whether the house was open for tours.

The three sisters wandered down the main hall until they came to one room that was cordoned off by a metal gate instead of a rope barrier. In this room, graced with a fireplace and a large portrait of a young lady over its mantel, they found another person at last.

The woman they saw was wearing a period dress and a white bonnet, and was standing with her back to the sisters, lighting candles on the mantle.

The girls called out to her, but the woman seemed oblivious to their presence and continued lighting the tapers. Not getting any response, the three continued down the hall and turned the corner, where they found another door with a metal gate which gave access to the same room. When they peeked back in, however, the woman in the costume had disappeared.

The sisters began to get a very eerie feeling, for the woman had been behind the gates just a moment before, and the two barred doorways were the only ways in or out of the room. The realization began to sink in that what they had seen was not a living being, but rather *something* not of flesh and blood.

Joan turned to her younger sisters and suggested that they cut short their tour and leave. She didn't need to ask twice; and all three dashed for the front door at once.

As they later discovered, their experience at Arlington mansion was not unique. Other visitors have reported similar experiences, and even the National Park Service personnel who work there have had their fair share of spectral encounters.

Staff members have reported candles blown out when no one was about. There is also a cat that inhabits the mansion, a unique feline, since it is said to have the ability to disappear into thin air right before one's eyes.

On occasion a teddy bear, normally displayed on a bed upstairs, will be found the next morning downstairs next to the fireplace—as if some spectral child had forgot to pick up after himself.

On another occasion, late one afternoon at closing time, a Park Service employee heard the sound of children laughing and playing in the Morning Room. He went to clear out these stragglers so he could begin to lock up for the day, but as he approached the room the voices began to trail off—and they stopped completely when he entered.

No one was in the Morning Room, nor was there a sign that anyone had been there recently, but as he turned back toward the exit, the sounds started again. The man went back a second time to check, and again the sounds faded away as he approached. No children were there.

Such goings on at Arlington would be curious enough; however, compounding the mystery is the fact that the two other homes most closely associated with Robert E. Lee and the Lees of Virginia are also haunted.

Stratford Hall, ancestral home of the Lees, was built during the 1730s by the patriarch of the clan, Thomas Lee. Thomas was a wealthy planter, a member of the Virginia governing council, and he even served as acting governor of the colony at one point. Crafted in solid brick two and a half feet thick, Stratford Hall lies in the center of a 1,600-acre estate that was even more opulent (if that was possible) than Arlington.

Stratford Hall would also be home to the famous cavalry leader "Light Horse Harry" Lee—the father of Robert E. Lee. Even though Richard Harry Lee was elected to high political office and was widely respected as a hero of the Revolution, his postwar life was marked by tragedy and tribulation.

When his first wife died in 1790, Harry was devastated, and though he later remarried, his financial affairs soon went from bad to worse, landing him in debtors prison. Later, Lee suffered serious injury in Baltimore while defending a friend from a mob.

That a member of one of the richest families in Virginia was sent to debtors prison would have been humiliating enough, but his older brother, Henry Lee—dubbed "Black Horse Harry"—brought further shame on the family. When "Black Horse" Lee's wife fell ill and lapsed into a coma, he found solace in the arms of her sister. The affair turned to public scandal when the sister-in-law became pregnant with his child.

With a cloud of scandal and tragedy shrouding the lives of many who dwelt at Stratford Hall, it shouldn't be surprising that reports have filtered out of paranormal activities on the venerable plantation.

On one occasion, a maid new to the estate was detailed to clean the library. No sooner had she gone inside the room than she emerged again. When her supervisor asked why she was not busy cleaning the room, the girl replied that she didn't want to disturb the gentleman already in there.

Puzzled by this, the supervisor went back into the room with the maid, only to find the library empty. The maid swore she had seen a man there, busy poring over business papers of some sort. When she realized that the man she'd seen was not a mortal being, she fled the house in terror and never returned.

Another employee, now retired, believes that this particular ghost may be the same one that has been spotted in one of the plantation's outbuildings. A man dressed in a long black coat, with knee-length stockings and a white ruffled shirt, has been seen by other staff members carrying a ledger book in his hands. Could it be "Light Horse" Harry is still concerned over his failing finances?

Either way, the gentleman ghost of Stratford Hall is not alone. A hostess at the estate, giving a guided tour, encountered the hooded figures of a woman and child, attired in eighteenth-century dress, in the upper level of the west wing of the main house. Mistaking the woman for another costumed interpreter, she thought little of it until after the tour.

When the hostess asked another interpreter about the guide and the little girl who had been with her upstairs, the woman gave a puzzled look, for no one else had been in that part of the house at the time. When the hostess described the woman and child, a shock of recognition came over the guide's face, and she told the hostess that she had "finally seen them."

Whom had she seen? The matron explained to her friend that there had been rumors circulating for years that Ann Lee and her daughter Margaret haunted the mansion. Ann, the wife of "Black Horse" Harry, had recovered from her illness and forgiven her husband, but the loss of her young child in an accident had compounded the family's tragedies and was widely regarded as something of a judgment from God.

Visitors and workers have occasionally heard the voice of a woman calling to a child, the sounds of children running, and two persons laughing—sounds, in fact, of a mother and daughter at play. But no one had actually seen the two ghosts until the tour guides encountered them in the west wing.

Other workers at the historic house have had psychic encounters— although generally of a less dramatic nature. At night, for example, strange noises are often heard—noises far different from the usual creaking and settling of an old house.

In the evening, noises akin to the sounds of furniture being moved have been reported, although nothing is ever found disturbed. The distinct sound of footsteps on the second-story floors also has been heard, as has an odd rustling sound—like that of petticoats and dresses rubbing against chairs and tables. Despite diligent searches, no one has ever been found in the mansion after closing time to account for such noises.

The ghostly sounds of a child at play seem to be a phenomenon common to yet another house connected with the Lees. When "Light Horse" Harry fell on hard times and could no longer afford to live in Stratford Hall, his family moved to more modest lodgings in Alexandria.

Commonly called the "Lee Boyhood Home," the Federal-style town house was ample even by modern standards. It was here that Robert E. Lee passed most of his youth, and despite his family's tribulations, these were perhaps the happiest years of his life.

Although the status of the Lee boyhood home as a museum is currently under a cloud, for some thirty years it has been a house museum open to the general public. Described by one historian as the "crown jewel" of historic Alexandria, its halls have not only been graced by the presence of the Lee family but also visits by the likes of George Washington and the Marquis de Lafayette. During the 1930s it was also home to renowned poet and author Archibald MacLeish.

During the 1960s the Lee boyhood home was still in private hands—the home to wealthy financier Henry Koch and his wife. At that time the house resounded to the patter of little feet—but not those of the Kochs.

One day in early June 1962 Mrs. Koch heard the sounds of a child running and of childish laughter emanating from upstairs. She naturally assumed the noise was made by her seven-year-old son, William, but to her surprise Mrs. Koch learned that Will was nowhere near the area from which the sounds came.

During the following weeks, the sounds of laughter and small feet running continued to be heard, but there was no one visible. The presence, whatever it was, was not frightening, and the Kochs came to regard their spectral visitors as "cheery" in nature.

After about six months of almost daily encounters with the phantom children, the sounds gradually faded away.

The Kochs later learned that their experiences were not unique. A local milkman asked Mrs. Koch whether she and her husband had heard "the Little Lees" yet. When she admitted she had heard them, the milkman reassured her that her phantom houseguests were a benign presence, a fact known by nearly all the neighborhood.

As it turned out, the spectral giggling and running sounds were not the only ghostly doings inside the house. Phantom music was often heard wafting down from the upper story at odd hours. Common household objects vanished and reappeared without any apparent cause. Then, too, there was the "black dog"—a phantom hound found wandering the grounds where no mortal dog could have gained entry.

While there is little doubt that all three Lee homes are haunted, what is curious is that the ghost of the clan's most famous scion—Gen. Robert E. Lee—has never been seen in any of them.

Perhaps the general, having fought the good fight and served with honor, went to glory with a clear conscience. In that case, his spirit would have no cause to remain bound to the earthly realm.

However, it may also be that Marse Robert's ghost manifests in a form not readily recognizable to living beings. It is known that Lee always cherished fond memories of his boyhood home in Alexandria. Directly after his surrender at Appomattox in April 1865, General Lee rode his horse Traveler to the home of his youth on Oronoco Street in Alexandria. His first thought was not to visit family or friends but to re-visit the scene of his youth once more—to see "if the snowballs were in bloom," as they had been when he lived there.

Some psychic researchers have theorized that the childish sounds and playful spirits in the "Robert E. Lee Boyhood Home" are actually manifestations of Robert E. Lee himself. His spirit, it is thought, has chosen to hearken back to the innocent and carefree days of his youth rather than dwell on the more painful memories of adulthood.

As is often the case with the paranormal, absolute certainty remains elusive. In any event, what is certain is that the First Family of Virginia—the Lees—can lay claim to being the preeminent family of phantoms in the Old Dominion as well.

Two of the three homes in which Robert E. Lee lived are currently open to the public. For hours and admission policies, contact:

McLEAN
ARLINGTON HOUSE
The Robert E. Lee Memorial
Turkey Run Park
McLean, VA 22101
(703) 235-1530
www.nps.gov.arho

STRATFORD
STRATFORD HALL PLANTATION
c/o The Robert E. Lee Memorial Association
Stratford, VA 22558
(804) 493-8038
www.stratfordhall.org

Also see:
THE ROBERT E. LEE BOYHOOD HOME VIRTUAL MUSEUM
www.leeboyhoodhome.com

32

The Trouble With Martha

HAVE YOU EVER WALKED INTO a room where an old portrait hung and thought that its eyes seemed to follow you wherever you went? Perhaps it was just a trick of the light, or the skill of the artist who painted the portrait. But what if something else were involved? What if the artist did his job too well and captured the very essence, the very soul, of his subject?

The Shirley Plantation is one of the oldest and most venerable estates in the Dominion of Virginia—a state renowned for its grand mansions and historic plantations.

Shirley Mansion was begun in 1723 by Edward Hill III as a wedding present to his daughter, Elizabeth.

The farm itself may have been in operation as early as 1613, and if so it can lay claim to being the oldest existing plantation in Virginia. It was at first called the West and Shirley Hundred, Shirley being the maiden name of Lord Delaware's wife, Elizabeth. She wed John Carter, son of the famed "King" Carter, who possessed vast holdings in the colony. Their marriage united two of the Old Dominion's richest families.

After the young couple moved into their new home, the Queen Anne-style manor house was soon filled with all manner of ornately carved furniture, handsome silver services, and assorted artwork—the latter consisting mostly of family portraits. Somehow in this odd lot of family heirlooms and assorted white elephants was the portrait of "Aunt Pratt."

No one is sure how she gained the nickname of "Aunt Pratt" (perhaps she was known to prattle about things), but her Christian name was Martha Hill. She was the sister of Elizabeth's father, Edward.

Martha had a commanding—some might say domineering presence—and her portrait displays a firm, resolute mouth and deep penetrating eyes. The eyes in particular seem to almost dare one to ignore her.

If local gossip is true, Martha was something of a royal pain. Her brothers, nieces, and nephews may well have heaved a sigh of relief when she went abroad to further her studies, leaving her elegant portrait behind.

While in England, Martha met an Englishman, Hugh Griffith, who became thoroughly smitten with her. In due course she consented to be Hugh's wife, and the two were married. "Aunt Pratt" stayed in England with her husband; thus, Martha never returned to Virginia and died overseas. Only her portrait remained as a reminder to her family.

Although no one realized it at first, Martha possessed a far stronger will than one could have imagined. Successive generations of the family would find out just how willful Aunt Pratt could be.

And those later generations were successful indeed. Elizabeth Hill Carter's daughter, Ann, married Revolutionary War hero "Light Horse Harry" Lee at Shirley Plantation in 1793—their youngest son was Robert E. Lee.

Other branches of the Carter line also excelled in public service, and descendants and relations of the Carters included three signers of the Declaration of Independence, two presidents of the United States, and eight governors of Virginia.

As for Elizabeth and her husband, John, the picture of Aunt Pratt eventually began to get on their nerves almost as much as Martha had in life. They removed the portrait from its prominent place in the sitting room and hung it in an upstairs bedroom.

A short while later one of their many distant relations paid a visit to Shirley Plantation, and John and Elizabeth put her up in the room with Aunt Pratt's portrait. After she spent several nights tossing and turning, the woman complained that Martha's image kept staring at her and it eyes following her around the room.

Finally, the relative, her nerves on edge from the penetrating gaze of Aunt Pratt, turned the portrait to face the wall. No sooner had she done so than she heard a low moan emerge from somewhere in the room and an armchair began to rock.

Apparently Aunt Pratt's antics finally persuaded the woman to cut short her visit. Martha's spectral presence at the time may have been regarded by the Carters as a blessing in disguise.

No doubt Martha continued to make her presence known to other members of the family, but the next recorded antics of Aunt Pratt occurred about 1858. By that time the painting of Aunt Pratt had been moved above the mantel in a third-floor bedroom.

For some unknown reason, the painting started rocking violently on the wall over the mantelpiece—perhaps the old girl was getting bored with her new abode. At any rate, Hill Carter, great-grandson of Elizabeth, was the master of Shirley Plantation at the time and resolved to banish Martha's portrait to the attic—thinking that if she were out of sight, she would also be out of mind. He was wrong.

Aunt Pratt's portrait did not take well to the attic. Knocking was heard all around the house, and soon word spread about the family's boisterous poltergeist.

During the Civil War Shirley Plantation was luckier than most estates. Hill Carter obtained a Federal "safeguard" from General McClellan, and the house and grounds were preserved from harm. In return, Shirley Plantation was turned into a field hospital, and thousands of Union casualties were brought there from battlefields throughout Virginia. Many of those who survived their wounds were transferred to hospital ships; those who died were buried on the plantation grounds.

Although Martha's antics were overshadowed by the tragedy of the Civil War, her spirit did not stay entirely quiet during the "Late Unpleasantness."

At one point during the war Lavinia Deas visited Shirley Plantation and stayed in an upstairs bedroom where the painting of Aunt Pratt had been hung. It was a dark and stormy night, and Martha's portrait began to jiggle about on the wall.

Lavinia, at first attributing the shaking to the storm, ignored it. But soon it became clear that the movement was unrelated to either wind or thunder, and Lavinia took the picture off its hook and set it down facing the wall. When Lavinia later sustained a serious injury, she was convinced that it was somehow related to the ill will of Martha Hill.

After the war, the portrait was again moved, this time to the mansion's main level, where it occupied a prominent place. But even here Aunt Pratt seemed restless, and after an initial quiet period, the painting started rocking again. Once more the portrait was moved upstairs.

After a restless spell on a bedroom wall, Aunt Pratt was again moved to the attic. She remained very cantankerous there, but at least her antics didn't embarrass the family by disturbing visitors on the main floor.

Several decades after the war a Mrs. Branford stayed at Shirley Plantation. Her efforts to go to sleep the first night were severely impaired by loud noises emanating from overhead—in particular the creaking of a rocking chair. The next morning the houseguest complained to her hosts about the racket in the attic.

The Carters explained that what Mrs. Branford had heard was the ghost of Martha Hill, who was still upset at having her portrait placed in storage.

For generations, Hill and Carter children who became fretful over noises in the attic were reassured by their parents that the disturbances were just Aunt Pratt acting up again.

In 1974 the Virginia Division of Tourism approached the owners of Shirley Plantation about borrowing the portrait of Aunt Pratt and displaying it at a tourism convention in New York. The agency's Travel Council had decided that Martha Hill's portrait would be an ideal item to include in its exhibit at Rockefeller Plaza.

But Martha soon was up to her old tricks. The painting began to swing back and forth like a pendulum in its display case, causing quite a sensation even among the most jaded New Yorkers. Aunt Pratt finally garnered national attention when an NBC-TV television crew stopped by and captured the picture's antics on tape.

The painting caused such a ruckus that authorities removed it from the exhibit and returned it to its shipping crate. That evening the night watchmen and others working late at Rockefeller Center reported hearing what sounded like crying sounds and an incessant knocking and banging coming from the storeroom. Some workers feared that someone inadvertently had been locked inside the strong room overnight.

By most accounts, when the room was unlocked the next morning, Aunt Pratt's portrait was found on the floor outside its shipping crate.

Apparently the painting had somehow broken out of a nailed wooden crate and moved close to the door. Could Martha have been trying to escape?

All the commotion in New York had damaged the portrait's antique frame, so when the picture was returned to Virginia, it was sent to the Linden Galleries in Richmond to undergo some needed restoration. While it was in the hands of the conservators, however, workers there reported hearing bells ringing—although there were no bells any-where in the galleries or workshop.

Aunt Pratt at last returned to Shirley Plantation, a place her portrait has called home for nearly three centuries. After much trial and error, it was finally found that the second-floor bedroom seems to suit her best—although she still acts up from time to time.

In the 1980s the latest Carter to occupy Shirley Mansion, C. Hill Carter, gave permission for two psychics to search the house for ghosts. In 1986 Jo O'Shields and Karen Benson visited Shirley Planta-tion with a journalist in tow.

Strangely, although they swept the entire house high and low, the investigators did not make active contact with any apparitions. One of the psychics claimed she felt a woman's presence in the dining room, but she said the contrary spirit didn't wish to communicate and had left. Perhaps Martha did not feel like talking that day.

The Shirley Plantation today is open to the public for guided tours and special events. In operation for some four centuries, it can justly lay claim to being the oldest family-owned business in North America. The Hill-Carter family still resides in their elegant ancestral home—and so, it seems, does Aunt Martha.

For hours and rates, contact:

SHIRLEY PLANTATION
501 Shirley Plantation Road
Charles City, VA 23030-29087
(800) 232-1613 • fax: (804) 829-6322
www.shirleyplantation.com
E-mail: information@shirleyplantation.com

If you go ...
More haints and haunts of Dixie to see in Virginia:

ABINGDON
THE BARTER THEATRE
127 West Main Street
Abingdon, VA 24212
(270) 628-3991
www.bartertheatre.com

At least two ghosts haunt this legendary theater. One is the shade of the founder, Robert Porterfield, reportedly an amiable sort; the other is more cantankerous.

ALEXANDRIA
GADSBY TAVERN MUSEUM
134 N. Royal Street
Alexandria, VA 22314
(703) 838-4242
www.oha.alexandriava.gov/gadsby

While this early American tavern is now a public museum, its old patrons still haunt the colonial era building and the adjacent modern restaurant of the same name.

CHARLOTTESVILLE
MONTICELLO
931 Thomas Jefferson Parkway
Charlottesville, VA 22902
(434) 984-9822
www.monticello.org

During recent renovations, workers had a number of strange encounters inside the mansion. Others have had similar experiences over the years. Whether it's the founding father himself or his servants who haunt the mansion is still uncertain, but someone—or something—haunts the famous home.

FORT MONROE
FORT MONROE
AND CASEMATE MUSEUM
P.O. Box 51341
Fort Monroe, VA 23651-0341
(757) 788-3391
www.monroe.army.mil

The oldest continuously occupied military base in the states, several former occupants of the fort make an appearance here from time to time, including Abraham Lincoln and Jefferson Davis.

WILLIAMSBURG
COLONIAL WILLAMSBURG
P.O. Box 1776
Williamsburg, VA 23187-1776
(757) 229-1002
www.history.org

Once the capital of colonial Virginia, it is still the capital for early American ghosts and haunts. Several locations throughout the village have had sightings at various times, and evening ghost tours are available to help the curious in seek of eek!

Virginia Ghost Tours

ABINGDON
ABINGDON GHOST TOUR
(Appalachian Ghost Walks)
(423) 743-9255
www.appalachianghostwalks.com

ALEXANDRIA
ALEXANDRIA'S ORIGINAL GHOST AND GRAVEYARD TOUR
March–November
(703) 519-1749

FREDERICKSBURG
GHOSTS OF FREDERICKSBURG TOUR
Candlelight tour by costumed guides.
April–November
623 Caroline Street
Fredericksburg, VA 22401
(540) 654-5414
www.ghostsoffredericksburg.com

LEESBURG
LEESBURG GHOST TOUR
(Operated by the Virginia Scientific Research Association—a paranormal investigation group. April-October)
Meets at:
The Georgetown Café
19 South King Street
Leesburg, VA 20178
(703) 901-8333 • (703) 899-4993
www.vsra.net

LEXINGTON
HAUNTING TALES: LEXINGTON'S GHOST TOUR
May–October
Lexington Visitor Center
106 East Washington Street
Lexington, VA 24450
(540) 464-2250

PETERSBURG
PETERSBURG GHOST TOUR
A tour of the city's downtown haunts, coordinated by the Petersburg Department of Tourism; a cemetery tour is also offered.
Halloween season only
(804) 733-2402

RICHMOND
HAUNTS OF RICHMOND
1914 East Main Street
Richmond, VA
(804) 343-3700 • (866) 782-2661

VIRGINIA BEACH
GHOSTS OF VIRGINIA BEACH
(Daily by Histories and Haunts Inc.)
P.O. Box 5372
Virginia Beach, VA 23471
(714) 498-2127
www.historiesandhaunts.com

WILLIAMSBURG
THE ORIGINAL GHOSTS OF WILLIAMSBURG CANDLELIGHT TOUR
(Nightly by Maximum Guided Tours)
5244 Olde Towne Road, Suite C
Williamsburg, VA 23185
(877) 624-4678
www.theghosttour.com

WILLIAMSBURG GHOST–LANTERN TOUR
Private tours; small groups only
(757) 897-9600
www.williamsburgprivatetours.com
/ghost

33

Cornstalk's Curse: The Mothman Enigma

THERE ARE MYSTERIES—AND THEN there are enigmas. Sir Winston Churchill once described the former Soviet Union as an enigma, which he defined as "a riddle wrapped in a mystery." For more than a year during the late 1960s, residents of the small West Virginia community of Point Pleasant were hip-deep in just such a puzzling mystery.

The Mothman enigma still defies rational explanation, and even the most elaborate theories fall short of accounting for all that was seen and experienced by scores of otherwise sober and sane inhabitants of northern West Virginia.

Point Pleasant, West Virginia, is a community with a long—and at times bloody—history. Just prior to the American Revolution, Point Pleasant was the scene of one of the largest battles of the frontier era. An alliance of western Indian tribes, led by the great Shawnee chief Cornstalk, engaged an American army of frontiersmen in a decisive struggle for control of the whole Ohio Valley.

The Indian alliance was defeated, and Cornstalk bowed to the inevitable and made peace with the "Long Knives." But the Shawnee chief and his young son were not allowed to live in harmony—they were ambushed and murdered in cold blood by vengeful white settlers. According to local tradition, with his dying breath Cornstalk laid a curse on the white settlers of the region, vowing that they and their descendants would be visited by death and disaster for two hundred years.

West Virginia saw much violence during the Civil War, not just involving opposing armies but also guerrilla bands that often vented their rage on unarmed civilians. And during the late nineteenth and early twentieth centuries, families in the region often engaged in bitter personal blood feuds as well.

World War II brought modernization—and the West Virginia Ordnance Works. This was a large reservation where all manner of munitions were stockpiled—and very likely where some classified military projects were carried out. After the war the depot was officially decommissioned; but the federal government leased portions of it to a number of chemical firms and bio-chemical companies.

Whether all this military-industrial activity had any direct bearing on the events that transpired there in the 1960s remains one of many disputed points. But the so-called "TNT Area" of the old ordnance works would be a major focus for all the weirdness that followed.

The complex adjoined the 2,500-acre McClintic Wildlife Station, home to all manner of animal life. Having a wilderness preserve in such close proximity to industrial plants manufacturing toxic chemicals is never a good idea—and researchers have suggested that this unfortunate mix may have led to some very strange events.

※ ※ ※

The first inkling that anything unusual was transpiring occurred in 1961. A locally prominent society matron and her father were driving along West Virginia's Route 2, close to the Ohio River, and as they began passing through part of the Chief Cornstalk Hunting Grounds, something suddenly appeared in the road ahead.

It was a tall figure, and as the woman came closer she could see that it was much larger than a normal man. It was big and gray and stood astride the road, blocking her way.

As she approached, the being unfolded a pair of wings from its back which spanned nearly the width of the road. Its wingspan was so wide, the woman later told a researcher, that "it almost looked like a small airplane."

This was odd enough; but then the creature took off—straight up! It ascended more like a rocket than a bird, she said, and was out of sight in less than a minute. The woman and her elderly father were both terrified by what they saw. She gunned the engine and sped out of the area as fast as she could.

The society matron chose not to report the incident at the time. It was so bizarre that she knew no one would believe it, and speaking of it would only make people think her crazy or a liar. It was only later, when others had come forward to tell of similar encounters, that she was willing to discuss the incident openly.

But the occurrence at Cornstalk Hunting Grounds would prove to be but a prelude of things to come. It was not until November 1966 that this strange entity entered the public consciousness.

On November 12 of that year five grave diggers were busy plying their trade at a small cemetery near the town of Clendenin. As they were digging a new grave, something in the nearby trees caught their attention.

What they saw looked like a "brown human being," and the thing fluttered from out of the trees and started buzzing the five men, swooping low over their heads. "It was gliding through the trees, and was in sight for about a minute," one of the men, Kenneth Duncan of Blue Creek, later told reporters. The five were bewildered more than frightened, for the creature seemed to be more man than bird.

The gravediggers discussed the curious encounter with their friends and neighbors. It probably would have gone no further, except for what happened in the following days.

On November 14 Newell Partridge, a building contractor from Salem, West Virginia, was relaxing at home, watching television. Around 10:30 that evening his television started going haywire for no apparent reason.

The screen suddenly went blank, then filled with a herringbone pattern. The set also started making a loud whining sound that rose in pitch, "like a generator winding up."

Just then, Newell's dog, Bandit, sitting out on the end of the porch, began to howl as the sound's frequency rose beyond the range of human hearing. The dog continued barking even after Partridge turned off the TV, so he went outside to investigate.

Partridge found his German shepherd, a trained hunting dog, staring at the hay barn, obviously roused by some foreign presence there. He shined a flashlight in that direction and saw two large red glowing circles. He described them as weird eyes, "like bicycle reflectors."

Newell knew his wildlife—"I certainly know what animal eyes look like," he told investigators—and these were far larger than any animal he knew of. It was over a hundred yards to the hay barn and those two eyes still appeared huge even at that distance.

An eerie feeling crept over Newell Partridge, a feeling the likes of which he'd never had before. He knew something was seriously wrong, but he couldn't quite put his finger on what.

Just then, Bandit bolted off the porch in pursuit of the thing by the barn. Partridge called out to the dog to halt, but the hound ignored him and disappeared in the direction of the barn.

Partridge went back into the house to get his shotgun, but as he reached for it, he broke into a cold sweat. Newell thought better of pursing the creature—whatever it was—in the dark. He slept with the loaded gun next to his bed that night.

The next morning Bandit was nowhere to be found. The only sign of the hound Newell could find were a set of tracks going round and round in a circle. It was almost as if the dog had been chasing his tail—yet Bandit had never been known to behave in that manner. Stranger still, there were no tracks leading away from the circle, not even Bandit's.

The night after Newell's encounter, ninety miles to the southwest, two young couples were driving through the TNT Area of the abandoned ordnance works, near Point Pleasant. It was close to midnight, and the four were looking for some friends who they thought might also be out there. The TNT Area was a favorite rendezvous for young lovers, drag racers, and others who wished to party out of sight of prying eyes.

Roger Scarberry was driving a 1957 Chevy he'd souped up for drag racing on the backroads. Also in the car with Roger and his wife, Linda, were Mr. and Mrs. Steve Mallete. As they passed the North Generator Building, Linda looked out the window and gasped.

The door to the power plant was off its hinges and out in front of it she saw a bizarre being. "It was shaped like a man, but bigger," she told newsmen, "and it had big wings folded against its back."

But what really caught her attention were its eyes. It had two big eyes, "like automobile reflectors," she said. For a moment, the two couples were mesmerized by the creature's stare.

The spell was broken when the creature turned to go back into the generator building. Panicked, the four young people hastened to depart.

Roger Scarberry floored the gas pedal and the Chevy roared toward the exit. As the four sped past a hill they saw the same—or a similar—creature standing there, and watched as it spread its wings and took off straight up into the air.

Roger jerked the steering wheel hard over and skidded onto Route 62, which led into Point Pleasant. By now the Chevy was doing well over 100 miles per hour.

For a moment the four thought they had gotten away safely. But suddenly one of the girls shrieked, "My God, it's following us!"

The thing was keeping pace with the car but was not even flapping its wings. The weird creature pursued the four all the way to the outskirts of Point Pleasant, making a weird squeaking sound, "like a big mouse," according to Mrs. Mallete.

Sheriff's Deputy Millard Halstead was on duty at the county courthouse that night. It had been a quiet evening for the most part (most were in Mason County in those days), when suddenly all hell broke loose.

The two couples came rushing into the sheriff's office, breathless and terrified out of their wits. They told a bizarre tale—of a headless, manlike creature with wings, a hypnotic stare, and incredible abilities.

Halstead had known the four young people since they were in diapers, and he knew their families as well. They had never been in trouble, and their fear was real enough, so the deputy agreed to accompany them to the TNT Area and investigate the strange encounter.

On the way, the Scarberrys noted something odd. On their mad dash into Point Pleasant, the two couples had passed the body of a large German shepherd lying by the roadside. Now, returning just a short while later, the dog was gone. They even stopped to search for it, knowing it should still be there, but to no avail.

They finally caught up with the deputy's car near the spot where they had spotted the winged creature. Halstead didn't see anything out of the ordinary; but when he tried to call in a report on his radio, a loud screeching sound came out of the speakers—a weird sound like a phonograph record being played at ultra-high speed. This weird sound, combined with the two couples' obvious terror, disturbed the deputy.

Other reports of a strange "birdlike" creature started to pour into the sheriff's office. By the next day, Sheriff George Johnson felt compelled to hold a press conference.

The Scarberrys and the Malletes recounted all that had happened the previous night, and the sheriff and Deputy Halstead added their comments as well. The newspapers and broadcast media picked up the story and ran with it.

An enterprising editor, trying to put a catchy spin to the story, tagged the creature with a name that was a parody of the popular *Batman* television series. Thus was born "Mothman." It was not a very accurate description of the strange entity, but the nickname stuck.

The next day, when Newell Partridge read the news reports in the paper, one detail leaped out at him: the description of the dog lying by the roadside sounded exactly like Bandit. His German shepherd had disappeared into thin air after chasing the red-eyed creature near the barn. The folks at Point Pleasant had reported a similar creature. Had Newell's dog had a fatal encounter with Mothman? Partridge was sure he had.

Bandit's disappearance and death was only the first in a series of canine disappearances and animal mutilations in the region. All were attributed to Mothman.

In the days after Sheriff Johnson's press conference, sightings and encounters with the creature multiplied.

On the evening of November 16, for example, Mr. and Mrs. Wamsley were traveling with a friend, Mrs. Bennett, and her baby to visit some mutual acquaintances, the Thomas family. Ralph Thomas and his family lived on the outskirts of the TNT Area, and he was a supervisor for one of the chemical companies that operated a plant at the ordnance depot. The area around the plant was sparsely inhabited, so there was no other home within sight of theirs.

On their way there, the trio spotted a funny-looking red light fluttering over the ordnance works, but they couldn't determine what it was.

Arriving at the Thomas household, the three adults got out of the car, Mrs. Bennett holding her baby in her arms. As they did, something arose slowly from the ground beyond the automobile: a big gray creature, larger than a man, with "terrible glowing eyes."

Marcella Bennett stood frozen by the sight, seemingly mesmerized by its beam-like eyes. Apparently in a trance, she dropped the infant from her arms. Mr. Wamsley, not under the creature's thrall, hustled his wife into the house. Marcella snapped out of her trance long enough to snatch up her baby and make a beeline for the front door of the house.

No sooner had they locked and bolted all the doors and windows than they heard the thing shuffling onto the porch and saw it peer through the front windows with its large, glowing red eyes. Wamsley phoned the police, but by the time they arrived the creature was gone.

There was no question that what the Wamsleys, the Thomases, and Mrs. Bennett experienced was real. Marcella was so traumatized by the event that she required medical attention for months afterward.

※ ※ ※

Predictably, these encounters also caught the attention of national media. Representatives not only from the tabloids but also from the more respected members of the fourth estate poured into Point Pleasant to cover the story. Film crews even camped out near the generator plant in the TNT Area in hopes of catching a prize shot of the beast.

Just as predictably, the professional debunkers and cynics tried to explain away the strange events—sight unseen. The usual suspects were trotted out—barn owls in flight, for example (they have big eyes, too, don't you know). One respected biologist from West Virginia University declared with some authority that what the witnesses had really seen was a sandhill crane.

Native to Canada, the sandhill crane is unknown in the Ohio Valley. Its long neck and long legs give it a height of close to six feet, and sometimes it has dull red patches around its eyes. To some, this seemed like explanation enough.

John Keel, a journalist whose investigation of the Mothman enigma soon approached near obsession, sought to test the "stray bird" hypothesis on the eyewitnesses.

He brought in a pictorial lineup of winged creatures—including not only a picture of a sandhill crane but even one of a pterodactyl.

The majority of witnesses overwhelmingly rejected all of these as possible candidates for the creature they saw.

Those who had actually seen Mothman unanimously agreed that the creature was not a crane; in fact, the long-necked bird looked just the opposite of the entity they saw, which had hardly any neck at all. Of all the interviewees, Keel determined that only three groups of contactees may have actually seen something resembling a bird. These few cases were the only ones where a misidentification may have occurred.

The one hundred other witnesses, however, had no doubt that they had encountered something far beyond the pale of known science. Even when re-interviewed ten years later, the witnesses stuck to their original accounts. Moreover, the testimony was consistent from one person to the other. Jerome Clark, a leading cryptozoologist, observed that "any 'rational' explanation for Mothman must first disregard all the testimony as wildly in error."

Admittedly, Mothman is a creature that challenges our preconceptions of reality. It even seems to defy attempts to pigeonhole it into any of the accepted categories of the paranormal—not that folks haven't tried.

The name Mothman itself is something of a misnomer. As described by eyewitnesses, the creature seems closer to a kind of humanoid bat than some overgrown insect. Standing about seven feet tall, it has a large human-like torso but an unusually small head—so small that it is not even distinguishable in the dark. Its most notable features are its red, glowing, hypnotic eyes.

Witnesses also agree that Mothman's wingspan is at least ten feet wide, and that the entity has little or no hair. Rather, its wings and body seem to be bare gray or brown flesh.

One theory holds that Mothman is a bizarre genetic mutation, brought about by industrial pollution leaking from the chemical plants located on the grounds of the old ordnance works. This real-life "toxic avenger" may have been using the abandoned munitions "igloos" as its roost.

The underground tunnels of the complex would have allowed the creature to move about unseen, and the woods and barns nearby would have provided an ample supply of fresh meat for this fey carnivorous creature.

A variant of this theory holds that, given the nature of the area it inhabited—a federal ordnance depot—it was no accidental mutation but rather a top-secret biological weapon developed during the cold war. Somehow the creature (or creatures) got loose from the labs (set up under the guise of "chemical plants," according to the theory) and that it took nearly a year for authorities to recapture them.

Some details gleaned from eyewitness accounts, however, cast doubt on whether Mothman was a living creature—mutant or otherwise—of any sort. There were oft-repeated reports of it taking off vertically, like a rocket or helicopter, and was capable of speeds in excess of 100 miles per hour, yet it never flapped its wings. Witnesses also reported that a high-pitched mechanical sound accompanied its appearances, which also coincided with electrical interference that garbled radio and television transmissions. All of this points to some sort of mechanical or robotic device—or at the very least a kind of exoskeleton or spacesuit—whose purpose may have been for extra-vehicular exploration of an alien world—planet Earth.

In fact, when John Keel arrived at Point Pleasant in December 1966—at the height of the Mothman flap—he was surprised to discover that neither the police nor the media in the area had received any reports of UFOs, but that thousands of people up and down the Ohio Valley had sighted UFOs throughout the year, although most had been hesitant to report them. Actually, there had been several UFO sightings around Point Pleasant—some in broad daylight.

The UFO sightings reached a peak in the spring of 1967, with strange craft reported almost daily over the TNT Area—the very same area where Mothman was seen lurking about. Sheriff Johnson and his deputies were among witnesses who saw UFOs but refused to go public with their sightings at the time.

As if all this weren't enough, many Mothman witnesses were also subsequently contacted by "Men in Black"—strangers who looked and behaved oddly, and who at times threatened individuals not to talk further about their experiences. Even the reporter for a local paper—Mary Hyre—was visited by these strangers, who seemed less interested in Mothman than in John Keel's investigation of it.

All this would seem to indicate some sort of UFO-related phenomenon—presumably a visitor from outer space. Yet, looking at the known facts from a different perspective, one has to admit that there is ample evidence for a supernatural explanation of Mothman as well.

After sighting Mothman in November 1966, the Scarberrys began to experience poltergeist-like phenomena in their own home. The disturbances became so upsetting that the couple moved into a basement apartment in the home of Linda's mother, Mabel McDaniel. Mabel had also seen the flying creature, on January 11, 1967. It was not long before the McDaniel household also began to experience paranormal activities.

Strange lights started appearing inside the McDaniel home, and the aroma of a burnt cigar was heavy in the air at times—even though no one there smoked. Then, too, household objects began to move of their own accord.

Finally, one morning, Linda Scarberry awoke to see the form of a large man in her bedroom, She screamed and the apparition disappeared. A thorough search of the house revealed no intruder; all the doors and windows were still locked tight, and there were no signs of forced entry.

In New Haven, West Virginia, the Carpenter family was similarly plagued by poltergeists. They also had had some uncanny encounters—with UFOs and Men in Black.

James Lilly and his family resided in Point Pleasant, just south of the ordnance works. During 1967-68 they experienced so much poltergeist activity that ultimately they had to sell their home and move out of the area. In these and other cases, locked doors opened and closed on their own, banging and thumping on walls were heard at night, and in some cases people even heard the ghostly sounds of a baby crying.

There was a local rumor current at the time (but never substantiated) that Mothman was in fact brought into being through black magic. According to this theory, an occult ritual conducted by an unknown—or at least undercover—warlock had summoned this being from the bowels of hell to bedevil the good folk of Point Pleasant. Some cited the creature's uncanny flying abilities, its hypnotic powers, and the increasing incidence of other strange events in the area to support this belief.

John Keel, who has delved into the mysteries of Mothman more than any other mortal, developed a unique theory of his own to try to explain the bewildering array of paranormal phenomena clustered in this region.

Keel believes the appearance of Mothman, UFOs, poltergeists, animal mutilations, Men in Black, and assorted phantoms and phantasms are all interrelated. Keel theorizes that UFOs do not come from outer space at all; rather, they are from a sort of inner space. He believes that "they and their occupants are inter-penetrating into our space-time continuum from some extradimensional universe beyond the range of our human perception."

According to Keel's "Unified Field Theory of the Paranormal," certain regions are particularly vulnerable to penetration from this other reality—what Keel calls a "window" area. Point Pleasant and the nearby areas of the Ohio Valley, he believes, constitute one such window.

Even Keel's explanation, however, does not seem to encompass all the weird happenings that occurred around Point Pleasant at the time. For one thing, even as sightings of Mothman mounted, many witnesses who saw it developed psychic abilities—apparently receiving messages and dreams that foretold the future. Keel estimated that as many as half of the Mothman witnesses had "latent or active psychic abilities." Not all their premonitions came true, but many were close enough to warrant serious examination.

Mary Hyre, who originally broke the story of Mothman to the national press, and also reported an encounter with Men in Black on November 19, 1967, told another reporter of her own strange dream.

In it, she saw large numbers of people drowning in the Ohio River: "Christmas packages were floating everywhere in the water . . . there were so many people." After waking from her dream, Mary remained very uneasy, feeling "like something awful is about to happen."

▨ ▨ ▨

The Silver Bridge spanned the Ohio, linking Point Pleasant, West Virginia, with Gallipolis, Ohio. Built in 1928, it was considered quite an engineering feat at that time, using a unique "eyebar" suspension system.

At 5 P.M. on December 15, 1967, the Silver Bridge was crowded with cars. It was rush hour and the lanes in both directions were jammed with workers hurrying home from their jobs and shoppers returning from a hectic day of Christmas shopping. Few people gave a thought to the bizarre events that had beset the area in the last year.

At 5:04 P.M., at the height of the holiday traffic, the beams of the eyebar bridge began to sway in the chill winter wind. Suddenly, a deep groaning sound was heard—a sound like nothing anyone had ever heard before.

Without warning, the entire span gave way and the roadway tore loose from its moorings, tumbling cars and trucks headlong into the icy river far below.

The bustling holiday scene was suddenly transformed into a vision of agony. The terror of people and steel plunging into the icy river; the silent horror of gaily wrapped presents floating slowly away from cars whose occupants would never see another Christmas; the agony of those onshore who could do nothing but watch the deadly scene unfold—Mary Hyre's dream had become a grim reality.

In the immediate aftermath, no one gave a thought to Mothman. Rescue operations were hastily organized at the disaster site, and a temporary morgue was set up in town for the victims. There were many of them—when the final count was tallied, 46 souls had died that night and many scores more were injured. It was the worst disaster in Point Pleasant's history.

Government investigators determined the reason for the bridge's collapse was the failure of a key support element—the No. 13 eyebar pin—which held together one of the suspension bars that supported the structure. The rest of the links were unable to stand the additional strain, and so the road gave way and the whole bridge with it.

Left unanswered, however, was the question of what exactly caused the No. 13 pin to suddenly fail. In the weeks and months following the disaster, many local folk thought they knew the answer.

For one thing, people living near the TNT Area reported unusually heavy activity there the evening of the bridge's collapse. At least a dozen eerie lights were spotted buzzing about at treetop level that night. After the bridge fell, sightings of Mothman tapered off dramatically—it was almost as if its mission had been accomplished and it had left the area.

John Keel believed that "it is completely erroneous to blame the collapse of the rickety old Silver Bridge on flying saucers or ÔMen in Black'"—or Mothmen. But local gossip had a far different view of the events of December 15 and also provided an explanation that accounted for Mothman and the *real* cause of the bridge collapse.

As one Gallipolis resident explained it to a visiting journalist, "The mothmen . . . got underneath the span of the bridge, right where it connects onto the road, and . . . flapped their wings until they reached the resonant point of the bridge. . . . That's what made the bridge fall . . . that was all part of Chief Cornstalk's Curse."

Long before the advent of Mothman, local misfortunes and fey events had plagued Point Pleasant. Devastating floods, fires, and other calamities had beset the town, and each time the run of bad luck was laid at the doorstep of Chief Cornstalk.

Two hundred years had not dimmed the infamy of the attack on the Indian leader and his son. Many in Point Pleasant felt that the sudden appearance of Mothman in their midst, if it had any relation to the events, was meant as the last, worst phase of the curse.

The fact that many who died in the bridge collapse had also had close encounters with the weird winged creature was cited as additional proof of Mothman's complicity in the catastrophe.

A failure of a lynch-pin may have caused the bridge's collapse, they said, but it was Mothman—and his master, Cornstalk—that caused the lynch-pin to fail. In fact, there existed two other bridges identical in construction to the Silver Bridge, and neither of them ever showed any signs of structural fault or failure. Did Cornstalk unleash his final revenge on the descendants of West Virginia's pioneers, and was Mothman but a creature summoned from the bowels of Hades to carry out this chastisement?

While we should not discount the beliefs of those who witnessed this mystery unfold, in fairness, there is evidence to suggest that Mothman actually may have tried to prevent loss of life that fatal December night.

Earlier on the eve of December 15, a young girl in Point Pleasant was looking out her bedroom window, when she saw a pair of glowing eyes looking back at her. Mothman was hovering outside of her window, studying her with his red hypnotic eyes. The girl's family was about to embark on a journey that evening—a trip whose route would take them over the Silver Bridge.

As their car pulled out of the driveway, the girl's father suddenly developed a splitting headache—a headache so severe that he was unable to drive a foot farther. Going back inside, her dad lay down until the pain eased. When he recovered, he turned on the radio to hear the traffic report. Instead, he heard late-breaking news of the Silver Bridge's collapse. The girl—today a grown woman—has ever since been convinced that her father's short-lived migraine was induced by Mothman, and that the purpose of the creature's visitation was to save her and her family from certain death that night.

In 1976 the UFO Ohio Investigation League went back to Point Pleasant and talked with many of the key eyewitnesses that John Keel had interviewed in the 1960s. All stood by their previous testimony. Some contactees, however, while admitting to being terrified at the time, confessed that, in retrospect, they felt Mothman had meant them no harm. "It just wants to communicate with you," one witness said.

Rather than seeking to harm the residents of Point Pleasant, could it be the Mothman was trying to warn them of impending doom? Far from fulfilling Cornstalk's Curse, was Mothman somehow seeking to avert it?

As with so many other questions surrounding the Mothman enigma, hard and fast solutions—even supernatural ones—are elusive. One thing is certain, though: whatever the truth behind Mothman, this being was quite real. Moreover, it possessed powers we cannot begin to fathom.

From whence Mothman came is a mystery; what its motives were remains a riddle; and where it went when it disappeared continues to be part of the great enigma. However, if Mothman visited us once, he may do so again.

For those who seek answers to the Mothman enigma, there is but one thing to say:

Look to the Skies!

34

Incident at Flatwoods: Close Encounter of the Weird Kind

I T WAS 7 P.M. ON September 12, 1952. Some local boys were playing a round of sandlot football in the Flatwoods school playground just before dark.

As they were tossing the ball around, the boys sighted a bright light in the sky. Soaring overhead, it seemed slow-moving and reddish in color, and to all appearances was spherical in shape. The glowing object seemed to sail about a nearby hill, hover, and then descend out of sight.

Soon, a bright glow arose from the opposite side of the hill—seemingly from the same object that had just passed overhead.

The boys felt excited and curious. Tommy Hyer and Ronnie Shaver, both ten, and fourteen-year-old Neil Mundy decided to investigate the strange glowing light. On the way, they stopped by the May home to tell Kathleen May and her two teenage sons about the sighting. The Mays agreed to help the younger boys look for the object, and on the way, Mrs. May enlisted the assistance of a neighbor, seventeen-year-old Gene Lamon, a member of the National Guard.

With Gene leading the way, flashlight in hand, the small expedition proceeded to the nearby Bailey Fisher property, where a weird glowing light was still visible.

Gene's dog came along as well. Barking in anticipation of a good hunt, the dog ran ahead of the group, disappearing quickly over the hill. In short order the dog came running back, its tail between its legs.

Nearing the crest of the hill separating them from the light, the group encountered an acrid odor in the air, accompanied by a gray mist that crept toward them along the ground like a ghostly snake. The mist—or smoke—was coming from the direction of the light. Mrs. May described the odor as a "metallic smell" that irritated eyes and nostrils.

Topping the hill, they saw what appeared to be an object of some sort. It was about "the length of a football field" from them at that point and glowing brightly. The object—whatever it was—was large and made a hissing sound, and as they drew nearer, they observed that it was at least ten feet in diameter and definitely spherical in shape.

Lamon and Nunley were leading the way, and everyone's attention was focused on the large glowing thing, when Gene's dog began to bristle and growl at something in the bushes off to their right. Responding to his dog's alert, Lamon shined the light in that direction.

A pair of small blue lights, side by side, glowed through the undergrowth from that direction. When Lamon's light hit the spot, it illumined something incredible: a creature staring back at the group from the dark.

The creature was large, standing over six feet tall, with a head (or headpiece) shaped like an "Ace of Spades." Inside this form was a sort of circular "window" from which the two lights shone. Illuminated by the flashlight, the creature had a reddish face and wore dark clothing—either blue-green or gray-green. The lower half of its body seemed to have clothing that hung in folds from the waist downward like a skirt. If it had arms at all, they were short and spindly and not easily seen.

Then, after what seemed an eternity but was only a few seconds, the creature started coming towards the onlookers. It did not so much walk as glide—as if it were hovering above the ground. A few seconds later, the creature changed direction and, oblivious to the watchers, headed toward the glowing orb at the bottom of the hill.

Needless to say, the boys and Mrs. May were absolutely terrified. Gene Lamon fainted, dropping his flashlight and plunging the scene into darkness and confusion. The others quickly grabbed hold of Gene and dragged him away. When he revived, the whole party beat a hasty retreat back over the hill and away from both the creature and the glowing orb.

The whole incident had lasted but a few minutes at most, the run-in with the creature even less time. But as anyone who has been in combat or a similar life-threatening situation can testify, during such peak experiences time seems to pass very slowly, and one's perceptions are significantly sharpened.

Although the encounter at Flatwoods was brief, the debate over what occurred has lasted nearly half a century.

As soon as Kathleen May returned to her home, she telephoned the county sheriff, Robert Carr. Judging from the number of people who then descended on the site, Kathleen and the boys must have gotten on the line with quite a number of other folk as well.

A. Lee Stewart, Jr., editor of the *Braxton Democrat*, arrived on the scene within half an hour and interviewed Mrs. May and the boys. Kathleen, understandably, was extremely upset, and most of the younger boys were so terrified they were unable to speak. Neil Nunley, however, was calm enough to give the journalist a coherent account of the encounter, while Gene Lamon recovered sufficiently to say he was willing to lead the newspaperman back to the site.

When Lamon and Stewart returned to the place they had encountered the "monster"—backed up, apparently, by an ad hoc posse of good ol' boys armed to the teeth—the creature and the large glowing orb were both gone. Stewart, however, also noticed a foul odor in the area—one that irritated his nose and throat.

Sheriff Carr and his deputy, Bunell Long, arrived on the scene sometime later that night. One gathers that the sheriff was not in a very good mood when he finally responded to Mrs. May's urgent call for help. He had spent most of the evening on a wild-goose chase.

It seems the sheriff had been several miles away, near Gassaway on the Elk River, responding to a reported sighting of a burning object in the sky, thought to be an airplane on fire and going down. No such downed plane was ever found, and in retrospect it seems clear that the "burning plane" and the fiery object that landed at Flatwoods were one and the same, interpreted differently by different observers.

But the sheriff's response to the two reports was very different. Carr took the report of the downed plane very seriously and expended a great deal of effort to try to find the crash site He regarded Kathleen May's call as a waste of his time, despite her urgent pleas.

From the evidence, it seems clear that Sheriff Carr never looked upon the Flatwoods incident as anything other than a hysterical woman and a bunch of impressionable kids imagining things.

In all fairness, though, the situation that greeted Sheriff Carr and Deputy Long when they finally arrived might well have had the atmosphere of a three-ring circus. There were, of course, Stewart and his armed companions, who had gone back to the scene of the landing, but nearly every other male resident of Braxton County—in varying states of sobriety—seemed to have descended on the Bailey Fisher property to have a look at the reported UFO.

Besides the very real danger from trigger-happy locals taking random pot-shots at anything that moved, all those curiosity-seekers had trampled on and driven over whatever evidence of alien visitation may have existed on the ground. If the sheriff was not amused by the airplane crash that never was, he was even less amused by the sudden invasion of little green men (in this case seven-foot-tall green men).

Given the circumstances, the sheriff was not inclined to take the word of teenagers, children, or a distraught woman seriously. In fact, it is Carr that we may credit with concocting the professional debunker's favorite interpretation of this incident: the meteor/animal theory.

Sheriff Carr—without any actual evidence—theorized that what the group had witnessed was simply a meteor passing through the atmosphere—that was the glowing orb they had all seen. And as for the creature, why it was just some animal—either a raccoon or an owl—its eyes reflecting in the light of the flashlight. Everything else must just be a figment of their imaginations.

The latest expression of Sheriff Carr's theory was published in November 2000 as an "investigative file" by everyone's favorite cynic, Joe Nickell. In essence, Nickell's article follows the sheriff's theory quite closely, with just the addition of some scholarly trappings.

On the surface, there is much to recommend this explanation for the close encounter at Flatwoods. There *was* a bright object that streaked across the heavens that night, and it was seen in at least three states. This celestial object that streaked across Pennsylvania and

Maryland was generally assumed to be a meteor, and its trajectory would indeed have placed it over West Virginia a little after 7 P.M. on September 12. The meteor, in fact, was described as "of considerable proportion."

The eyewitnesses on the ground at Flatwoods did see a large celestial object pass overhead, but they saw this same object slow down, maneuver, and make a soft landing. Moreover, they were able to trace it to its impact point.

The globe or "big ball of fire" the witnesses saw on the ground is dismissed by Nickell as merely distant flashing of airplane beacons already present in the neighborhood. He not only dismisses the "monster" as an owl but even asserts that he can identify the species of owl, based on the eyewitness accounts—a common barn owl.

How a six- to ten-foot red and green creature can become transformed into a two-foot barn owl in Nickell's eyes seems largely based on the fact that a barn owl's face is "heart-shaped" and because of the owl's "unbridled noise." So when the creature started floating eerily toward Mrs. May and the boys, it was really just the barn owl attacking them to defend her nest. Like Sheriff Carr, Nickell believes overactive imagination and hysteria did all the rest.

On the face of it, this explanation seems quite pat. But the theory was constructed by a highly selective choice of facts—and by almost completely ignoring first-hand testimony.

Not even the biggest skeptics have ever claimed that the Flatwoods encounter was a hoax. The eyewitnesses encountered something that terrified them, and their testimony was both truthful and sincere—this much is agreed upon by all.

That an object was sighted over the eastern seaboard on September 12 is also a fact not to be doubted. That it was very large may be deduced from its brightness in the heavens and the fact that it was always described as a meteor.

The notion that what was seen over Flatwoods was a meteor did occur initially to the eyewitnesses who saw it land. The boys on the ball field described what they saw as a "shooting star" to start with—*not* a UFO.

Mrs. May and the boys' interpretation of what came to earth changed radically, however, when they actually approached the object. According to witnesses, it was large, spherical, and glowed as though it was either on fire or red-hot. Size estimate varied somewhat—ten feet to twenty feet in diameter, or "as big as a house"—but on the whole, the witnesses were substantially in agreement.

The regularly flashing airplane beacons were there both before and after the incident, and would hardly have been mistaken for such a large glowing object. Likewise, the witnesses' estimates of their distance from the object—"the length of a football field"—while approximate, were consistent from one observer to another. Their distance from the object thus was "indeterminate" only in the minds of skeptics not present at the time.

The acrid odor present would also be consistent with a crash site—either of a meteorite or a spacecraft—as would be any mist or vapor arising from the site.

The acrid, "metallic" odor was said to be overpowering soon after the landing, yet it was little in evidence later when the sheriff arrived. This, too, is consistent with a meteorite impact or spacecraft landing. The fumes could hardly have been expected to wait around until it was convenient for the local constabulary to arrive. Nickell's suggestion that the grass there always smells "funny" seems a far-fetched rationalization.

The sheriff and Nickell dismiss the vapor as simply ground fog; but the sheriff did not arrive on the scene until very late, when the air had cooled considerably. At dusk, earth and air were still warm, and the vapor the boys and Kathleen encountered would not have been the fog the sheriff later saw.

Beyond the willful misinterpretation of eyewitness testimony, however, there is one other fundamental problem with the meteor theory: there was none.

If a meteor that large and traveling as fast as has been described had struck the ground (thus becoming a meteorite), the impact would have been felt for miles around and it surely would have created a large crater. In all likelihood such an impact might well have set off a major forest fire. Yet none of this occurred.

In fact, if the physical evidence for a UFO's landing is scanty, the evidence for a meteorite impact is nonexistent. No meteorite, or fragments of a meteorite, were ever found at Flatwoods or at any other place in the area.

First-hand accounts of the Flatwoods object describe it as slow-moving, sailing around a hill, hovering briefly, and then landing behind the crest of a hill. Meteors simply do not behave in that manner. The ability to swerve, slow down, remain stationary, and make a soft landing are characteristics of a piloted craft.

If that were not enough, there is the fact that Gene Lamon, Kathleen May, and the boys were not the only ones to spot the creature—or the vessel—near Flatwoods.

In June 2000 Joe Nickell was very diligent about interviewing everyone in Flatwoods who *never* saw anything that night—and hence did not believe that anything abnormal happened. Nickell studiously avoided interviewing anyone who could have corroborated the Flatwoods Seven's story.

The same night as the landing at Flatwoods, Bailey Frame, a resident of Birch River, witnessed a bright-orange object circling the Flatwoods area. He observed it maneuvering for about fifteen minutes before it flew away—a most un-meteoric thing to do.

Eleven miles away, near Weston, West Virginia, a woman and her mother had seen a similar creature while driving to church a week before. They, too, reported a foul odor. The driver was so terrified by her experience that she required hospitalization.

In the 1960s John Keel, who became famous investigating another bizarre West Virginia close encounter, looked into the Flatwoods incident and uncovered a couple who saw a similar ten-foot monster, accompanied by a horrible stench, the next night, September 13.

Their car stalled out for no apparent reason as they were driving, and it was then that they sighted the creature approaching their vehicle. After a short time it returned to the woods from which it had emerged. A few minutes later, they saw a large luminous sphere rise rapidly from among the same woods. This occurred fifteen miles southwest of Flatwoods. The Flatwoods encounter did not occur in a vacuum, therefore.

Certainly the incident at Flatwoods was unusual, even in the annals of UFO sightings. Theories have been advanced that the creature may actually have been something other than a being from outer space, coming from *inner* space instead. It may also be that the creature was not even a living being at all, but some sort of robotic device probing the earth environment.

But whatever interpretation one subscribes to, a few things are certain. The seven residents of Flatwoods did encounter something real.

What they saw was neither meteor nor barn owl nor anything else within the realm of human reckoning. Moreover, the creature they saw was borne in a vessel of indeterminate origin, whose handling characteristics were far beyond the capabilities of any known earth vessel of that time.

UFO sightings, strictly speaking, do not fall within the realm of the supernatural. But insofar as such experiences fall outside the realm of normal human experience, and challenge the parameters of our consensus reality, they may be considered as falling within the general sphere of the paranormal.

Certainly the Flatwoods "monster" encounter falls within this category. By any standards, the run-in with the spade-headed creature in the forest near Flatwoods constitutes a close encounter of the weird kind.

If you go ...

More haints and haunts of Dixie to see in West Virginia:

HARPERS FERRY NATIONAL HISTORICAL PARK
P.O. Box 65
Harpers Ferry, WV 25425

The most famous ghost here is John Brown, who has been seen in broad daylight; numerous other ghosts of the Civil War era also haunt the town.

WIZARD CLIP
Adam Livingston Farm
Highway 11, Jefferson County
Middleway, WV

The farm was host to a series of bizarre poltergeist visitations starting in 1794; supposedly the "wizard" ceased tormenting mortals in 1802. Although not open to the general public, a religious retreat house, the Priest Field Pastoral Center, currently occupies part of the property. There are reports of modern-day poltergeist incidents happening to some groups on retreat there. Locals also report a headless ghost nearby along the Opequan River.

West Virginia Ghost Tours

HARPERS FERRY
GHOST TOURS OF HARPERS FERRY
Route 1, Box 468
Harpers Ferry, WV 25425
(304) 725-8019

PARKERSBURG
HAUNTED PARKERSBURG
GHOST TOUR

Seasonal fall walking tours (includes info on Mothman)
(304) 428-7978

Appendix

Haunted Hotels of Dixie

For those to whom spending only an hour or two at a haunted site is not enough, the following inns, hotels, and bed and breakfasts offer overnight stays at documented haunts. Some locations are more forthcoming about their ghosts than others. Many hotels formerly did not like to publicize their resident haunting for fear of driving away customers, but in recent years it has become more fashionable to play up their haunted heritage, and some will even give private ghost tours for their guests. It would be advisable to check the hotel's attitude toward its resident spirits before booking a reservation.

ALABAMA

THE PICKWICK HOTEL
1023 20th Street South
Birmingham, AL 35205
(205) 933-9555
www.pickwickhotel.com

The eighth floor is haunted

THE TUTWILER HOTEL (1913)
2021 Park Place North
Birmingham, AL
(205) 322-2100
www.thetutwilerhotel.com

Colonel Tutwiler haunts here

KENDALL MANOR INN (1872)
534 West Broad Street
Eufaula, AL 36027
(334) 687-8847

ST. JAMES HOTEL (1837)
1200 Water Avenue
Selma, AL 36701
(334) 872-3234 • (800) 678-8946

"Lucinda" and a ghost dog

ARKANSAS

BASIN PARK HOTEL (1905)
12 Spring Street
Eureka Springs, AR 72632

Two female ghosts

OLD VAN BUREN INN (1889)
633 Main Street
Van Buren, AR 72956
(479) 471–5584 • (479) 461–4186

*Friendly but unseen spirits on the
second floor*

GEORGIA
THE PARTRIDGE INN (1892)
2110 Walton Way
Augusta, GA 30904
(800) 476–6888

*A Civil War ghost has taken up
residence here*

BONNIE CASTLE (1896)
2 Post Street
Grantville, GA 30220
(770) 583–3090 • (800) 261–3090

*Ghosts haunt the second floor
of this b&b*

EARLY HILL INN (1840)
Lick Skillet Road
Greensboro, GA 30542
(706) 453–7876

Two ghosts reported at this b&b

JEKYLL ISLAND CLUB HOTEL (1886)
371 Riverview Drive
Jekyll Island, GA 31527
(912) 635–2600 • (800) 333–3333

*"Spencer's Suite" occupied by a
coffee-sipping spirit; other ghosts
also vacation here*

17HUNDRED90 INN AND TAVERN
(1790)
307 East President Street
Savannah, GA 31401
(912) 236–7122 • (800) 487–1790

*At least three ghosts, including
"Anna" who sometimes doubles
as valet to guests*

THE MARSHALL HOUSE (1851)
122 East Broughton Street
Savannah, GA 31401
(912) 644–7896 • (800) 589–6304
www.marshallhouse.com

*Having served as a hospital for war
wounded and yellow fever victims,
the venerable hotel's rooms have
seen much suffering over the years;
Civil War ghosts, a mischievous little
girl and assorted unexplained noises
have all been reported*

KENTUCKY
THE TALBOT INN (1790)
P.O. Box 365
107 West Stephen Foster
Bardstown, KY, 40004
(502) 348–3494 • (800) 4-TAVERN

*In addition to poltergeist activity, a
"lady in white" and Jesse James have
been seen roaming the halls of the
historic b&b*

GRATZ PARK INN (1916)
120 West Second Street
Lexington, KY, 40507
(606) 231–1777 • (800) 752–4166

*Converted from an old hospital, while
the Laundry Room was formerly the
county morgue; most of the ghosts
are thought to date to that era*

THE BROWN HOTEL (1923)
335 West Broadway
Louisville, KY, 40202
(502) 324–1389
www.brownhotel.com

SEELBACH HILTON HOTEL (1905)
500 Fourth Avenue
Louisville, KY, 40202–2518
(502) 585–3200
www.seelbachhilton.com

A "Lady in Blue" roams the hotel, as well as a male ghost on the eighth floor; the hotel offers ghost tours for guests

LOUISIANA
LLOYD HALL (1820)
292 Lloyd Bridge Road
Cheneyville, LA 71325
(318) 776–5641 • (800) 240–8135

A Civil War ghost haunts this cozy b&b

T'FRERE'S HOUSE AND GARCONNIERE (1880)
1905 Verot School Road
Lafayette, LA 70508
(800) 984–9347

Located in the heart of Cajun country, the resident spirit here is named Amelie

THE BOURBON ORLEANS HOTEL
717 Orleans Street
New Orleans, LA 20116
(504) 523–2222
www.bourbonorleans.com

This antebellum hotel has at least one Civil War era ghost; it may have as many as 17 ghosts in total

THE PLACE D'ARMES HOTEL
625 St. Ann Street
New Orleans, LA 70116
(504) 524–4531 • (800) 366–2743
www.placedarmes.com

Said to be the most haunted hotel in the Big Easy, apparitions of both children and adults have been sighted throughout this three-diamond hotel

OAK ALLEY PLANTATION
3645 Highway 18 (Great River Road)
Vachere, LA 70090
(225) 265–2151 • (800) 44ALLEY
www.oakvalleyplantation.com

Celina and Louise Roman, mother and daughter, are both believed to haunt their ancestral home; the ghost of another owner, Mrs. Stewart, also watches over the mansion

MISSISSIPPI
RIVER'S INN
1109 River Road
Greenwood, MS 38930
(662) 453–5432

An unseen ghost raises a ruckus in different rooms of the house

MONMOUTH PLANTATION
36 Melrose Avenue
Natchez, MS 39120
(601) 442–5852 • (800) 828–4531
www.monmouthplantation.com

The sound of spurs and heavy footsteps are heard, along with occasional poltergeist activity

HARBOUR OAKS INN
126 West Scenic Drive
Pass Christian, MS 39571
(228) 452–9399 • (800) 452–9399

*Antebellum hotel and Civil War
hospital; several Civil War
ghosts reported*

CEDAR GROVE INN (1840)
2200 Oak Street
Vicksburg, MS 39180
(601) 636–1000 • (800) 862–1300
www.cedargroveinn.com

*The sound of a woman sobbing and
phantom footsteps are heard*

1902–08 STAINED GLASS MANOR—OAK HALL
2430 Drummond Street
Vicksburg, MS 39108
(601) 638–8893 • (800) 771–8893
www.vickbnb.com

*"Fannie's Room" has the most
spectral activity here*

MISSOURI
THE ELMS RESORT AND SPA
401 Regent Street
Excelsior Springs, MO 64024
(816) 630–5500 • (800) THE-ELMS
www.elmresort.com

*Several ghosts stay here, including
one murdered by Al Capone*

BASS COUNTRY INN
2610 North Glenstone Avenue
Springfield, MO 65803
(417) 522–7700 • (417) 866–6671

*"Carl," thought to be a former busboy,
is most often seen; a female ghost is
also present*

NORTH CAROLINA
THE GROVE PARK INN RESORT AND SPA
290 Macon Avenue
Asheville, NC 28804
www.groveparkinn.com

*"The Pink Lady" is one of three ghosts
known to frequent this resort*

ELIZABETH INN
307 Front Street
Beaufort, NC 28516
(252) 728–3861
www.beaufort.net/elizabeth1

*The spirit here has been identified as
"Captain John"*

GLENDALE SPRINGS INN AND RESTAURANT
7414 Highway 16
Glendale Springs, NC 28629
(336) 982–2103 • (800) 287–1206
www.glendalespringsinn.com

*"Rosebud," the resident ghost,
resides in Room 5*

THE LODGE ON LAKE LURE
P.O. Box 519
361 Charlotte Drive
Lake Lure, NC 28746
(828) 625–2789 • (800) 733–2785
www.lodgeonlakelure.com

*Rooms 2 and 4 seem the most
spectrally active*

NEW BERNE HOUSE INN
709 Broad Street
New Bern, NC 28560
(252) 636–2250 • (800) 842–7688
www.newbernehouse.com

*Two of this b&b's guest rooms are
already occupied: Rooms 4 and 6
are haunted*

SOUTH CAROLINA
JASMINE HOUSE (1843)
64 Hassell Street
Charleston, SC 29401
(843) 577–5900 • (800) 845–7639
www.jasminehouseinn.com

*The Chrysanthemum guest room
is the most haunted of the ten
rooms available*

MEETING STREET INN
173 Meeting Street
Charleston, SC 29401
(843) 823–1882 • (800) 842–8022
www.meetingstreetinn.com

*Of the 56 rooms available, at least
two—Rooms 107 and 303—have
ghosts in them*

ROSE HOPE PLANTATION (1840)
206 Rice Hope Drive
Monck's Corner, SC 29461
(843) 849–9000 • (800) 569–4038
www.ricehope.com

*The resident ghost here is
"Mistress Chicken"*

THE OLD VILLAGE POST HOUSE INN
(1888)
(Formerly Guilds Inn)
101 Pitt Street
Mount Pleasant, SC 29464
(843) 388–8935 • (800) 549–POST
www.oldvillageposthouse.com

*The ghost of Captain Guild is said
to visit here during a full moon or
a storm*

THE INN AT MERRIDUN
199 Merridun Place
Union, SC 29379
(864) 427–7052 • (888) 892–1020
www.merridun.com

*This antebellum manse has no less
than ten ghosts, who have been
known to throw their own Christmas
party. The owner's blonde tabby cat
can frequently be seen talking to
unseen specters*

TENNESSEE
WOODLAWN
110 Keith Lane
Athens, TN, 37303
(423) 745–8211 • (800) 745–8213
www.woodlawn.com

*The identity of this b&b's resident
ghost is unknown, but he is thought
to be a Civil War soldier*

MAGNOLIA MANOR (1849)
418 North Main Street
Bolivar, TN, 38008
(731) 658–6700
www.magnoliamanorbolivartn.com
/Ghosts

*The ghosts in this b&b are fairly
active; their presence has been
documented by ghost hunters out of
Memphis and they even offer ghost
tours in October*

THE READ HOUSE HOTEL
827 Broad Street
Chattanooga, TN 37402
(423) 266–4121
info@readhousehotel.com

*The present hotel replaced one that
stood on the same spot during the
Civil War, but apparently one of the
former hotel's residents decided to
stay put. Room 311 is haunted by a
Yankee soldier who murdered a pros-
titute in the same numbered room of
the old hotel. Reportedly, he is not a
happy trooper*

FALCON MANOR
2645 Faulkner Springs Road
McMinnville, TN, 37110
(931) 668–444
www.falconmanor.com

*Watches stop ticking in one of the
guest rooms, phantom footsteps are
heard in the hallway, and the resident
spirit has even been known to pose
for wedding photographs*

THE HERMITAGE HOTEL
231 Sixth Avenue North
Nashville, TN, 37219
(615) 244–3121

*The oldest hotel in Nashville, the Her-
mitage has played host to everyone
from famous presidents to the legendary pool champion Minnesota
Fats; currently, the venerable hotel is
host to several ghost, believed to be
former tenants*

UNION STATION HOTEL
1001 Broadway
Nashville, TN,
(615) 726–1001

*A former train station converted to a
small but elegant hotel, several
ghosts roam its halls, including Major
Lewis, the man who oversaw the
building's construction in 1898*

VIRGINIA
THE MARTHA WASHINGTON INN (1830)
150 West Main Street
Abingdon, VA 24210
(540) 628–3161
www.marthawashington.com

*Just before the Civil War, the inn was
a finishing school for young ladies,
but when war came, the building was
commandeered for use as a military
hospital; it is believed at least two of
the ghosts—a young violin-playing
girl and a Yankee soldier—died here
during the war*

CHAMBERLIN HOTEL (1928)
2 Fenwick Road
Hampton, VA,23651
(757) 723–6511 • (800) 582–8975

Overlooking scenic Chesapeake Bay, the Chamberlin's ghost is called "Ezmerelda," whose favorite haunt seems to be the eighth floor

WAYSIDE INN OF 1797
7783 Main Street
Middletown, VA 22645
(540) 869–1797 • (877) 869–1797
www.waysideofva.com

The oldest inn in America in continuous operation, the Wayside has been host to many famous folk, including George Washington. Periodically, a low moaning is heard from a loft in the oldest section of the inn; whether George's teeth are still hurting him, or some other shade from the past, is not known

BELLE GRAE INN
515 West Frederick Street
Staunton, VA 24401
(703) 368–9999 • (888) 541–5151
www.bellegrae.com

The former owner, Mrs. Bagby, is thought to haunt Room 7

THE ORELL HOUSE
Colonial Williamsburg
302B Francis Street (check-in)
Williamsburg, VA 23185
(757) 229–1000 • (800) HISTORY
www.colonialwilliamsburg.org

This historic village has over two dozen places to stay the night, at least two of which are haunted; poltergeist activity has been reported in the Orell House by guests